Refutation of Confab "ideas" – p xvii
unusual muscular powers
"Unconscious" Perception p 9 – justified by the "Hidden Observer" – p 9
Medical cos + ucs - ideas 30-50 yrs behind the times p 11
Hyp not role playing for stupid reasons p 39
Imp. of Pre Induction posture p 51

HANDBOOK OF INVESTIGATIVE HYPNOSIS

Other books by Martin Reiser
　The Police Department Psychologist
　Practical Psychology for Police Officers

HANDBOOK OF INVESTIGATIVE HYPNOSIS

By

Martin Reiser, Ed.D.
Director, Behavioral Science Services
Los Angeles Police Department
Director, Law Enforcement Hypnosis Institute, Inc.

with Forewords by

David B. Cheek, M.D.
Co-author, *Clinical Hypnotherapy*

Ronald L. Katz, M.D.
Professor and Chairman,
Department of Anesthesiology,
School of Medicine, UCLA

Daryl F. Gates
Chief of Police
Los Angeles Police Department

LEHI Publishing Company
Los Angeles, California

Reiser, Martin, 1927 —
 Handbook of Investigative Hypnosis
  Bibliography
  Includes Index
 1. Hypnosis 2. Investigative Hypnosis
 3. Policy Psychology 4. Criminal Investigation
 Library of Congress Catalog Card Number: 79 - 53215
 ISBN 0 - 934486 - 00 - X

Printed in the United States of America

Copyright © 1980 by Martin Reiser

All rights reserved. No part of this book may be reproduced or utilized in any form or by any means, electronic or mechanical, including photocopying, recording or by any information storage and retrieval system without permission in writing from the Publisher. Inquiries should be made to LEHI Publishing Company, 303 Gretna Green Way, Los Angeles, California, 90049.

To those law enforcement practitioners of investigative hypnosis who are making a significant contribution to society.

CONTENTS

    ACKNOWLEDGMENTS viii
    FOREWORD — David B. Cheek, M.D................ ix
    FOREWORD — Ronald L. Katz, M.D................. xi
    FOREWORD — Chief Daryl F. Gates............... xii
    PREFACE....................................... xiii
    INTRODUCTION xiv

1. History and Present Status of Hypnosis...............3
2. Basic Psychodynamics............................7
3. Emotional Development and Mental Health..........14
4. The Nature of Hypnosis and the Role of
   the Hypnotist....................................30
5. Myths, Misconceptions; Dangers and
   Contraindications................................34
6. Theories of Hypnosis.............................38
7. Principles of Suggestion; Feelings and
   Motives of the Hypnotist.........................42
8. Who is Hypnotizable: Susceptibility Tests...........46
9. Preparation of Subject; Induction Methods;
   Deepening Techniques and Dehypnotization.........51
10. Laws of Hypnosis................................58
11. Ethical and Professional Considerations............60
12. Hypnosis and the Truth; Machines and Drugs.........65
13. Hypnosis and Crime — Social and
    Anti-Social Aspects..............................70
14. Criminological versus Psycho-therapeutic
    Uses of Hypnosis................................75
15. Eyewitness Testimony............................78
16. Interviewing Techniques; Body Language...........81
17. Role of the Composite Artist......................86

18. Additional Induction Techniques, Direct and Indirect 89
19. Trance Depth Phenomena 97
20. Victimology and Traumatic Reactions 102
21. Transference and Countertransference Reactions 106
22. Waking, Hypnotic and Post-Hypnotic Suggestions 109
23. Memory, Amnesia and Time Distortion 114
24. Difficult Subjects and Rapid Techniques 119
25. Self-Hypnosis 125
26. Hypnosis With Children and Elderly Persons 129
27. Legal Aspects and Status of Hypnosis 132
28. Expert Witness Considerations 142
29. Age Regression and Automatic Writing 151
30. Ideomotor and Ideosensory Techniques, Pendulum and Fingers 154
31. T.V. and Other Memory Retrieval Techniques 158
32. Witness Identification Procedures; Lineups, Photos 163
33. Office Procedures 166
34. Administration and Coordination of a Hypnosis Program 169
35. Experiences and Problems of an Investigative Hypnotist 173
36. Checklist of Procedures with a Witness/Victim 178
37. Research Needs and Methods 180
38. Results to Date — Statistics and Cases 183
39. A Representative Case (with photos) 189
40. Transcript of a Hypnosis Session 193
    SAMPLE FORMS 223
    GLOSSARY 232
    BIBLIOGRAPHY 235
    INDEX 247
    ABOUT THE AUTHOR 256

ACKNOWLEDGMENTS

I am indebted to the administration of the Los Angeles Police Department for its openness and support in encouraging the demonstration of the feasibility and cost-effectiveness of police-conducted investigative hypnosis sessions.

I would also like to thank some of the original LAPD consultant-faculty panel for their professional endorsement and assistance:

Gerald Cohen, J.D.; Ira Greenberg, Ph.D.; Ronald Katz, M.D.; William Kroger, M.D.; Perry London, Ph.D.; Ward McConnell, J.D.; Chaytor Mason, M.A.

My faculty colleagues of the Law Enforcement Hypnosis Institute have been a continuing source of inspiration, innovation and delight. They have all contributed importantly to this book: Gerald Cohen, J.D.; Jerry Dash, Ph.D.; Lt. Richard King; Raymond La Scola, M.D.; Chaytor Mason, M.A.; Captain Michael Nielsen; Fernando Ponce, B.F.A.; Lt. Keith Ross; Susan Saxe, Ph.D.

I am grateful to my secretary, Beverly Marrone, for her patience and conscientiousness in assisting me on a daily basis and with the manuscript.

As always, my wife, Enid, has given me continuing support, encouragement and inspiration.

FOREWORD

Martin Reiser, Ed.D., Director of Behavioral Science Services for the Los Angeles Police Department and Director of the Law Enforcement Hypnosis Institute is eminently qualified as the author of the HANDBOOK OF INVESTIGATIVE HYPNOSIS which may soon become better known as the "Bible" on this subject. It will be a valuable asset to law enforcement officers, lawyers, judges and those experts in knowledge of hypnosis who may be called upon to set up teaching programs comparable to the excellent ones offered by Reiser and his associates in the Los Angeles Police Department.

Victims of crime and witnesses to violence may be so horrified that they repress all conscious memory for important details. Sometimes a victim or a witness to a crime may be unconscious. Life threatening events are recorded in primitive parts of the brain that are not eliminated by drugs or head injury. Although not consciously remembered the stressful events will be rehearsed in sleep with continuing harmful effect until the dreams are recalled and exposed to conscious reason. Newer methods of subconscious repetitive review with subjects in hypnosis are of great value not only for releasing important information but for relieving the anxieties produced by consciously unremembered stressful dream sequences.

From his long experience Doctor Reiser has recognized that police officers trained for criminal investigation are better qualified to use hypnosis in their field of work than are psychologists and physicians who may have great knowledge about hypnotic behavior but are untrained in criminal investigation.

This book is composed of three major divisions that are closely related. It starts with a discussion of the human nervous system and the fundamentals of human behavior. The second division is concerned with fundamentals of semantics, suggestion and the phenomena of hypnosis. Its values and limitations are carefully explored. Doctor Reiser stresses that hypnosis is used by investigators only for memory improvement. It is not a tool for extracting "truth" from criminals or for coercing witnesses into fabricating information. He stresses the fact that a police investigator is not a "therapist" although victims and witnesses may derive much emotional benefit from releasing troubled memories that have been kept from conscious recognition.

The third major division spells out ways in which hypnosis can be integrated into investigative work. Past and present applications of hypnosis in police work have been documented to offer a valuable reference reservoir of information. Ethical principles regarding the welfare and needs of the victim or witness are given careful consideration. Steps in the process of producing a composite picture of a suspect are given in detail with a verbatim account of an interview. Forms for documentation, release of information and assessment of the investigative work are all there in the book which is a must for libraries of law, forensic medicine and hypnosis.

DAVID B. CHEEK, M.D.
Co-author, *CLINICAL HYPNOTHERAPY;*
Fellow, American Society of
Clinical Hypnosis; Diplomate,
American Board of Obstetrics
and Gynecology

FOREWORD

In the early 1970's I was approached to help design and teach a course in hypnosis for Los Angeles Police Department officers. My initial reaction was one of total opposition to the proposed project. However, after meeting Dr. Martin Reiser and others I agreed, reluctantly, to participate. My main reason for participation was to provide a critical view of the study. I subsequently learned that many of the other health care professionals teaching the course had similar negative views.

In my first session with the students, who were specially selected police officers, I was favorably impressed but still wondered about possible abuses of hypnosis by police officers. After the course was completed I was asked to occasionally observe these officers using hypnosis to aid victims of crime. I have been impressed with the professional manner and expertise of these officers. After viewing this project for several years, I believe that the abuse of hypnosis, which I feared, has not occurred. Hypnosis has been shown to be a valuable tool in aiding crime victims.

Dr. Reiser in this book reviews the history of the project and details the value of hypnosis in police investigation. Some of his case histories will have a familiar ring since they were previously reported in newspaper articles. Dr. Reiser has also written an excellent basic text on hypnosis per se. Thus this book will be of value not only to those interested in investigative hypnosis but also the general reader with an interest in hypnosis.

Although my initial feelings about this project were mostly negative, time and experience have made it clear that the victims of crime and the general public have benefited from investigative hypnosis. I am glad that I initially participated in the project as a devil's advocate. Now I believe that investigative hypnosis, when properly used and with appropriate safeguards, can be an important tool of law enforcement agencies.

RONALD L. KATZ, M.D.
Professor and Chairman, Department of Anesthesiology, School of Medicine, UCLA

FOREWORD

The pressing need for effective crime control in our complex society could not be any more intense than it is today. As one of the leading law enforcement agencies in the world, the Los Angeles Police Department continues to be innovative and progressive, developing new methods and techniques that will increase our effectiveness and make our community safer.

Several years ago, my Department was considered a pioneer in the application of psychology to the practice of professional policing when the position of Department Psychologist was created. Under the leadership of Dr. Martin Reiser, the Department's psychological program began as a small but vital service to employees and their families. That program has continued to grow in stature and, more recently, has found its way into effective crime control application in the form of investigative hypnosis. Its usefulness as an investigative tool is amply demonstrated by the fact that between July of 1975 and December 31, 1978, investigative hypnosis was utilized on 357 occasions resulting in additional information of value being obtained in 229 cases. Additionally, eight major cases would not have been solved had hypnosis not refreshed the memory of the victim or witness. Those figures become more significant when viewed in context; in all cases where this non-therapeutic technique has been used no negative psychological side effects have resulted.

Dr. Reiser has skillfully outlined this developing technique in his publication *Handbook of Investigative Hypnosis,* a book which is now a tool law enforcement can use to provide better service to the community.

DARYL F. GATES
Chief of Police
Los Angeles Police Department

PREFACE

This book was motivated by the many requests from graduates of the Law Enforcement Hypnosis Institute and the need for a pragmatic and focused text in the new specialty of investigative hypnosis.

There are many differences of opinion and variations in technique among researchers and practitioners of this specialty. The points of view and approaches presented here represent a distillation from many authoritative sources. However, there is no one "right" answer in hypnosis and each practitioner needs to evolve his or her own views and style. This book represents some of mine.

Los Angeles, California   Martin Reiser, Ed.D.

INTRODUCTION

Beginning in the 1950's attempts were made to train law enforcement investigators in hypnosis techniques and to interest police departments in developing in-house capability in this area.[1] Apparently the time wasn't right and investigative hypnosis was given only sporatic application, mainly by consultant mental health professionals and lay hypnotists.

In spite of an occasional dramatic report of success in a major crime case where hypnosis was used and improved the recall of a witness, investigative hypnosis lay relatively dormant as an investigative tool until the mid 1970's when the Los Angeles Police Department developed its investigative hypnosis project.[6]

Beginning in 1972 the author began receiving occasional requests from LAPD homicide detectives to try hypnosis in cases where witnesses should have revealed more information than they were able to recall on routine interrogation. As a result of some early success,[5] word began circulating more widely about the efficacy of hypnosis in these cases. Over the next several years hypnosis requests from investigators increased to the point of being difficult to handle and keeping up with other assigned duties.

As Department Psychologist the author had the responsibility for therapy and counseling with officers and family members, teaching at the academy at various levels, designing, implementing and evaluating research projects within the Department, consulting with middle and upper management on organizational systems problems, and consulting with investigators in crime cases for a psychological profiling of a suspect, and being on call as a crisis negotiation team member in hostage situations. It became apparent that some better way would have to be found to handle the burgeoning hypnosis requests.

In collaboration with an investigative captain, the author designed a one-year research demonstration project to test the feasibility of training experienced police investigators to use hypnosis teachniques with volunteer witnesses and victims to enhance their recall. This concept was based on the author's several years of personal experience and the realization that professional investigators could easily be taught to use this tool relatively independently.

After legal clearances with the City Attorney and District Attorney offices, it took about a year for this research proposal to get Departmental administrative approval and to begin. Preliminarily, meetings had been held with a group of outside health professionals, also experts in hypnosis, to gain their inputs, their support for the project, and their participation in the training and consultation phases.

The one-year research design consisted of three phases. Phase one involved a basic training program for the eleven lieutenants and two captains selected for training. The outside faculty-consultant panel and in-house experts provided the initial basic training on six successive Saturdays at the police academy. The training included theory and practice, ethical and professional considerations, as well as legal questions and cases.

During phase two the trainee lieutenants, working in teams of two, were assigned a major crime case for hypnosis by the investigative captain coordinating the project. One of the lieutenants functioned as the hypnotist and the other lieutenant as the recorder-evaluator in each case. Every session was completely tape-recorded and data were collected for statistical and evaluation purposes. During phase two an outside consultant was usually involved in each of these cases along with the investigator trainees.

In phase three of the project, which usually occurred at about eight-months into the program for most of the hypno-investigators, the teams worked on cases more autonomously with a consultant on call but not necessarily present.

The one-year project officially began in June of 1975 and ran until June of 1976. Of the approximate 70 cases in the data base at that point, it was estimated that in approximately 77%, information was elicited under hypnosis of importance to the case investigator that was not previously available on routine interview. The LAPD project was continued and is now a regular part of the investigative procedures within the Department. In December of 1977, the project was given the American Express/International Association of Chiefs of Police Award as the year's outstanding contribution to the field of international police science and technology.[2]

Because of the many requests that began coming in from other police agencies for training people in investigative hypnosis techniques, the author established the Law Enforcement Hypnosis Institute, Inc. in 1976. An independent educational training organization, the Institute makes the training available to those criminal justice agencies interested in adding this useful tool to their investigative resources.

The original 48-hour training program given to the LAPD trainees was distilled into a tight, comprehensive program of four days consisting of 32 class hours of theory, demonstration and practice. Feedback from the trainees suggests that the format is about right. The seminar compares favorably with the typical two or three day seminars given to beginners from the health professions who have to learn the more complex psychotherapeutic applications of hypnosis.

Basically, hypnosis induction is relatively easy to teach and the person of average intelligence can usually learn in an hour or two. The extended training time is required to teach individuals how to utilize the hypnosis state once it is achieved. This requires knowledge, skill, and practice in applied areas as well as in inducing the hypnotic state.

Experience indicates that many hypnosis trainees neglect to practice in their areas of specialization and eventually discontinue using hypnosis because it involves hard work, continuing education, and regular practice. It has been estimated that of those health professionals who attend a weekend seminar in hypnosis, over two-thirds will lose interest in it because it is time consuming and personally demanding. Therefore, it is important for those who complete the basic training in investigative hypnosis to practice, to continue learning, and to refine techniques. One's education begins with the completion of the basic seminar and then becomes a life-long process as in any other area of training or specialization.

It is recommended that criminal justice professionals arrange for consultation in their local communities with licensed health professionals, particularly in the beginning of their practice with volunteer witnesses and victims. This may enhance the confidence level of the beginning hypno-investigator and also communicate to others in the criminal justice system and the community that investigative hypnosis is a professional enterprise in which specialists in areas such as law enforcement, medicine, psychology and dentistry collaborate. With added experience and increased confidence the hypno-investigator will likely find that a consultant is not needed in each case, that one can be called on in those cases where there are relevant questions.

Investigative hypnosis is a subspecialty within hypnosis and requires specialized training, even for those who may have had hypnosis training for hypnotherapy purposes or for dental applications. Although licensed health professionals can be very useful in a consultant role, they are not automatically expert or competent in the area of investigative hypnosis since most have not been trained specifically with that focus. The trained hypno-investigator is the expert in his area and will need to familiarize and educate consultants from the health professions in those technical aspects of investigation, information retrieval and the relevant legal parameters.

There has been some criticism of the investigative hypnosis movement for training detectives, prosecutors, defense attorneys, and others in these specialized hypnosis techniques. Much of this criticism seems to center around the fear that law enforcement personnel may wittingly or unknowingly coerce, shape or lead a subject into giving desired answers and that the investigator will be unable to maintain objectivity during the hypnosis session.

It has also been asserted that witnesses to crimes are likely to fantasize, confabulate, and give misleading information under hypnosis.[3]

In four years of experience using investigative hypnosis in over 350 cases at LAPD, we have found that these fears and prognostications are unfounded. Our experience is that most volunteer witnesses and victims of major crimes are motivated to cooperate and assist in the investigation and have no need to lie, confabulate, or distort. Over 90 percent of the time where follow-up information is available, we do corroborate details elicited during the hypnosis session. These details include license numbers, suspect description, names mentioned during the crime, vehicle descriptions, and a host of other information which is subject to validation.

If a subject is motivated to lie, it would be as easy to do under hypnosis as it would be for that person in a non-hypnotic state. It is the author's impression that the underlying issues being reacted to by the critics of investigative hypnosis are not those having to do with hypnosis, but about the ethical and professional standards of professionals in the criminal justice system. That, of course, is a separate question from the hypnosis one.

Because of the desire to keep investigative hypnosis on a high professional and ethical level, the hypno-investigators of the Los Angeles Police Department, in 1977, founded The Society for Investigative and Forensic Hypnosis. As do other professional associations, the Society establishes ethical standards and experience requirements. It also encourages in-service training, research, and provides for the sharing and dissemination of information about investigative hypnosis.

Developments to date indicate that the future of investigative hypnosis is bright. Follow-up inquires have revealed that subjects do not report negative effects resulting from participating as a subject in investigative hypnosis. In fact, many of the subjects have reported feeling better after the hypnosis session. This included sleeping more soundly, having fewer nightmares, and feeling less guilty about being a victim of or a witness to a violent crime.

The use of investigative hypnosis by law enforcement and other criminal justice professionals will likely continue to evolve, because it works. Experience shows that it is a safe, high payoff community service. Investigative hypnosis likely reduces crime by quicker apprehension of suspects and by saving some of the man hours and dollars required to clear particular cases. As one psychiatrist put it, "I am certain . . . that our studies and those of 200 others, are going to contribute importantly to hypnosis and criminology. I can see the time when the science of hypnosis will become just as valuable in our fight against crime as fingerprinting is today."[4]

References

1. Arons, H. *Hypnosis in Criminal Investigation.* Springfield, Illinois: Thomas, 1967.
2. Award winners for 1977. *The Police Chief,* December, 1977, p. 22.
3. Dellinger, R.W. Investigative hypnosis. Tapping our cerebral memory banks. *Human Behavior,* April, 1978, 36-37.
4. Gerber, S. Hypnotism - new weapon against crime? *This Week Magazine,* January 25, 1959.
5. Reiser, M. Hypnosis as an aid in a homicide investigation. *The American Journal of Clinical Hypnosis,* October, 1974, 84-87.
6. Reiser, M. Hypnosis as a tool in criminal investigation. *The Police Chief,* November, 1976, 36-39.

HANDBOOK OF INVESTIGATIVE HYPNOSIS

CHAPTER 1
BRIEF HISTORY AND PRESENT STATUS OF HYPNOSIS

Early History

Hypnosis is a human phenomenon and is as old as man. For centuries it has been used by tribal medicine men and other religious practitioners to influence behavior and to achieve cures. There is evidence that hypnotic states were induced in primitive peoples by their own dreams, by chanting rituals, and by ceremonial dances.

Hypnosis was used by Egyptian soothsayers over 3,000 years ago. It was also practiced by the Greek Oracles, the Persian Magi, the Hindu Fakirs, and the Indian Yogi. The earliest medical records of the applications of hypnosis appear to be those describing the Aesculapian sleep temples in Egypt and Greece.[10]

The Bible alludes to touch and the laying on of hands in order to cure certain ailments. The concept of laying on of hands is also associated with authority figures such as rulers and this "royal touch" was used by Edward the Confessor in England and by Francis I in France in helping subjects with a variety of ailments.

In the seventeenth century Valentine Greatrakes was called "The Great Irish Stroker" and was famous for curing individuals by his touch. Paracelcus in the sixteenth century introduced the concept of the healing effects of magnetism emitted by astral bodies. Later, Father Maximillian Hell, a Jesuit priest in Vienna, became famous for applying magnetic plates to the body of sufferers in order to heal them.[14]

Modern History - First Phase

Franz Anton Mesmer (1734-1815) first gave a naturalistic explanation for hypnosis and did much to eliminate the notion of the occult in explaining trance behavior. He used a theory of animal magnetism. His doctoral dissertation at the University of Vienna in 1773 was entitled, "The Influence of Stars and

Planets as Cureative Powers." He experimented with magnets and eventually designed a tub called a *Baquet* filled with iron rods and fillings for his patients to sit in.[4]

"In one room, under the influence of rods issuing from tubs filled with large bottles, the said rods applied upon different parts of the subjects' bodies, the most extraordinary scenes took place daily. Sardonic laughter, pitious moans and torrents of tears burst forth on all sides. The subjects were thrown back in spasmotic jerks, the respirations sounded like death rattles, and terrifying symptoms were exhibited. Suddenly, the actors of these strange performances would frantically or rapturously rush toward each other, either rejoicing and embracing, or thrusting away their neighbors with every appearance of horror. Another room was padded and presented a different spectacle. There, women beat their heads against the padded walls or rolled on the cushion-covered floor in fits of suffocation. In the midst of the panting, quivering throng, Mesmer, dressed in a lilac coat, moved about, halting in front of the most violently excited, and gazing steadily into their eyes, while he held both their hands in his, bringing the middle fingers into immediate contact to establish the communication. At another moment he would, by a motion of open hands and extended fingers, operate with the great current, crossing and uncrossing his arms with wonderful rapidity to make the final passes."[5]

Mesmer, a charismatic and controversial person, caused many people to become disturbed at his approach to the cure of his patients. A French commission was established to determine the validity of animal magnetism as propounded by Mesmer, and Benjamin Franklin was a prominent member of that commission. They concluded that there was no validity to the theory of animal magnetism. Ironically, they said that hypnosis was *only* a result of suggestion and imagination and dismissed it out of hand.

The Marquis de Puységur (1751-1825), a former student of Mesmer, was the first to discover that the "magnetic" effects in the hypnotic trance are produced by the relationship between the magnetist and patient and could be produced by employing only talk and suggestion and leaving out the rods, magnets and other trappings used by Mesmer.

James Braid (1795-1860), a Scottish physician, introduced the term "neurohypnosis" which was later shortened to "hypnosis." He adopted a psychological theory of hypnosis and attributed hypnotic phenomena to the effect of mental concentration on one dominant idea which he called "monoideism."[2]

James Esdaile (1808-1859), a Scottish surgeon in India, performed over 300 major operations and countless smaller ones using hypnosis as the only anesthetic. He reported a mortality rate of only five percent, which is significantly lower than that when chemical anesthesias are used for surgery. The introduction of chloroform as an anesthetic in 1858 contributed to the decline in the use of hypnosis for that purpose.[6]

Modern History - Second Phase

The interest in hypnosis remained at a fairly low level until the 1880's when the work of Charcot, perhaps the most distinguished neurologist of the nineteenth century, equated susceptibility to hypnosis with pathology, especially in hysterical neurotics.[7]

Liébeault and Bernheim in France did much to popularize the use of hypnosis for therapeutic purposes. They considered hypnosis in the range of normal behavior, emphasizing the power of suggestion.[1]

Josef Breuer (1842-1925), used hypnosis in developing his cathartic method to directly cure hysterical symptoms. He found that in hypnosis the patient remembered painful emotions, could ventilate them and in some cases resolve the conflict. He was also interested in looking for the causes of disturbance rather than in merely treating the symptoms.[3]

Sigmund Freud, in 1885, went to France to study with Charcot and also with Liébeault and Bernheim. His early studies were influential in his development of the concepts of repression and of the unconscious part of the mind. He later dropped hypnosis for the technique of free association and the structure which he called psychoanalysis.[9]

Hadfield originated the term "hypnoanalysis" during World War I in working with cases of amnesia and paralyses. He utilized age regression techniques to help his patients to uncover and relive early traumatic experiences.

After a long history of rejection and of skepticism by the medical professions, in 1955 the British Medical Association endorsed the teaching of hypnosis, and in 1958 the American Medical Association and the American Psychological Association followed suit.

Interest in hypnosis seems to be cyclic and there is a current resurgence of interest in the psychotherapeutic uses of hypnosis as well as its uses in education[12], in sports[8], relaxation[11], and in criminal investigation.[13]

References

1. Bernheim, H. *Hypnosis and Suggestion in Psychotherapy.* New York: University Books, 1964.
2. Braid, J. *Neurypnology.* New York: Arno Books, 1976.
3. Breuer, J. and Freud, S. *Studies in Hysteria.* New York: Nervous and Mental Disease Monographs, 1950.
4. Darnton, R. *Mesmerism.* Cambridge, Mass.: Harvard University Press, 1968.
5. Deleuze, F. *Histoire Critique du Magnetism.* Paris: Hipolyte and Bodiere, 1813, p. 34.
6. Esdaile, J. *Natural and Mesmeric Clairvoyance.* New York: Arno Books, 1975.
7. Frankel, F. *Hypnosis. Trance as a Coping Mechanism.* New York: Plenum Medical Book Co., 1976.
8. Galwey, T. *The Game of Inner Tennis.* New York: Random House, 1964.
9. Kline, M.V. *Freud and Hypnosis: The Interaction of Psychodynamics and Hypnosis.* New York: Julian Press, 1958.
10. Kroger, W.S. *Clinical and Experimental Hypnosis.* 2nd Edition. Philadelphia: Lippincott, 1977.
11. LeCron, L.M. *Self-Hypnotism.* Englewood Cliffs, N.J.: Prentice Hall, 1964.
12. Lozanov, G. *Suggestology and Outlines of Suggestopedy.* New York: Gordon and Breach, 1978.
13. Reiser, M. Hypnosis and its uses in law enforcement. *The Police Journal (British),* January-March, 1978, 24-33.
14. Tinterow, M. *Foundations of Hypnosis.* Springfield, Ill.: Thomas, 1970.

CHAPTER 2
BASIC PSYCHODYNAMICS

Brief Neurology

The average adult brain weighs about 3½ pounds. It is a vast electro-chemical system which manufactures its own electricity by "burning" sugar. Composed of some 10-12 billion cells, it is capable of storing and handling some 10-quadrillion facts, ideas, images and bits of information. The brain has the capacity to process, store, or utilize more than 600 memories per second for a hundred years. That totals 51,840,000 bits of information per day handled by the mental computer. Its infinite storage and cybernetic capacity can out perform a dozen of the most modern computers combined. With fantastic speed it accepts and transfers messages, codes and stores information, makes decisions, learns, modifies information and sends instructions to all parts of the body continuously.[8]

The brain can be divided into three basic systems:
1. The Sensory Input System — receives information from the senses: the eyes, ear, skin, muscles, tongue, and nose.
2. The Modulation or Control System — evaluates new information with respect to other incoming and outgoing signals as well as to memories and past experiences. It determines how this information affects a person's activity and immediate survival and makes decisions as to what course of action may be necessary.
3. The Motor Output System — controls the brain's emotional and motor response to any stimulus. It puts into action what it is told to do by the control system.

The interaction between these three systems is very complex and rapid involving a multitude of neuronal interconnections, both electrical and chemical.

Brain Waves

The brain's electrical activity reflects its state of arousal or quiescence. During stage 3 and 4 sleep the brain produces slow waves called delta waves with a frequency of 1 to 3 cycles per second. Normal wakefulness is characterized by relatively fast brain waves called beta waves with a frequency of 18 to 30 cycles per second. Alpha waves, 7 to 13 cycles per second are associated with relaxation and can be brought under conscious control to some degree by biofeedback techniques. Similarly, theta waves, 4 to 8 cycles per second, are associated with an introspective, restful state conducive to creativity. Studies of brain waves and hypnosis suggest that sleep and hypnosis are quite different states. The electroencephalograph tracings of hypnosis are similar to those of the waking state.[13]

Recently some interesting discoveries have been made about the brain's two distinct hemispheres. The left hemisphere of most peoples' brains (most left-handers excepted) deal with logical thinking processes involving language. It processes information sequentially, one bit after another in an orderly fashion. In contrast, the right hemisphere is specialized for simultaneous processing in a holistic, relational way. Right hemispheric consciousness appears to be involved in meditation, intuition, imagery, art and creativity. In the past, Western psychology has been primarily concerned with left hemisphere consciousness and with logical thought. However, activities involving altered states of consciousness including hypnosis and subconscious motivations, likely involve right hemisphere functions.[10]

Dr. Wilder Penfield, a Canadian neurosurgeon at McGill University, did some important brain probe research beginning in 1951 while working with epileptic patients and made some very important discoveries. Perhaps his most significant finding was that past events are recorded in detail in the brain along with the associated feelings that accompanied the event. Penfield concluded that whenever a normal person is paying attention to something he is simultaneously recording it in the temporal cortex of each hemisphere. He concluded that the brain functions much like a high fidelity recorder, putting on tape, as it were, every experience from the time of birth, possibly even before birth, and that these experiences and associated feelings are available for replay today in as vivid a form as when they first occurred.[11]

The Nervous System

The brain and spinal cord constitute the central nervous system which sends and receives sensory and motor impulses.

Nerves running out from the central nervous system can be classified into two groups, those running to the striped or striate muscles, usually grouped with the central nervous system, and those running to smooth muscles and glands which are grouped together as the autonomic nervous system (self-regulating). The autonomic nervous system controls such activities as digestion and circulation which go on even when a person is asleep or unconscious. The autonomic nervous system has two divisions, the sympathetic division which is dominant in fear, violent and excited activities, and the parasympathetic division which functions to conserve and protect bodily resources and is dominant in quiet states. Although they often act antagonistically, the two systems interact in complex ways which are not fully understood.[9]

The autonomic nervous system is very important, since in the altered state of consciousness known as hypnosis, the individual may transcend customary limits of neuromuscular control as seen in ideomotor responses and in physiological and biochemical changes which can occur through subconscious mediation.[14]

Penfield's original observation that perceptions require one's conscious attention in order to be recorded in the brain needs to be altered in light of more recent research. Hilgard's work on the "hidden observer"[6], and recent research at the Medical Center of the State University of New York[4], confirm that perception occurs simultaneously at conscious and subconscious levels. This has tremendous implications for investigative hypnosis in that it is possible in some instances that a witness or victim may insist that nothing was perceived consciously and yet may have perceived and recorded key information at a level outside of conscious awareness.

An interesting case which tends to confirm the dual recording hypothesis involved a homicide committed while the key witness was extremely intoxicated on alcohol and other drugs. When questioned by detectives she could not remember any significant details, however, under hypnosis she was an excellent witness recalling numerous conversational details and providing an excellent composite description of a suspect. All of this information was later corroborated as to accuracy.[12]

Psychodynamics

One system of explanation of the mind uses the concepts of conscious, preconscious, and unconscious ego systems.[7]

Conscious

Much like the beam of a flashlight, only a small portion of experience can be conscious at any one time. The rest fades into the background outside of conscious awareness. One moment we are aware of doing, feeling, thinking, imagining or remembering and the next moment it disappears into the preconscious background while we become aware of something else. This usually results from a shift in attention or a change in environment.

Preconscious

The scope of the preconscious is relatively large. It includes present and past perceptions and memories as well as representations of drive states and pressures of conscience. A vast reservoir of the preconscious is available to consciousness on demand but a great deal of it is not readily available because of defenses against recall imposed by the individual's ego.

Unconscious

Much of the unconscious part of the ego has been conscious or preconscious at one time, however, unconscious material is barred from consciousness or preconscious representation by the ego's use of the defense of repression. Unconscious ego elements are usually subjected to primary processes so that they become fantastically illogical. The primary process of the unconscious involves primitive symbols, the coexistence of opposites, condensation (combining of drives), displacement (transfer of energy) from one idea to another.

The repressed unconscious ego contains many active infantile fantasies, day dreams, wishes, hopes, expectations, fears and conflicts. Material from the repressed unconscious appears in dreams, in neurosis and psychosis, drug intoxication and in sensory deprivation situations.

Conscious and preconscious systems operate according to the reality principle which utilizes secondary processes that are reality oriented. This involves the uses of reason and logic. One of the functions of the normal ego is to maintain optimal tension throughout the entire psychodynamic system. The child's mind can be seen as being mostly unconscious at birth and gradually differentiating as development slowly proceeds. Gradually, reality testing improves and the capacity for conscience develops.

Conscious and Subconscious

For purposes of simplicity the mind can be divided into two main components.
1. The conscious mind, which contains about one-eighth of the total. It deals with cognitive functions and external reality using logic and reason. It has partial control over nervous system and muscle functions.
2. The subconscious, which contains about seven-eighths of the total. It includes both the preconscious and unconscious levels as described above. It controls the sympathetic division of the autonomic nervous system which in turn controls the involuntary muscles, organs and glands as well as the actions of the vital organs. This is why a person who is unconscious continues to breathe and maintain vital functions including basic metabolism.

The subconscious mind is alert and on duty 24 hours a day, seven days a week; it never sleeps. Common examples are the new mother who becomes immediately alert when hearing her infant's cry while sleeping through a thunder storm; the effect of comments of operating room personnel on patients as they may influence normal, speedy or slow recovery. Cheek's work in recovering memories around the birth experience suggests that both pre and perinatal experiences are recorded reflexly by the active subconscious of the baby.[3]

PERSONALITY DEVELOPMENT

A useful and comparatively simple conceptualization of personality development is that proposed by Eric Berne[1,2] and popularized by others.[5] This system views the personality of the individual as consisting of three parts, the parent, the adult, and the child. The various conflicts and interactions among these three parts can help explain many defenses, symptoms and behaviors.

The Parent

The parent consists of the huge collection of recordings in the brain made essentially during the first five years of life. These are messages and events involving real or symbolic parents and are recorded in the parent part. These inputs are recorded verbatim without editing and include all of the rules and taboos, the do's and don'ts, the criticisms and the praise.

As the child develops, more complicated injunctions are internalized such as, "eat everything on your plate," "never trust a cop," "women are devious," etc. Whether positive or negative, these rules are recorded as truths from the powerful authority figures who pronounce them.

Some of the parental "never" and "always" rules and generalizations may become the origins of later compulsions and eccentricities in the individual. Early parent data is supplemented by outside authority figures such as teachers, movie stars and other celebrities, as well as older siblings. The parent part is recorded from a very dependent position with the child feeling small, helpless, dependent and vulnerable.

The Adult

The adult part begins to develop as the child increases its contact with the environment, beginning with locomotion, exhibiting of curiosity and attempting to master the environment. As this occurs the child no longer feels helpless and gains a sense of separateness and independence. This results in a feeling of control over the environment. The child can begin to compare what is taught by parents with its own experience. It begins to gather its own data and develop a thought concept of life. However, this early adult is fragile and easily overpowered by dominant parent commands and by residual fears of the child part. As the adult matures, there is more self-direction. Parent data is updated, either validated or rejected. The adult part gains the capability of turning off inappropriate recordings and developing its own value system. However, under stress overloads, the adult can regress back to the helpless dependent child state, experiencing and behaving at that level.

References

1. Berne, E. *Transactional Analysis in Psychotherapy.* New York: Grove Press, 1961.
2. Berne, E. *Games People Play.* New York: Grove Press, 1964.
3. Cheek, D.B. Unconscious perceptions of meaningful sounds during surgical anesthesia as revealed under hypnosis. *American Journal of Clinical Hypnosis,* 1959, *1,* 101-113.
4. Frank, J. and Levinson, H. Report on non-conscious learning. *Academic Therapy,* Winter 1976-77, 133-153.
5. Harris, T. *I'm OK, You're OK.* New York: Avon Books, 1967.
6. Hilgard, E.R. *Divided Consciousness.* New York: Wiley Interscience, 1977.
7. Kline, M.V. *Psychodynamics and Hypnosis.* Springfield, Ill.: Thomas, 1967.

8. Maltz, M. *Psychocybernetics*. New York: Prentice Hall, 1960.
9. McCleary, R.A. and Moore, R. *Subcortical Mechanisms of Behavior*. New York: Basic Books, 1965.
10. Ornstein, R. *The Psychology of Consciousness*. New York: Viking Press, 1972.
11. Penfield, W. and Roberts, L. *Speech and Brain Mechanisms*. Princeton, N.J.: Princeton University Press, 1959.
12. Reiser, M. Hypnosis is an aid in a homicide investigation. *The American Journal of Clinical Hypnosis,* October, 1974, 84-87.
13. Schwartz, G.E. and Shapiro, D. *Consciousness and Self-Regulation*. New York: Plenum Press, 1976.
14. Zinberg, N.E. *Alternate States of Consciousness*. New York: The Free Press, 1977.

CHAPTER 3
EMOTIONAL DEVELOPMENT AND MENTAL HEALTH*

Police officers and other criminal justice professionals deal with mental health problems on the job every day. The professional person knows that in addition to the problems of citizens and suspects, his own inner security and emotional state profoundly influence the outcome of routine transactions. Increasingly, the modern officer is not only interested in how to handle the emotionally disturbed person, but also in the dynamics of the problem. These are legitimate and necessary knowledge areas in deepening his evolving professionalism.

Influences on Personality Development

Although there are influences throughout life which affect personality development, the process can be viewed as analagous to a pyramid structure. The wide base of the pyramid represents the earliest years of life and forms the basic foundation for emotional stability.

There is considerable evidence that as early as age six or seven much of one's permanent personality structure has been built. The structure is added to, modified and sometimes renovated over the years, but the basic architecture remains.

Inner Drives, Values, Self, Conscience and Value System

Human beings have survival motives, social motives and ego-integrative motives. Survival motives or drives are related to bodily needs such as hunger, thirst and fear. Social motives include drives such as maternal, sex, dominance and submission, and aggression. Ego-integrative motives include a drive for achievement, sometimes called achievement-motivation and other goal-directed behavior. An important fact is that motives

*From Reiser, M. *Practical Psychology for Police Officers.* Springfield, Ill.: Thomas, 1973.

are not only conscious but also unconsciously based.
Unconscious motivation sometimes leads to irrational or unusual behavior. Drives such as manipulation, activity, and curiosity are not directly related to physiological bases, but still seem to be important needs in human beings. Those drives which emanate from within the individual not only insure his survival, but also the development of more complex behavior. The self-integrative drives are essential to the development of one's self-concept which results in a personal identity and the ability to differentiate oneself from other organisms.

Conscience is a mix of internalized limits and restrictions residing in the individual. As these become elaborated and are juxtaposed against ego-integrative drives, a value system emerges whose function is to allow the individual to live with minimal internal and environmental conflict.

Outer — Important Adults, Wider Environment

A person exists and grows in a particular environment. Many significant environmental influences impinge on and help to shape some of the internal structure. Parents and other important adults in the child's environment are crucial in this regard. As models for the child they gratify survival needs, set standards and limits and also supply the basic learning which the child emulates and internalizes as part of his developing personality structure.

Parents represent the world and ensure physical and emotional survival to the child. As the child develops, becomes less dependent on parents and exercises his new social skills, he can move away from the home situation and begin to explore and learn from the wider environment. But he can do this only after he has established a sense of confidence and adequacy based on what he has learned earlier in his own family situation.

Interesting work by Spitz[20] has indicated convincingly that the first year of life is critical. What follows is based on the many important emotional events occurring in the infant's early life. In extreme cases, it can become a life and death question based on the amount and quality of emotional gratification of basic affectual needs of the infant. Without adequate mothering, arrested development or even death may occur.

Physical Factors — Hormones, Diet and Exercise

Hormone imbalance caused by physiological malfunction,

diet, or trauma can result in physical and psychological dysfunction. The proper balance of male and female sex hormones appears to be necessary if the individual is to develop adequately.

In cases of hormone imbalance or malfunction, it is possible to supplement or balance body chemistry by prescribed medication. This is commonly done to counter hormone deficiency when testicles or ovaries are removed, and for menopausal conditions resulting from diminished female hormone output.

Both sexes seem to have cycles over the month. Periods of high energy and well-being may alternate with apathy and indifference. However, the critical factor seems to be basic life style rather than the fluctuations in it.

Diet has come under increasing scrutiny lately in terms of its role in maintaining physical and emotional health. Not only amounts of food, but kinds of food seem to be significant in maintaining equilibrium.

Nutritionists today[22] feel that refined sugar is a culprit which leads to tooth decay, to excess weight and cardiovascular problems. Protein foods on the other hand provide long-range energy and the necessary building blocks for maintenance of life.

Increasingly, the trio of smoking, sugar, and coffee are being looked upon as harmful and disruptive of healthy functioning.

Overweight is a common problem in our society and is frequently related to emotional frustration with overeating as a compensatory mechanism. There are many fads and forms of diet propounded and many of them will work on a short-term basis. However, the reality is that for long-range success, diet is not effective without a change in one's eating habits. This means accepting the nutritional importance of protein foods and minimizing sugar and starches, the carbohydrate group.

In addition to eating patterns, maintaining a desired weight is related to one's self concept and sense of worth. If a person feels worthwhile and deserving of looking attractive, he is willing to do what is required to achieve that goal. However, if he unconsciously feels unworthy, guilty or unacceptable, in spite of conscientious dieting and daily weighing, his long-range goal will probably be frustrated because of his unconscious need for self-criticism and punishment.

The lack of exercise may well kill us in the long run. As members of the animal kingdom we were provided with muscles which must be exercised in order to remain healthy.

However, our way of life in Western society with its technology, urbanization and emphasis on leisure and non-exertion have led to serious muscular disuse and consequent development of a variety of psycho-physical symptoms.

There is some evidence to suggest[12,16] that adequate exercise can have beneficial effects on a wide range of psychosomatic disturbances. These include such ailments as migraine headaches, ulcers, backaches, colitis, asthma, arthritis, skin conditions and hypertension.

Some interesting research recently[1] has shown that we tend to operate on the basis of a circadian rhythm. This means that man and other animals are affected by day and night, and biologically adapt by developing certain cycles or rhythms. One of the interesting findings was that male sex hormone production seems to be at its maximum early in the morning rather than late at night, although we are accustomed to thinking of nighttime for sexual activity.

Diet and exercise appear to be closely related to the problem of heart attacks in our society.[18] More and more men and women are being affected earlier in life by disabling cardiovascular disturbances. One of the culprits in the development of atherosclerosis or fatty deposits on the walls of the arteries, is cholesterol.

Although cholesterol is a necessary substance manufactured by the body, its concentration in the blood can also be increased by diet, stress, and lack of exercise. In addition to cholesterol, fatty substances called triglycerides seem to be involved. Although excessive amounts of cholesterol in the blood correlate positively with probability of coronaries, when cholesterol and triglycerides are both high, the likelihood increases significantly.

One prediction table indicates that at age forty with increased cholesterol and triglycerides the probability of a coronary is 75 percent and at age fifty-five there is a 91 percent chance of an attack. A simple test called phenotyping can determine whether the rise in these substances is caused by diet, physiological dysfunction, or genetic inheritance. In many cases, proper diet, exercise and perhaps medication can halt or reverse this process.

MENTAL HEALTH — WHAT IS NORMAL?

The term normal has been misunderstood over the years. It

isn't simply the presence or absence of something. Normality is hard to describe because it is a statistical concept which is based on the rule of the majority. What most people are like in a society constitutes the norm. This varies in difference subcultures.

The Continuum of Mental Health

Although it is easier and appears to save energy to put labels on people, and to view mental health as being either absent or present, emotional or mental health is actually a range or continuum of behaviors. In the center of the mental health continuum is normality which represents the majority of people with a wide range of individual traits and idiosyncrasies.

Rather than asking if someone is normal, the essential question is, can the person cope adequately in his daily life? How well-adjusted is he inwardly and in his interpersonal relationships in the environment? All people have problems of one kind or another. The issue is not the presence of problems but how the problems are coped with that determines one's mental health.

At the extreme low end of the mental health continuum are severe disturbances in internal and environmental coping reflected in poor reality-testing, an inability for adequate self-care, or being a danger to self or to someone else. The gravely disabled individual may be labeled psychotic or borderline psychotic, or with somewhat better coping, a neurotic.

At the upper end of the emotional health continuum are those individuals who are extremely emotionally stable, who have had just the right combination of factors in their early environment genetically and developmentally to predispose them to handling stress in an optimal way with minimum interference in their everyday functioning. This group has been studied very little.

It is important to conceptualize mental health not as a static state, but as a fluid process. A person's functioning level varies on a day-to-day, weekly or monthly basis, particularly under stress situations. It is possible for any individual, no matter how stable, to crack mentally under certain circumstances with sufficient stress and tension being applied.

However, most of us establish an equilibrium and stablize our functioning, so that we operate within a particular range of the mental health continuum. Unless some unusual trauma or stress situation develops to temporarily displace us from our accustomed adjustment, we usually maintain our established coping pattern.

Love and Hate, Conscience and Reality

The main forces which tend to influence our emotional state and behavior are love and hate, our inner sense of right and wrong, and our striving for mastery over the environment. Love and hate are strong forces that operate at both conscious and unconscious levels.

It is common to love and hate someone simultaneously or have one side of the ambivalence predominating. In extreme situations the love-hate conflict may be so severe that killing with kindness may emerge as a symptom.

Theoretically, warmth, tenderness and affection derive from the constructive drives which include the self-preservative needs. Hate emanates from the destructive drives which relate to rage, self-punishment or death. Ideally the constructive and destructive drives are fused and help to control and channel each other. This allows some of the energy from both drives to be used to the individual's advantage.

The content and quality of one's conscience is largely learned. Infants and small children require outside limit setting, guidance and protection because they are not able to provide it for themselves. As they grow, they model themselves after significant admired or feared people in the environment. They internalize some of the personal traits, taboos, prohibitions and values and incorporate them into a personal conscience.

If the environmental influences have been positive, the values and rules of society will be adopted and adhered to by the individual and he will feel guilt if he transgresses these limits. He will also be more self-directed and will value other people's rights as much as he does his own. He operates by his own inner control system.

The individual who has had poor models in the environment may internalize few controls and is less likely to generate guilt to prohibit him from behavior that is detrimental to himself or others. This type of individual remains more outer-directed and like the child will expect someone to stop him from behaving in an undesirable way, to provide external limits since he doesn't have enough inner control or self-motivation.

Small children are curious and need to explore the environment. This need for mastery continues as a drive in people throughout life. When the drive for mastery has been positively reinforced, the individual develops a sense of adventurousness, optimism and looking forward to challenges in order to gain satisfaction from exercising his ability to master new situations.

However, if he has been traumatized in the past by being punished or discouraged from exploring, he will probably develop fears and anxieties about new situations and the unfamiliar. This will inhibit and shackle him in later life.

Insecurity coupled with the drive for mastery can lead to a dilemma, the desire for certainty in all things. In this individual, ambiguity or uncertainty causes tension and anxiety and is felt to be intolerable. He may then try to prevent anxiety by using absolutes. He must see things concretely as good or bad rather than exploring further to seek more accurate answers. The ability to tolerate uncertainty and ambiguity is one measure of a person's self-assurance and maturity. This is open-mindedness.

Because much of what we are is learned, we are all very dependent on our unique environment for what we eventually become. The environment includes significant parents and parent substitutes with their ability to provide optimal amounts of love and discipline, and additional influences such as total family situation, school, diet, friends, interpersonal relationships, and value systems. All of these influences interact in various ways to contribute to personality, character structure, and lifestyle.

Some Healthy Qualities

Although mental or emotional health is very difficult to define and is often characterized by an absence of illness, there are some traits related to a healthy state of functioning.

A. A wide variety of sources of gratification.

This involves a variety of interests, ways of satisfying basic needs rather than having all eggs in one basket. It suggests a broad dimension, being well-rounded rather than narrow in regard to sources of satisfaction in life.

B. Flexibility under stress.

Stresses are inherent in living and vary from situation to situation and from month to month. How stresses are handled is the important measure of our emotional stability. If every small and stressful event is perceived and reacted to as a major crisis, then we are constricted and self-limiting. If we can continue to cope flexibly under stress, we retain our perspective and judgment resulting in more constructive options for handling the stress situations.

C. Recognizing and accepting our own limitations and assets.

We tend to be our own worst enemies. Although most of us have tremendous potential, we utilize only a small portion of it. We tend to limit our own functioning and downgrade our assets. False humility or modesty is a self-limiting attitude with grandiosity as an opposite side of the same coin. By being able to accept our own worth-whileness and value as a human being, we can come to recognize our potentials and aptitudes more realistically and have less need to live in fantasy, feel frustrated and angry.

D. Treating other people as individuals.

If we value ourselves, we also value other people. If we accept ourselves, we accept others. Putting people into pigeonholes and labeling them is convenient, but a highly inaccurate and unfair process. Others must be seen and evaluated as individuals rather than stereotyped.

E. Being active and productive.

All of the genius and potential in the world means very little when it is not used constructively. Extremely high I.Q. is not genius if it is not implemented. In order to achieve we must put into practice our philosophy and our values. When we live what we believe, a sense of well-being and satisfaction results.

STRESS, ANXIETY AND DEFENSES

Stresses are ever present in life, both from internal and external sources. Anxiety is an alerting mechanism and also a measure of our ability to handle tension in a particular stress situation.

Because of the constant bombardment of stimuli from our internal and external environment, we need defenses to protect us from being overwhelmed. The kind and amount of defenses that we utilize are important in successful coping and vary according to personality and how much stress we are attempting to deal with.

Adapting to Stress — The Vital Balance

One measure of emotional health is how we adapt to stress. Typically we try to maintain a balance among inner and outer forces which allows us to function in a state of equilibrium. In this state we are able to cope with the usual kinds of stresses on a day-to-day basis without becoming emotionally upset of unbalanced. Menninger calls this the vital balance.[13]

Selye[19] has described what he calls the general adaptation syndrome which outlines the general bodily responses to stress. First, an alarm reaction occurs, with some shock, and consequent reduction in activities of the individual, which is followed by a large mobilization of forces to meet the threat. In the second stage, there is resistance to the stress and this state is maintained if the adaptation to the threat is adequate at this level. Third, is the stage of exhaustion where the previously acquired adaptation is lost and the person is no longer able to cope.

Cannon[14] has described homeostasis as a state of equilibrium between subsystems in any organism. This balance protects the body and allows the individual to function without the need to constantly attend and expend energy on the subsystems while external work is being accomplished.

Under an excessive amount of stress, the individual will go into a state of crisis.[10] The previous balance is upset, he feels confused, anxious, overwhelmed and temporarily unable to cope. At this point he can go either way, in a downward spiral emotionally, or he can reconsitute, rearrange his focus and establish an even better emotional adjustment than before. In this regard, a crisis state can have positive value.

Anxiety — Real, Neurotic, and Anticipatory

Anxiety can serve a useful self-preservation function or it can also become an inhibiting interference. Real anxiety is a result of real danger. In this context it is hard to separate fear from the real anxiety someone experiences when facing an attacking animal.

Anxiety can also be lifesaving in alerting us to a potentially dangerous situation and permitting us to take the necessary steps to avoid injury. This anticipatory anxiety stimulates adrenalin flow and the arousal network to put us at the maximum level of efficiency. However, this type of signal anxiety can develop into a problem when felt in a situation which does not justify the signal.

This happens when we react with extreme fear to situations that realistically do not present real danger. Phobias, which are exaggerated learned fears are examples of this. Neurotic anxiety tends to be uncontrolled and usually emanates from fears and unconscious conflicts within the person.

Symptoms — Problems in Coping

When the emotional balance has been upset by excessive stress, our normal defenses are breached and we are no longer able to cope adequately, we develop symptoms or signs of emotional disturbance. Symptoms are not primary causes, but indicators of distress. The individual may develop psychosomatic symptoms such as headache, backache, stomach-ache, diarrhea, ulcers, depression, feelings of being persecuted and in extreme cases, hallucinations and delusions.

Symptoms are idiosyncratic. Why a person develops specific symptoms is difficult to answer. It is likely that there are certain predispositions within organ systems of the individual as well as learned ways of reacting based on models in the early environment and on past successful defensive maneuvers. Although over-determined, symptoms are useful indicators of the kind of distress and can be interpreted by a trained person. The symptom is a symbolic condensation of the basic underlying conflict, including the wish, the fear and the self-punishment.

Defenses — normal and Exaggerated

All human beings normally employ a variety of defenses in coping with the ordinary stresses and problems of everyday life. However, if under high stress, our normal defenses are unable to cope with the situation, we will call in additional defenses or intensify those already in operation.

Some of the more common defenses are suppression, repression, displacement, projection, rationalization, reaction-formation, denial, and turning-on-the-self.

These defenses are activated and maintained on an unconscious level. However, it is possible for a person to become aware of his defenses. Suppression is the control of certain impulses and emotions. It may involve keeping in angry or sexual feelings habitually or in situations where they are deemed inappropriate.

Repression is the unconscious forgetting and keeping out of awareness ideas or emotions which are too difficult to handle or are unacceptable. Displacement is the controlling of emotion toward one person and expressing it toward a substitute person or thing. An example of this would be feeling angry at the boss and going home and kicking the dog or yelling at the wife.

Projection is a defense which attempts to get rid of unacceptable feelings by externalizing them onto somebody else in the environment and then attributing the ideas or the feelings to the other person. An extreme example of projection is that of feeling anger and hate toward someone, but because the emotions are unacceptable, they are attributed to the person that one is angry with. The defense become, "He is angry at me, and wants to do me in. Therefore, I am justified in feeling some animosity toward him."

Rationalization is the process of making excuses for what we want to do to alleviate our guilt feelings about doing them. For example, a man who gets involved in an extramarital affair may rationalize it by saying all his friends are doing it, so why shouldn't he.

Reaction-formation is the turning of a feeling into its opposite. An example is the Milquetoast person who behaves in a very subdued, passive and mild way rather than show his underlying anger and hostility which would make him feel guilty and unworthy. The person who is overly polite and saccharine is also using a reaction-formation defense.

Denial is a defense in which one refuses to accept the reality of a situation. An example is the husband who denies that his wife really means it when she says she wants to divorce him. He is unable to cope with this truth, so he will either not hear what she is saying or interpret it as he wants in order to maintain his equilibrium.

Compensation is another interesting defense because it can be used in a constructive way. The use of this defense helps to make up for shortcomings by developing compensating skills in other areas. An example of this is the boy who has seriously-injured his legs and is told he will never walk again. He compensates by rigorous daily exercising and becomes an Olympic runner.

Defenses are useful and necessary in order to help us maintain our emotional equilibrium. However, when they are overused constantly, without an adequate readjustment in emotional balance, our mental economy is strained and chances of emotional upset increase. However, it is important to realize that people generally do the best they are capable of at that point in time.

EMOTIONAL UPSET

Under sufficient stress even the most stable individual will become emotionally upset, and in extreme prolonged situations even mentally ill.

Types of Disorders

There are four main categories of emotional disorders. The first group are the psychoneuroses, or neuroses, which are unsuccessful attempts to handle anxiety. Second, the personality disorders which attempt to displace conflicts toward the outside world and then act-out in a repetitive pattern of behavior. Third, the psychosomatic disorders which are bodily ailments resulting from the attempt to drain off emotional tension into physical channels. The fourth category includes the psychotic level disorders in which there is ego fragmentation and a significant loss of ability to face reality.

The psychoneuroses are classified according the nature of the defenses against anxiety.[3]

A. Anxiety Reaction — chronic, diffuse anxiety, palpitations, sweating, nausea, breathing difficulties, diarrhea, indigestion, headaches.

B. Conversion Reaction — inner conflict represented by symbolic somatic disturbances. Hysterial blindness or leg paralysis.

C. Dissociative Reaction — avoids anxiety by walling off consciousness. Amnesia, state of confusion, sleepwalking, multiple personality.

D. Phobic Reaction — one or more severe unrealistic fears such as of animals, dirt, enclosed spaces, heights, water, etc.

E. Obsessive-Compulsive Reaction — persistent unpleasant thoughts (obsessions) and strong impulses to perform repeated ritualistic acts (compulsions). Uses defenses of reaction-formation and undoing.

F. Depressive Reaction — chronic dejection and self-depreciation. Complains and withdraws from social activities.

Personality disorders are known as Character Disorders.

A. Personality Pattern Disturbances — deep-seated problems of personality.
  1. Inadequate Personality — responses to the world are below par — dull.
  2. Schizoid Personality — cold, aloof, daydreams and fantasies without any real emotional relationships.
  3. Cyclothymic Personality — wide mood swings from elation to severe depression.
  4. Paranoid Personality — overly sensitive and suspicious of everyone's motives — complains loudly that world is

against him. "Nobody pushes me around."
  B. Personality Trait Disturbances.
    1. Emotionally Unstable Personality — low frustration, tolerance, self-centered and childish.
    2. Passive-Aggressive Personality — may be passive-dependent with clinging and parasitic orientation, or passive-aggressive using passive resistance as in being stubborn or obstinate or aggressive with open hostility and rebelliousness such as in temper tantrums.
  C. Sociopathic Personality Disturbances (Psychopathic) — lack of conformity to society's rules and regulations.
    1. Anti-social Reaction — self-centered and pleasure oriented, lacks guilt and doesn't learn from experience — lies, steals, and cheats.
    2. Dyssocial Reactions — relatively mature and stable but comes from environment with distorted values and is in conflict with the law.
    3. Sexual Deviation — sexual immaturity including homosexuality, transvestism, exhibitionism, voyeurism, sadism and masochism.
    4. Addictions — alcohol and drugs.
  D. Transient Situational Personality Disorders — acute responses to stress in normal individuals.
    1. Gross Stress Reaction — combat fatigues.
    2. Adult Situation Reaction — react to new situations such as marriage, school, new job, as traumatic.

Psychosomatic Disorders can be categorized as follows:
  A. Skin Reactions such as rash, itching anus or vulva.
  B. Musculoskeietal Reactions — headache, backache, cramps.
  C. Respiratory Reactions — hyperventilation, asthma.
  D. Cardiovascular Reactions — migraine, hypertension, chest pains.
  E. Gastrointestinal Reactions — dyspepsia, ulcers, obesity, diarrhea.
  F. Genito-urinary Reactions — menstrual dysfunctions, impotence, frigidity.
  G. Endocrine Reactions — infertility.
  H. Nervous System Reactions — chronic fatigue.

The Psychotic Reactions are as follows:
  A. Schizophrenic Reactions — severe difficulty in interpersonal relations, withdrawal from reality, personality disorganization.
  B. Affective Reactions — severe disturbance of affect with

thought, behavior and mood changes, manic-depressive symptoms.
   C. Involutional Reactions — depression with physical complaints, usually late in life.
   D. Paranoid Reactions — ideas of persecution or grandiose delusions.
      1. Paranoid State — generalized oversuspiciousness.
      2. Paranoia — an encapsulated delusion with relatively normal functioning in other areas.
   E. Organic Brain Disorders.

Levels of Dysorganization — The Downward Spiral

Some of the most common stresses which tend to precipitate emotional upset are marital conflicts, job problems, guilt feelings, and threats to the self-image.

Common early warning signs of emotional upset are:
1. Changes from usual behavior.
2. Anxiety and irritability.
3. Sleep disturbances.
4. Depression, withdrawal, comments about suicide.
5. Excessive drinking, not under the individual's control.
6. Sexual problems.
7. Excessive altercations.
8. Accident prone — physical or traffic accidents.
9. Argumentative — feeling persecuted.
10. Physical complaints of a chronic nature.
11. Excessive discussion of home problems.
12. Deterioration in work performance.
13. Loss of interest and self-confidence.

   Menninger[13] has outlined the downward spiral to levels of dysorganization as one becomes emotionally upset.
   1. First level — Slight impairment of control and some failure in coping, resulting in nervousness. Symptoms are a conscious effort at self-control. Inhibitions, exaggerated perception, tearfulness, over gaiety, restlessness, instability, worry, denial, minor somatic and sexual dysfunctions. This is a reversible or transitional state. Some cases recover, some get worse.
   2. Second level — Development of neurotic level symptoms. There is subjective discomfort and anxiety — a sense of failure, uselessness, incompetence and of being a disappointment to oneself and others. Work

becomes drudgery and friends seem perverse or provocative.
  3. Third level — Outbursts of aggression and destructive impulses — assaults and social offenses. Indicates greater weakness than second level disturbances. This level is generally characterized by loss of control of aggressive impulses and lashing out, may be homicidal.
  4. Fourth level — Abandonment of the will to live, psychological death, which may lead to successful suicide.

Skeletons From The Past

Missildine[15] describes the inner child of the past and how we are all influenced in varying degrees by our childhood experiences.

All too frequently unsatisfied childhood needs, frustrations and fixations remain active in us as adults and on an unconscious level tend to influence our behavior as if we are still living in the past. Many of these childhood needs are no longer appropriate. Environment has changed and our needs and capabilities as adults have changed as well.

In order to avoid the repetitive kinds of emotional conflicts that constitute the broken record syndrome, a person must come to terms with his old skeletons. This involves psychological separation from parents and the development of a self-image as an equal and valuable adult to replace the old self-image of helpless, dependent, unequal child.

When this change is achieved, one should have the conviction of being on a par with any other adult regardless of the title or station in life. Equality is now measured in terms of human value rather than by status or material goods.

Another relic from the past which can cause serious difficulty is the internalized parent skeleton. This is the harsh, overly punitive conscience which is based on outmoded comparisons and values. This is the dinosaur skeleton that administers self-punishment and evokes depressive feelings, isolation and despair.

In order to open the closet and remove the skeleton, it is necessary to evaluate one's parents from the perspective of adult rather than from the vantage point of the child.

By seeing parents as fallible human beings who have weaknesses and faults, the old sense of awe and reverence can be replaced by a realistic acceptance of parents as people who are no better or worse than most others. One can reevaluate himself more realistically from the stance of equality toward other adults rather than from the position of inferiority. Among men in police work, one of the common symptoms of the parent skeleton is the ambivalence felt toward people in authority. There is usually a mixture of reverence and awe toward high ranking officers along with underlying resentment and anger. This is reminiscent of the feeling that children have toward when they are vulnerable, helpless and resentful of their dependency.

References

1. *Biological Rhythms in Psychiatry and Medicine.* Chevy Chase, Md.: National Institute of Mental Health, 1970.
2. Brodsky, S. *Psychological Training Techniques in Law Enforcement and Corrections.* Ann Arbor, Mich.: Center for Forensic Psychiatry, 1970.
3. Cameron, N. *Personality Development and Psychopathology.* Boston: Houghton Mifflin, 1963.
4. Cannon, W. *The Wisdom of the Body.* New York: Norton, 1939.
5. *Emotions and Physical Health.* Metropolitan Life Insurance Company, 1959.
6. Fink, D. *For People Under Pressure.* New York, Simon and Schuster, 1956.
7. Hilgard, E.R. *Introduction to Psychology.* New York: Harcourt, Brace and World, 1962.
8. Hollander, E.P. and Hunt, R. *Current Perspectives in Social Phychology.* New York: Oxford University Press, 1963.
9. Jersild, A.T. *Child Psychology.* Englewood Cliffs, N.J.: Prentice Hall, 1960.
10. Levi, L. *Stress: Sources, Management and Prevention.* New York: Liveright, 1967.
11. Levinson, H. *Emotional Health in the World of Work.* New York: Harper and Row, 1964.
12. Lewis, H.R. and M.E. *Psychosomatics.* New York: Viking Press, 1972.
13. Menninger, K., et al. *The Vital Balance.* New York: Viking Press, 1963.
14. *Mental Illness and Law Enforcement.* St. Louis, Mo.: Washington University, 1970.
15. Missildine, W. *Your Inner Child of the Past.* New York: Simon and Schuster, 1963.
16. *Physical Fitness for Law Enforcement Officers.* Washington, D.C.: Federal Bureau of Investigation, 1972.
17. *Recognizing and Supervising Troubled Employees.* Washington, D.C.: U.S. Civil Service Commission, July, 1967.
18. Rodale, J.I. *Your Diet and Your Heart.* Emmaus, Pa.: Rodale Press, 1969.
19. Selye, H. *The Stress of Life.* New York: McGraw Hill, 1956.
20. Spitz, R. *The First Year of Life.* New York: International Universities, Press, 1965.
21. Storr, A. *Human Aggression.* New York: Atheneum, 1968.
22. Watson, G. *Nutrition and Your Mind. The Psychochemical Response.* New York: Harper and Row, 1972.

CHAPTER 4
THE NATURE OF HYPNOSIS AND THE ROLE OF THE HYPNOTIST

Hypnosis is an altered state of consciousness[10] involving focused attention, heightened awareness and concentration[7], which can be achieved by most subjects having proper motivation and attitudes. The hypnotic state may be produced by a process of relaxation, the misdirection of attention, beliefs and expectations, all of which are influenced by the subject's imagination. Hypnosis is just one of the wide spectrum of altered states of consciousness which allow suggestions that are acceptable to become more effective[9]. The conviction of hypnosis leads to hypnosis resulting in a pyramiding effect for additional suggestions.[2]

Paradoxically, physical relaxation combined with the superconcentrated state of mind leads to what Van Pelt calls an increase in the units of mind power[11]. He uses the following diagram:

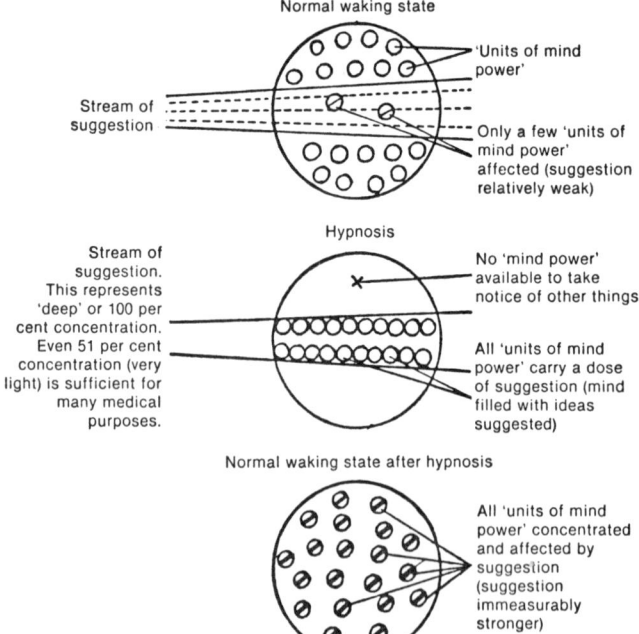

Fig. 1 — The mechanism and nature of hypnosis, and the reason for increased suggestibility in this state.

Hypnosis is a naturally occurring phenomenon and has been experienced by almost everyone in a variety of every day circumstances. These situations range from total absorption in a television program or music to automatic highway driving in the reverie state of "highway hypnosis".[12] Benson describes this innate capability which all humans possess as the relaxation response, which, unfortunately, many have forgotten how to utilize so the basic mechanisms remain dormant.[1]

In a hypnotic state the subject increases his capacity to restructure reality by reorganizing to some degree his usual perceptual and object relationships.[4] The degree to which this occurs is significantly related to the nature of the relationship between the subject and hypnotist.

Repetition is an important factor in the achievement of the hypnotic state. Suggestions, repeated many times, establish neuronal pathways leading to a conditioned reflex which then utilizes these associated pathways in the brain.[5]

Employment of physiological mechanisms such as muscle relaxation and eye fatigue are coupled with suggestions that give the subject the impression that the hypnotist is influencing the resultant feelings. These may include heaviness, lightness, warmth, coolness or tingling sensations. As each suggestion is experienced physiologically and as each physiological manifestation is observed by the hypnotist and re-suggested, the reinforcement process confirms to the subject that the hypnotist is indeed inducing these and other responses by his suggestions.[5]

There are certain conditions capable of bringing about or enhancing the hypnotic state: 1. A fixation or concentration of attention. 2. Monotony and repetition. 3. Limitation of subject's voluntary movements. 4. Limitation of the subject's field of consciousness. 5. Inhibition of usual responses. 6. Successive response to suggestions.[7]

Reflex ideomotor action underlies primary suggestibility. This action accumulates with multiple repetition leading to psycho-physiologically learned reactions as a conditioned response. General suggestibility within the context of the relationship with a trusted and influential person is another component of hypnosis. A third factor is dissociation of awareness by the subject, and this is essential to the achievement of a deep state of hypnosis.[4]

Orne and Hilgard have discussed some important variables of hypnosis. One is the concept of trance logic exhibited by subjects in a deep hypnotic state.[8,6] This phenomenon supposedly differentiates genuinely hypnotized persons from those who are simulating hypnosis. Trance logic involves a combination of the subject's reality-derived perceptions which are combined with contradictory ones suggested by the hypnotist. An example would be the suggestion of a positive hallucination of a person not actually present, the acceptance of the suggestion by the subject and the rationalization of it subsequently. The fact that the hallucination typically has a transparent quality would not bother the hypnotic subject. A second issue discussed by Orne is an important one and involves the demand characteristics of the experimental situation.[8] In essence, it involves the subject complying with what is expected by the trusted authority figure. The subject will perform seemingly harmful acts, but with the underlying realization of being protected from real harm by the trusted hypnotist.

Role of the Hypnotist

The hypnotist is an authority figure to the subject and should inspire confidence and trust, maintaining an aura of prestige. As in other professional roles, status as an expert tends to enhance the interaction and the subject's responsiveness. Imagine how a person would feel who went to a new physician and was very anxiously told that this was his first case, but that he would try to do the best that he could. The new hypnotist typically tends to be unsure of himself and tries to convince himself as well as the subject that hypnosis really does work. This uncertainty gets communicated to the subject in a variety of ways.

The main task of the hypnotist is to establish rapport with the subject, to build a sense of trust in the hypnotist and in the hypnotic process.[3] Resistances are to be expected and may be revealed by itches, restlessness, laughing, lack of attention or concentration. They need to be focused on and resolved when possible before proceeding with the hypnotic induction. The hypnotist continues to motivate the subject to accept the beliefs and expectations which are necessary to establish the conviction of hypnosis.[13]

The investigative hypnotist should reassure the subject that there will be no personal questions asked and no secrets will be revealed. The questioning during the interview should cover only previously agreed-upon material, usually involving the crime under investigation. The subject needs to know that there will be no loss of control and that nothing embarrassing will likely emerge or happen during the hypnosis session. It is important for both the hypnotist and the subject to accept the fact that all hypnosis is really self-hypnosis and that the hypnotist is only a guide or teacher who helps a motivated and cooperative subject to experience the altered state of consciousness, which is labeled "hypnosis".

References

1. Benson, H. *The Relaxation Response.* New York: Morrow, 1975.
2. Bowers, K.S. *Hypnosis for the Seriously Curious.* New York: Jason Aronson, 1977.
3. Gill, M.M. and Brenman, M. Data on the nature of the hypnotist. *The Nature of Hypnosis* (Shor, R.E. and Orne, M.T., Eds.). New York: Holt, Rinehart & Winston, 1965, 448-452.
4. Gill, M.M. Hypnosis as an altered and regressed state. *International Journal of Clinical and Experimental Hypnosis,* 1972, *20,* 224-237.
5. Hilgard, E.R. *The Experience of Hypnosis.* New York: Harcourt, Brace & World, 1965.
6. Hilgard, E.R. A critique of Johnson, Maher and Barber's "Artifact in the essence of hypnosis: an evaluation of trance logic." *Journal of Abnormal Psychology,* 1972, *79,* 221-233.
7. Kubie, L.S. and Margolin, S. The process of hypnotism and the nature of the hypnotic state. *The Nature of Hypnosis* (Shor, R.E. and Orne, M.T., Eds.). New York: Holt, Rinehart and Winston, 1965, 217-233.
8. Orne, M.T. The nature of hypnosis: artifact and essence. *Journal of Abnormal and Social Psychology,* 1959, *58,* 277-299.
9. Reyher, J. *Hypnosis.* Dubuque, Iowa: William C. Brown, 1968.
10. Tart, C. *Altered States of Consciousness.* New York: Wiley, 1969.
11. Van Pelt, S.J. *Hypnotic Suggestion.* New York: Philosophical Library, 1956.
12. Williams, G.W. Highway hypnosis: an hypothesis. *The Nature of Hypnosis* (Shor, R.E. and Orne, M.T., Eds.). New York: Holt, Rinehart and Winston, 1965, 482-490.
13. Wolberg, L.R. *Hypnosis: Is it for you?* New York: Harcourt, Brace and Jovanovich, 1972.

CHAPTER 5
MYTHS AND MISCONCEPTIONS, DANGERS AND CONTRAINDICATIONS

A common image of hypnosis is that portrayed in the 1894 novel *Trilby* by George Du Maurier.[4] In this book, a masterful musician, Svengali, who is also a frustrated singer, uses mesmerism with a promising female singer, Trilby, who has tone deafness, and influences her to develop into a successful performer. This story depicts hypnosis as mind control, with almost complete power over the subject. The media have since capitalized on numerous thrillers using the Svengali stereotype and helped to perpetuate the myth of losing control in hypnosis in the minds of the general public. The fact is that rather than mind control, hypnosis involves trust and cooperation on the part of the subject.

A common misconception is that a person in a state of hypnosis loses conscious awareness or falls asleep. The fact is that hypnosis involves a more alert state than usual with increased physical relaxation. The hypnotized person may hear and be aware of everything that is happening while in hypnosis and can terminate the hypnotic state at will.

In the past the ability of a person to go into hypnosis has been linked to weakmindedness or having a weak will. The fact is that intelligent persons who are motivated make better hypnotic subjects.

A frequent misconception is that the hypnotized individual will reveal dark secrets and thus be in jeopardy later. The truth is that the individual in hypnosis is aware of what is being said and will not say or do anything against his will. People in hypnosis continue to protect their self interest.

A common fear associated with hypnosis involves a misconception that a person can get stuck in hypnosis indefinitely and not be able to come out of it. The fact is that the person in a hypnotic state can terminate hypnosis at any time and those who elect to remain in hypnosis have their own personal reasons for doing so, such as feeling very relaxed, engaging in a contest with the hypnotist, or some other underlying reason.

Another misconception is the equating of hypnosis with

gullibility. These are actually quite different. The gullible person is usually taken advantage of by designing individuals without hypnosis being used at all, as are the victims of confidence games and get-rich-quick schemes.

A more recent misconception voiced by some attorneys and health professionals is that law enforcement hypnotists will coerce a subject or shape the hypnotized person's responses in order to get a predetermined answer. The issue here isn't really hypnosis, but the ethical and professional practices of the hypnotist.

Dangers

Pierre Janet[3] said that, "Even in bad hands, suggestion and hypnotism do not seem to have been able to do much harm." Similarly, Cheek[1] asserted that more harm is done with ignorance of hypnosis than can be done by intelligently using the forces of suggestion. The issue of dangerousness is still tinged with the notion of magic and mysticism. However, there is no real evidence of hypnosis being dangerous aside from a few instances of misuse usually in a psychotherapeutic setting or for entertainment purposes.[2,5] As with any tool, the only danger with hypnosis lies in its misuse. Conn gives an unqualified "no" to the question "Is hypnosis dangerous?"[1]

Considerations for the Operator

The interpersonal relationship between the hypnotist and subject is of crucial importance and involves the eliciting of transference reactions on the part of the subject. The hypnotist needs to be aware of these phenomena and their handling. These issues are discussed in Chapter 21.

In a few instances, usually involving medical or dental hypnosis, a charge of unethical conduct has been made by female patients alleging sexual improprieties on the part of the medical or dental hypnotist. This is not a likely problem for law enforcement hypnotists since the session will be completely taped and there will usually be other persons present.

The hypnotist may develop or get enhanced feelings of omnipotence and the need to manipulate other people and tend to rationalize this in the context of the hypnotist-subject relationship. If this occurs to any noticeable degree, it may suggest a personality problem of the hypnotist and would likely require some help to overcome.

Hypno-investigators need to be aware of the lines of demarcation between therapeutic and law enforcement hypnosis and not engage in any form of therapy or entertainment which would detract from the ethical-professional role.

Considerations Regarding the Subject

It is important that the operator remember to remove suggestions given during the hypnosis session that are not intended to be effective post-hypnotically. Otherwise, subjects may report physical and emotional feelings of discomfort.

Subjects in deep hypnosis tend to take suggestions literally and it is important for the hypnotist to be aware of phrasing and semantics. However, this is not usually a big problem in the criminological uses of hypnosis.

It has been alleged by some health professionals who have proprietary interests in hypnosis that law enforcement practitioners may precipitate a psychosis, neurosis, or suicide in a subject. However, as Conn points out, hypnosis doesn't cause mental illness, the process must already be there. There have been a few instances reported in the literature of psychiatrists and psychologists encountering psychotic reactions while doing hypno-therapy with severely disturbed patients.[2] This is not likely to be a problem for law enforcement practitioners since the demand characteristics are very different from those of hypnotherapy. Subjects seem to maintain their adaptive defenses with little difficulty.

It is desirable to avoid sudden shocks to the subject and it helps to inform the person in advance of what will be said, what will be done, and what will be expected.

It is important that the subject be fully dehypnotized before being dismissed from the hypnosis session. It sometimes takes individuals several minutes or longer, even though appearing to be fully alert and conscious.

Contraindications

Overtly psychotic individuals, those deeply emotionally disturbed, those severely depressed or suicidal, should be avoided by the hypno-investigator.[5] Where a hypnosis session may be desirable, a mental health consultant should be employed in these situations.

In cases where subjects have a history of serious physical or emotional illness, medical clearance should be gotten before proceeding with the hypnosis session. This includes cardiac cases, asthmas, epilepsies and other types of life-threatening conditions. In extremely severe cases it may be desirable to have a physician present during the session as a safeguard. Because hypnosis involves increased relaxation, it is unlikely that any problem will be precipitated, but these precautions may be reassuring to the hypnotist and subject alike.

References
1. Cheek, D.B. and LeCron, L.M. *Clinical Hypnotherapy.* New York: Grune & Stratton, 1968.
2. Conn, J.H. Is hypnosis really dangerous? *The International Journal of Clinical and Experimental Hypnosis,* 1972, *20,* 61-79.
3. Janet, P. *Psychological Healing.* London: Allen and Unwin, 1925, P. 346.
4. Schneck, J.M. Henry James, George Du Maurier and Mesmerism. *International Journal of Clinical and Experimental Hypnosis,* 1978, *26,* 76-80.
5. West, L.J. and Deckert, G.H. Dangers of hypnosis. *Journal of the American Medical Association,* 1965, *192,* 9-12.

CHAPTER 6
THEORIES OF HYPNOSIS

Many theories have been advanced over the years to account for hypnosis, but no one theory accounts for all of the hypnotic phenomena.[8] Hypnotic experience and behavior depend on the subject's expectations, the depth of the hypnotic state, and on the nature of the the relationship between subject and hypnotist.

Rather than being a steady state, hypnosis is more often a fluctuating process with the subject experiencing lighter to deeper alterations of consciousness, much like a sine wave.

In hypnosis, cortical areas of the brain can be conditioned to become more alert or to become inhibited, a form of selective inattention. With the proper mental set, new neuro-psychological pathways can be established, new responses conditioned, which are based on acceptance and belief.

Immobilization Theories

These explanations[9,18] involve the subject's regression to the animalistic response of "freezing" in order to become immobile and avoid danger. Using this defense mechanism, some animals feign death in an attempt to survive.

Hypnosis Equated with Hysteria

Charcot[3] had suggested that only hysterical individuals were hypnotizable, and the more hysterical, the more the individual is subject to deep hypnosis. However, in light of present knowledge, this theory is no longer supportable.

Changes in Cerebral Physiology

These theories[13,18] are based on notions of shifts in nervous energy and arousal of different parts of the brain and related blood flow changes. As yet, there is not conclusive data to support these hypotheses.

Conditioned Reflex

Pavlov[10] thought that hypnosis is a partial sleep state and essentially a conditioned response learned by the individual. However, we now know that hypnosis and sleep are quite different states and that rapid induction techniques don't require a conditioning process.

Dissociation Theory

Both Pierre Janet[6] and Morton Prince[11,12] proposed that the subconscious has functional independence and is able to circumvent consciousness. Prince's classic studies in multiple personality, the most notable being the case of Miss Beauchamp, provided important data on the process of dissociation as it occurs in certain altered states of consciousness. However, in some altered states there is often a hypersensitivity to and awareness of reality rather than an amnestic or splitting of ego response as described in the multiple personality.

Role Playing Theory

Barber[1,2] and others[15] have argued that there is no special state of hypnosis. They suggest that the "hypnotized" subject is playing a role based on what is expected. However, this theory doesn't explain the changes that occur in the subject's sensory responses to heat and cold, pupillary reflex or reversal of the Babinski reflex when the person is regressed beyond age two.

Regression Theory

According to this theory,[4,16] the subject regresses to earlier developmental levels of functioning and responds to the hypnotist as a parent figure. Partial regressions can occur cortically and psychologically if suggested.

Hypersuggestibility

This theory[5] suggests a narrowed attention span by the subject, and increased gullibility is also implied. However, this theory does not explain the spontaneous amnesias which may occur in hypnosis. Increased suggestibility is only one variable in the altered states of consciousness.

Psychosomatic Theories

These theories[19,20,21] suggest that hypnosis is based on psychosomatic processes. Suggestibility is explained as ideomotor action, a result of conditioning.

Psychoanalytic Theory

These theorists[7,14,17] suggest that in hypnosis the subject regresses to childhood and unconsciously associates the hypnotist with a strong father or a nurturing mother. Transference reactions commonly occur and unresolved oedipal conflicts may be activated. This theory leans heavily on the experience of Freud, and Breuer's experiences with hysterics in the 1890's. This theory does not adequately account for self-hypnosis phenomena.

References

1. Barber, T.X. The concept of hypnosis. *Journal of Psychology*, 1958, *45*, 115-131.
2. Barber, T.X. *Hypnosis: A Scientific Approach*. New York: Van Nostrand Reinhold Co., 1969.
3. Charcot, J.M. *Lectures on the Diseases of the Nervous System*. London: New Syndenham Society, 1877.
4. Gill, M.M. and Brenman, M. *Hypnosis and Related States: Psychoanalytic Studies in Regression*. New York: International Universities Press, 1959.
5. Hull, C.L. *Hypnosis and Suggestibility: An ͫ perimental Approach*. New York: Appleton-Century, 1933.
6. Janet, P. *The Major Symptoms of Hysteria*. New York: Macmillan, 1907.
7. Kline, M.V. *Psychodynamics and Hypnosis*. Springfield, Ill.: Thomas, 1967.
8. Kroger, W.S. *Clinical and Experimental Hypnosis, 2nd Edition*. Phila.: Lippincott, 1977.
9. Meares, A. *A System of Medical Hypnosis*. Phila.: Saunders, 1960.
10. Pavlov, I.P. *Experimental Psychology*. New York: Philosophical Library, 1957.
11. Prince, M. *The Dissociation of a Personality*. New York: Longmans, 1925.
12. Prince, M. *The Unconscious*. New York: Macmillan, 1929.
13. Roberts, D.R. An electrophysiologic theory of hypnosis. *International Journal of Clinical and Experimental Hypnosis, 1960, 8*, 43-55.
14. Rosen, H. *Hypnotherapy in Clinical Psychiatry*. New York: Julian Press, 1953.
15. Sarbin, T.R. and Coe, W.C. *Hypnosis: A Social Psychological Analysis of Influence Communication*. New York: Holt, 1972.
16. Schilder, P. *The Nature of Hypnosis*. New York: International Universities Press, 1956.
17. Schneck, J.M. *Principles and Practice of Hypnoanalysis*. Springfield, Ill.: Thomas, 1965.
18. Volgyesi, F.A. *Hypnosis of Man and Animals, 2nd Edition*. Hollywood, Calif.: Wilshire Book Co., 1968.
19. Weitzenhoffer, A.M. *Hypnotism: An Objective Study in Suggestibility*. New York: Wiley, 1953.

20. Weitzenhoffer, A.M. *General Techniques of Hypnotism.* New York: Grune & Stratton, 1957.
21. Wolberg, L.R. *Medical Hypnosis, Volume I.* New York: Grune and Stratton, 1948.

CHAPTER 7
PRINCIPLES OF SUGGESTION: FEELINGS AND MOTIVES OF THE HYPNOTIST

Every individual is suggestible to some degree. We may become hypersuggestible in certain altered states of consciousness, including hypnosis. In general, the deeper the trance state, the greater the suggestibility of the subject, assuming trust on the part of the hypnotized individual and no major conflict with the individual's value system.[6,10] Individual suggestibility appears to be strongly related to the person's belief system.[12]

There are cases reported of individuals literally being "scared to death" because of their belief in voodoo.[1,2] There are also countless examples of miraculous healings that have occurred on the same basis. Scientific medicine as well as religious and faith healers acknowledge the importance of beliefs in recognizing the individual's will to live and the primacy of natural healing processes of the mind-body.[3,5,7,8,9,11]

Common examples of suggestion are seen in the operation of the placebo effect which results in patients feeling less pain and actually getting better because of their belief in a new treatment or drug, which may actually be inert or ineffective.[4] The tremendous power of commericial advertising on television, radio, and in the printed media shows very clearly that hypnosis is not necessary for suggestions to be effective. Yawning in a crowded room or looking upward at a tall building often have a group contagian effect. The subconscious association of running water and urinating is often used to assist a person with related medical procedures or problems.

Suggestibility can be increased by the subject's mental set and motivation. It is also highly dependent on the nature of the rapport in any interpersonal relationship.

Types of Suggestion

Hypnotic suggestion is usually dichotomized into either authoritative and command kinds of suggestion, or the permissive non-command type. In actual practice, most experienced hypnotists find themselves using a combination of these approaches or adapting their style to the particular situation and subject on an almost intuitive basis. During the typical induction and deepening procedure, the hypnotist will generally follow a permissive mode, with occasional firm and even forceful comments at particular times as needed.

The authoritarian approach traditionally has been used by stage hypnotists and others who perceive the subject as one to be dominated and manipulated. Suggestions are typically phrased to include "you will..." or, "I want you to...". This approach may be useful with individuals who have an unconscious need to be dominated based on early childhood experience and conditioning. However, a generally permissive approach utilizing phrases such as "you can" or "you may" is suggested for investigative hypnosis work. This approach is frequently more effective with subjects who are resistant to authority and who have some anxiety about being controlled.

Suggestions may be direct or indirect. The hypnotist's office dress, reputation, voice quality and personal mannerisms constitute indirect suggestions to the subject. They may also include tangential or symbolic kinds of communication. Direct suggestions are those given directly and in undisguised form as part of the hypnosis procedure.

Suggestions may be verbal in nature, visual, or conveyed through any of the other senses, such as touch. Positively worded suggestions are more effective than negative ones. It is best to avoid words like "not", "don't", "won't", and "can't". Negatively phrased suggestions tend to have negative effects with some hypnotized subjects. Instead of saying "You won't have a headache when you are dehypnotized", the hypnotist should phrase the suggestion positively, such as, "You will feel clear headed, refreshed, relaxed and perfectly normal in every way when you come out of the hypnotic state".

There is often a time lag between the suggestion given and the response of the subject. This lag varies from person to person and may involve seconds or minutes. The hypnotist needs to be patient and allow the subject adequate reaction time. Otherwise, the hypnotist may misinterpret the delay as a lack of response and consequently upset a nicely developing hypnotic state.

The subject's likely reaction to hypnotic suggestion may be inferred from how the individual reacted to suggestions from significant others in the past. It will also depend on how the suggestions are structured by the hypnotist, the prestige of the suggestion given, and the kind of rapport that exists in the relationship.

There are individuals called paradoxical reactors who believe they aren't susceptible to hypnotic suggestion. However, this is sometimes a form of stubbornness, and the subject usually reacts to the hypnotic suggestions quite well.

Feelings and Motives of the Hypnotist

Freud once remarked that hypnosis endowed the hypnotist with considerable authority which involves the alteration of the mental and physiological state of the subject. The subject places trust in the hypnotist and cooperates to an unusual degree. It tends to place the subject in a somewhat vulnerable position and the hypnotist in a position of great responsibility, before, during and after the hypnosis session.

The hypnotist may react to the subject's responses with irritation, anger, pleasure, or affection, and needs to be aware of the reason for these feelings. The hypnotist's motives for engaging in hypnosis are important. Is there a need for adulation? Are there feelings of omnipotence and magical power? Is there a need to feel in control of another person? If so, these affects will likely constitute problems that may become manifest with the subject as well as with the hypnotist.

There is no perfect hypnotist nor are there ideal personal qualities. These vary with the intended use of hypnosis and the particular style of each individual involved. The traits that are desirable for doing hypnotherapy, which requires considerable intimacy, may not be required for investigative purposes. What may be substandard in one area of practice may be quite satisfactory in another. Thus, it isn't possible to equate the requirements of a psychotherapeutic relationship with those desirable in the hypnosis investigation of a major crime. Certainly professionalism is required in both areas.

The hypnotist needs to be aware of his increased importance to the subject especially following dehypnotization. He should pay attention to his speech as well as his actions and their potential effect on the subject after hypnosis since subjects vary in the time required to become fully dehypnotized.

Post-hypnotic or hypnotic suggestions should not be used to coerce a subject into any kind of compliant behavior. An example would be telling the subject that "You will definitely remember the detail in question tomorrow morning and call the investigator on the phone at 2:00 p.m." A permissively-worded suggestion about future recall is desirable.

The hypno-investigator may go into a state of hypnosis while working with the subject and may also find the case investigators present slipping into hypnosis during the induction and deepening procedures. This is usually not a serious problem and many hypnotists feel that operating in a light state of hypnosis facilitates their rapport and communication with the subject.

References
1. Barber, T.X. Death by suggestion. *Psychosomatic Medicine*, 1961, *23*, 153-156.
2. Bowers, M. Hypnotic aspects of Haitian voodoo. *International Journal of Clinical and Experimental Hypnosis*, 1961, *9*, 269-283.
3. Bromberg, W. *From Shaman to Psychotherapist*. Chicago: Regnery, 1975.
4. Conn, J.H. Cultural and clinical aspects of hypnosis, placebos and suggestibility. *International Journal of Clinical and Experimental Hypnosis*, 1959, *7*, 179-
5. Daim, W. *Depth Psychology and Salvation*. New York: Ungar Publishing Co., 1963.
6. Derman, D. and London, P. Correlates of hypnotic susceptibility. *Journal of Consulting Psychology*, 1965, *29*, 537-545.
7. Eddy, M.B. *Science and Health With Key to the Scriptures*. Boston: Stewart, 1875.
8. Frank, J.D. *Persuasion and Healing: A Comparative Study of Psychotherapy*. Baltimore: Johns Hopkins Press, 1961.
9. Lewis, H.R. and Lewis, M.E. *Psychosomatics*. New York: Viking, 1972.
10. Melie, J.P. and Hilgard, E.R. Attitudes toward hypnosis, self-predictions and hypnotic susceptibility. *International Journal of Clinical and Experimental Hypnosis*, 1964, *12*, 99-108.
11. Reiff, P. *The Triumph of the Therapeutic: Uses of Faith after Freud*. New York: Harper and Row, 1966.
12. Rokeach, M. *Beliefs, Attitudes and Values*. San Francisco: Jossey-Bass, 1968.

CHAPTER 8
WHO IS HYPNOTIZABLE?; SUSCEPTIBILITY TESTS

That almost every one is hypnotizable to some degree is evidenced in the every day experiences of altered states of consciousness and suggestibility.[13] Hypnosis has been achieved with subjects as young as age three as well as those in old age.[4] Generally, intelligent people make better hypnotic subjects, but motivation is probably overriding. The best hypnotic subjects seem to be those between the ages of seven and fourteen, with a gradual tendency to decrease in hypnotizability with age.[7,8] As mentioned before, the relationship of the hypnotist to the subject is a critical variable of hypnotizability. There are very few differences between the sexes or among races as to hypnotic response.[9]

Numerous attempts to estimate hypnotizability have been made.[2,3,6,10,11,13] One interesting approach involved the first session response with a hypnotist of average skill. The following predictors resulted: five percent of subjects are unhypnotizable: forty-five percent of subjects will achieve a light state; thirty-five percent of subjects will achieve a medium state; fifteen percent of subjects will achieve a deep state of hypnosis.[14]

An advantage in investigative hypnosis is that the volunteer witnesses and victims of major crimes have usually experienced considerable emotional trauma and are therefore more likely to have recorded significant details at a conscious or subconscious perceptual level and be motivated to remember in the safe structured environment provided by the hypnoinvestigator. The hypnotist should keep in mind that hypnotizability has no direct correlation with truthfulness. Veridicality is more a function of motivation and the desire to cooperate in an open, honest way.

Susceptibility Tests[1,5]

Although many experienced hypnotists do not utilize susceptibility tests because they are time consuming and may be perceived as a challenge by the subject, the experienced hypno-investigator should be familiar with some of the more common tests. They may possibly be used in special situations such as conducting group orientation and familiarization training with detectives and attorneys attending a demonstration session. Many of the susceptibility tests described below can be adapted for either individual or group administration.

Finger Pull Test

The subject is instructed to clasp hands together in front with fingers interlocked. With hands remaining tightly clasped together, the two index fingers are separated and held apart vertically, pointing at the ceiling. The subject is told to clasp hands together tighter and tighter and attempt to keep the two index fingers apart, parallel to each other. But that the tighter the hands are clasped, the harder it will be to keep the two index fingers apart, that very shortly they will come together as the subject focuses his attention on the tips of the two index fingers. With each passing second as the fingertips are watched, it will becme harder and harder to keep them apart and it seems as if the muscles in the arms, hands, and fingers are becoming more tense, stiff and rigid and forcefully pulling the two index fingers together.

This test, like many others, utilizes natural neuromuscular effects to help achieve the desired result. Because it requires a tremendous amount of counterpressure to not have the fingers touch, it is usually an indication of resistance if the subject doesn't allow them to touch after a few minutes.

Hand Clasp Test

The subject is instructed to clasp hands and fingers tightly together and then invert the hands over the head with palms facing upward, keeping the fingers interlocked. Suggestions are given that the subject close his eyes and feel the fingers growing thicker and thicker, like sausages, as they interlock tighter and tighter and very shortly the fingers will feel as if they are tightly glued together with epoxy cement, thick and tight. The glued together sausage fingers would be very difficult and perhaps impossible to pull apart. After additional reinforcing suggestions, the subject is asked to *try* for just a second to pull the fingers apart but to find it extremely difficult or impossible. Very quickly the instruction is given to stop trying and to relax. Those individuals whose hands remain tightly clasped together are considered more susceptible.

Hands as Magnets Test

The subject is instructed to put both arms straight out in front with hands a foot apart facing each other. He is told to close his eyes and to imagine that his two hands are electromagnets that will be pulled very tightly together when the current is allowed to flow into them, on the count of three. A slow count of three is made and the subject is then told that the current is now flowing into his hands which are electromagnets; he can feel the electricity developing a strong positive attraction in each of them. The electromagnets are being pulled toward each other more and more strongly all the time, stronger and stronger, coming together more and more all the time. A rheostat is going to be turned up which increases the current flowing into these electromagnets and the increased charge is pulling them even more strongly together. The closer they come together the stronger the magnetic charge, increasing the pull tenfold as they come together more and more.

The susceptible subject will usually comply, hands coming together and touch after a relatively short number of repetitions of the instructions and images.

Arms Rising and Falling Test

The subject is instructed to put both arms straight out in front with the left palm facing down and the right thumb facing the ceiling. He is told that very shortly a large 25-pound dictionary will be placed on the back of his left hand and at the same time a large helium-filled balloon will be tied to the thumb of his right hand. On the count of three both the book and balloon will be in place and the subject will experience the interesting and powerful results of the attached forces, with the left hand being pushed down very strongly by the heavy book, and the right hand being pulled upward by the lighter-than-air balloon, tugging it upward toward the sky. Repeated suggestions of heaviness in the left hand with perhaps an additional book or two being piled on as needed, with instructions of lightness and being tugged upward on the right hand being given also. This should result in the subject's left hand being lowered while the subject's right hand is moving upward. The susceptible subject will comply with these suggestions after just a few minutes. The noncompliant subject is usually exhibiting resistance.

The Eye Roll Test

Spiegel has described the eye roll as part of his hypnotic induction profile.[12] In this test the subject is asked to look straight ahead and then roll the eyes upward as high as possible as if looking right through the top of the head. The more upgaze the greater the susceptibility of the subject. If very little pupil is showing during the upgaze, the subject is likely very hypnotizable.

The Odors Test

A bottle with colored water is unstoppered in the room and vivid descriptions of a strong perfume or aroma contained in the bottle are given to the audience with the instruction that the odor is wafting its way toward the back of the room and very soon everyone in the room will be able to detect the odor. As soon as the odor is detected, the person should raise his hand to indicate that he smells the odor. He is asked to identify it. Of course, the liquid in the bottle is odorless, so that the people who smell it and identify the scent are susceptible.

The Pencil Drop Test

This is also a group test in which individuals are instructed to rest their right elbow on a table and hold a pencil lightly in the writing position. They are asked to focus attention on the tip of the pencil and continue to gaze at it while instructions are given for increased relaxation, eye heaviness and hand and finger lightness. They are told that ultimately the pencil will drop to the table as the fingers gradually pull apart, and when the pencil hits the table the eyes will close and they will become very deeply relaxed. The sound of other pencils dropping will increase the state of relaxation.

References

1. *A Syllabus on Hypnosis and a Handbook of Therapeutic Suggestions.* Des Plaines, Ill.: American Society of Clinical Hypnosis, 1973.
2. Bowers, P. Hypnotizability, creativity and the role of effortless experiencing. *International Journal of Clinical and Experimental Hypnosis,* 1978, *26,* 184-201.
3. Burns, A. Changes in hypnotizability following experience. *International Journal of Clinical and Experimental Hypnosis,* 1976, 269-279.
4. Cooper, L.M. and London, P. Children's hypnotic susceptibility, personality and EEG patterns. *International Journal of Clinical and Experimental Hypnosis,* 1976, 140-147.
5. Duke, J.D. Intercorrelational status of suggestibility tests and hypnotizability. *Psychological Record,* 1964, 14, 71-80.
6. Hilgard, E.R. and Lauer, L.W. Lack of correlation between the CPI and hypnotic susceptibility. *Journal of Consulting Psychology,* 1962, *26,* 331-335.
7. Hilgard, E.R. *The Experience of Hypnosis.* New York: Harcourt, Brace & World, 1965.

8. Hilgard, J.R. *Personality and Hypnosis: A Study of Imaginative Involvement.* Chicago: University of Chicago Press, 1970.
9. Kroger, W.S. *Clinical and Experimental Hypnosis, 2nd Edition.* Phila.: Lippincott, 1977.
10. Moore, R.K. Susceptibility to hypnosis and susceptibility to social influence. *Journal of Abnormal and Social Psychology,* 1964, *68,* 282-294.
11. Perry, C. Is hypnotizability modifiable? *International Journal of Clinical and Experimental Hypnosis,* 1977, *25,* 125-145.
12. Spiegel, H. *Manual for Hypnotic Induction Profile.* New York: Soni Medica, 1976.
13. Stukat, K.G. *Suggestibility: A Factorial and Experimental Analysis.* Stockholm: Almqvist and Wiksell, 1958.
14. Weitzenhoffer, A.M. *General Techniques of Hypnotism.* New York: Grune & Stratton, 1957.

CHAPTER 9

PREPARATION OF SUBJECT, INDUCTION METHODS, DEEPENING TECHNIQUES, AND DEHYPNOTIZATION CONSIDERATIONS

The preparation of the investigative hypnosis subject begins with the first police contact from which the person will infer information, develop attitudes, and draw conclusions. For this reason, it would be very desirable for all patrol officers and investigators who may have initial contact and subsequent communication with witnesses and victims of crimes to receive relevant familiarization training in regard to the investigative hypnosis process. This will enable them to communicate in positive ways in preparing potential subjects.

Assuming that the case investigators have properly described the hypnosis process, enlisted the subject's cooperation, and have contributed to the person's motivation, the next main phase will be the hypnosis session proper. This begins with the subject meeting the hypno-investigator during the pre-induction hypnosis phase.

The pre-induction part of the hypnosis session is important in that it can determine the entire outcome.[5] Rapport building begins with the pre-induction talk, continues throughout the hypnosis session and afterward.

During this time, the hypno-investigator discusses with the subject any physical or mental illnesses or treatments, any prior hypnosis experiences, and the subject's reactions to them. The subject's ideas about hypnosis, including the myths and misconceptions are very important. The subject should be given factual information about hypnosis including a comprehensive preview of what will occur during the hypnosis session, questions to be asked, topics to be avoided, such as non-relevant sexual details already in the crime report. The subject should be told that he will be aware of everything that happens, will maintain control over verbal and physical responses, and may remember as much or as little as is comfortable after the session.

The hypno-investigator may deem it desirable to increase the subject's motivation by pointing out the community service value of cooperating in the investigation of a major crime. This includes the possibility of other victims being spared if the criminal can be apprehended sooner.

If fear of revenge or retribution is a significant resistance factor for the subject, protective measures should be discussed. It may also be motivating to mention that witnesses and victims frequently feel better after a hypnosis session because of having confronted their feelings about the crime in a positive way. They often find themselves sleeping better, feeling more relaxed, and having less guilt feelings that before.

Prior to beginning the induction, the hypnotist should ask the subject about bathroom needs, contact lens discomfort, and other physical or environmental considerations. In a particularly noisy hypnosis environment, it can be suggested to the subject that any noises including typewriters, air conditioning, telephones, fire engines or sirens, may be noted but not paid attention to. If anything, they may help to increase the sense of relaxation and comfort.

INDUCTION METHODS

Unless an authoritarian approach has been decided on for a particular subject, the induction should begin in a permissive way. Typically, it may involve eye closure, either by an eye fixation method or direct suggestion for eye closure. It can be followed by suggestions for breathing and then muscle relaxation utilizing progressive relaxation, tensing and relaxing specific muscle groups of the body.[3] There are numerous induction techniques described by Kroger[4] and Teitelbaum.[7]

A few common induction techniques are outlined below:[1]

TRADITIONAL EYE-FIXATION METHOD:

Instructions: Have the subject fixate some point or object overhead, which causes him to roll his eyes upward.

"As you stare at the object, your eyes will become tired. The natural thing to do when one's eyes are tired is to close the lids to rest them. Soon your eyelids will become heavier and heavier. When your eyes close, just let them stay closed. That is right. Now you become more and more relaxed."

HAND-LEVITATION TECHNIQUE:

Instructions: Have the subject sit comfortably in a chair with his hands resting lightly on his thighs. Instruct him to look at his hands, stare at an object on the wall, or close his eyes. Having selected one, he should continue to do that until asked to do otherwise.

"Please pay attention to all the feelings that you become aware of in your right hand and fingers. You can feel the texture of the cloth, the warmth of your skin, and perhaps a little tingling sensation in the fingers. Your fingers may move back and forth a little bit in order to increase the feeling.

"Soon you may notice a feeling of lightness in your fingers which will spread to your hand. Soon you will be aware of and fascinated by the fact that your hand is moving up from your thigh. You can help this movement by imagining, if you wish, that a huge balloon is tied to the wrist. When the hand has moved high enough so that you feel that your arm will relax and the rest of your body is relaxed also, the hand will drop back to your lap and your eyes will close. Let your hand move up until your muscles are all ready to relax completely."

RELAXATION TECHNIQUE:

Instructions: Have the subject sit in a chair suitable for complete relaxation. Have him loosen any clothing which may be tight.

"Now take a deep breath, which will help relax the muscles as you let your breath out again. Soon you will notice that your eyelids begin to feel heavy and they will have a tendency to blink. They may blink more and more. They will grow heavier and heavier, heavier and heavier. You will find it harder and harder to hold them open. You may find your vision growing somewhat blurred. You may find that you have to swallow from time to time. The eyelids are becoming heavier and heavier now. Soon the eyes will want to close and to shut out the light. They are getting so heavy now, so awfully heavy, you can hardly hold them open. Let them close whenever they are ready. Heavy. Still heavier, and they can close now. (If the eyes have not closed now, continue with more suggestions, and if they do not close, tell the subject to close them.)

"You are probably feeling a listlessness now, a drowsy, listless feeling. It is very pleasant to feel so listless and drowsy. Let yourself relax still more. A feeling of well-being gradually comes over you, as though all your cares have rolled away, as though nothing matters, nothing at all. A feeling of 'I don't care'. You are so listless now. Give way to the feeling, as it is so pleasant. Just let yourself go, drifting deeper and deeper. Deeper with every breath you take. Deeper and still deeper. You are going still deeper now.

"Pay attention only to my voice - nothing else seems to matter and nothing will disturb you. Let yourself relax completely, now, let every muscle go loose and limp. You will notice a growing feeling of heaviness in your arms and legs, perhaps over your whole body. There may be tingly feelings here and there, perhaps a numbness. And your breathing is getting slow and easy now. Slow and easy. (Call attention to abdominal breathing if present) Give way to the drowsy listlessness. Let go completely. You are going deeper and still deeper now.

"Let all your muscles relax, relax them completely. Begin with your feet and your legs. Let the muscles go loose and limp. Relax them all. Now your thighs, and your hips. Let them relax. Your stomach and abdominal muscles, now, can relax too. Let those muscles relax. Your shoulders, your arms and your hands. Relax them. Now your neck. Let it relax. Do not mind if your head bows forward or to the side. It will be perfectly comfortable. Your facial muscles can relax, and particularly the eye muscles and the lids. Relax now, completely. Every muscle in your body will relax."

CHIASSON'S TECHNIQUE

Instructions: Help the subject to put his hand directly in front of his face, about 12 inches from his nose, and the back of the hand toward the face with the fingers pressed together, elbow bent.

"You and I will look at your fingers. Soon we will see them begin to spread apart. Keep your eyes on your fingers as long as your eyes are open. Now that we see your fingers spreading, your hand will begin to approach your face. When you feel the touch of your hand on your face, usually the tip of your nose, your eyes will close if they are not already closed. Often they become so tired that they close before your hand gets to your face. Once the close, let them stay closed. When your hand touches your face you will become completely relaxed and your hand will fall to your lap and you will go deeply relaxed."

SPIEGEL EYE ROLL - LEVITATION TECHNIQUE[6]

"Get as comfortable as possible with your arms resting on the arms of the chair. Now look toward me. Get as comfortable as you can. As you hold your head in that position, look upward toward your eyebrows - now toward the top of your head. As you continue to look upward, close your eyelids slowly. That's right. Keep your eyelids closed and continue to hold your eyes upward. Now take a deep breath, hold it. Now exhale, let your eyes relax and let your body float. Concentrate on a feeling of floating, floating down right through the chair. There will be something pleasant and welcome about this feeling of floating. Now while you concentrate on this floating, I am going to concentrate on your left arm and hand. In a while I am going to stroke the middle finger of your left hand. After I do, you will develop movement sensations in that finger. Then the movements will spread, causing your left hand to feel light and buoyant and you will let it float upward. Ready? (Stroke middle finger from nail to elbow.)

"First one finger and then another. As these restless movements develop, your hand becomes light and buoyant, your elbow bends and your forearm floats into an upright position. Just let it go. This is an exercise in your imagination. Imagine your hand feels like a balloon. When you were a seven-year-old child, you had this ability to imagine. Try to recover this feeling. If necessary, help it along. That's right, all the way up.

"Now I am going to position your arm in this manner so, and let it remain in this upright position. (Gently cup the elbow with both hands and position it in comfortable alignment on the chair arm.) In fact, it will remain in that position even after I give you the signal for your eyes to open. When your eyes are open, even when I put your hand down, it will float right back up to where it is now. You will find something pleasant and amusing about this sensation. Later, when I touch your left elbow, your usual sensation and control will return. In the future each time you get the signal for the trance experience, at the count of one, your eyes will roll upward and by the count of three your eyelids will close and you will be in a relaxed trance state. Each time you will find the experience easier and easier.

"Now I am going to count backwards. At two, your eyes will again roll upward with your eyelids closed. At one, you let them open very slowly. Ready, three, two, with your eyelids closed roll up your eyes and, one, just let them open slowly. (Gently lower arm holding wrist. Touch left elbow to end post-hypnotic suggestion.)

DEEPENING TECHNIQUES

Although considered separately for discussion purposes,

deepening is actually an extension of the induction process and occurs naturally as the subject becomes more relaxed. Common techniques involve counting down suggesting the subject go deeper and deeper with each count. This may be combined with the image of going down in an elevator, escalator or stairs, descending and deepening with each number mentioned.

Imagery is very effective as a deepening technique. The suggestion is given that the subject imagine being in the most relaxed place in the world, carefree, worry-free, anxiety-free, feeling perfectly wonderful. This can be a beach scene, a mountain scene, a snow scene, a country scene, a desert scene, floating on a raft, swimming in a pool; whatever the subject finds compatible with relaxation and comfort.

Physical touch can reinforce deepening. After informing the subject first, the hypnotist presses down on one or both shoulders while telling the subject, "As I press down, you can feel yourself going deeper and deeper, becoming more and more relaxed as you feel the pressure of my hand on your shoulder".

Post-hypnotic suggestions can also be used for deepening purposes either during the present session or in preparation for subsequent ones.[2] The subject is told that each time the induction procedure is used he will be able to more easily and comfortably go deeper and deeper until he reaches an optimal level of hypnosis. He will find this to be a very interesting experience.

DEHYPNOTIZATION

Dehypnotization should be done slowly with the awareness that many subjects may take considerable time because of the residual hypnotic effect, in spite of the eyes being open again. Prior to dehypnotization all suggestions which were given, not intended for post-hypnotic effects, should be cancelled, or reinforced if they are intended to remain. The subject may be counted out of hypnosis slowly or told that he can count himself out at his own rate of speed. He is told that on reaching the normally alert and conscious state, he will feel perfectly relaxed, physically and mentally, feeling clear-headed, refreshed, finding the hypnosis process an interesting, positive experience. Prior to dehypnotization, cues for quicker rehypnotization and increased depth may be given as post-hypnotic suggestions if future sessions or self-hypnosis are anticipated.

Difficulties in dehypnotization are usually indicative of

resistance and should be explored directly with the subject by asking about the subject's feelings and reactions to what is happening. The subject will tell you the reason in most cases. In a very few, unusual cases reported in the literature, subjects who elected not to come out of hypnosis as suggested, fell asleep instead and awakened naturally some hours later.[8] Since all hypnosis is really self-hypnosis, the subject will decide when to come out of hypnosis just as he decides to go into the hypnotic state.

References
1. *A Syllabus on Hypnosis and a Handbook of Therapeutic Suggestions.* Des Plaines, Ill.: American Society of Clinical Hypnosis, 1973.
2. Cheek, D.B. and LeCron, L.M. *Clinical Hypnotherapy.* New York: Grune & Stratton, 1968.
3. Jacobson, E. *Anxiety and Tension Control.* Phila.: Lippincot, 1964.
4. Kroger, W.S. *Clinical and Experimental Hypnosis, 2nd Edition.* Phila.: Lippincott, 1977.
5. LeCron, L.M. and Bordeaux, J. *Hypnotism Today.* North Hollywood, Ca.: Wilshire Book Co., 1972.
6. Spiegel, H. *Manual for Hypnotic Induction Profile: Eye-roll Levitation Method.* New York: Soni Medica, 1976.
7. Teitelbaum, M. *Hypnosis Induction Technics.* Springfield, Ill.: Thomas, 1969.
8. Weitzenhoffer, A.M. *General Techniques of Hypnotism.* New York: Grune & Stratton, 1957.

CHAPTER 10
LAWS OF HYPNOSIS

Because people are naturally suggestible they will normally take the path of least resistance. In this connection, there are four "laws" of hypnosis or suggestibility that the hypno-investigator should be aware of.

1. **Law of Dominant Effect**

    This law developed by Pierce,[6] states that the imagination is much stronger than conscious willpower. Following Coue,[2] he asserted that imagination always wins when there is a conflict with the will. Essentially, this is analogous to the subconscious being stronger than the conscious mind.

    Strong emotion tends to increase suggestibility. This is seen in the powerful and longlasting effects of the early programming during childhood. A poor self-concept, lasting a lifetime, may have its origin in constant criticism and demeaning of the child by parent figures and other authorities.[5]

    A stronger emotion will counteract and take precedence over a weaker emotion. Anyone in a state of strong emotion is already in an altered state of consciousness. A common example is the person who is injured and automatically goes into a hypnoidal state as part of the organism's protective defenses.

    The laying on of hands, touching, reinforces suggestions of relaxation. A typical example is a mother's kissing her child's hurt part and instantly "making it better".

2. **Law of Reversed Effect**

    Baudouin[1] says that the harder you consciously try, the less likely you are to succeed. Examples are: trying hard to fall asleep when you have insomnia, or attempting to recall a familiar person's name that is on the tip of your tongue. In hypnosis procedures, the law of reversed effect can be used to increase the subject's responsiveness. For example, the subject may be told, "The harder you try to keep your fingers apart, the more they will come together; the harder you try to keep your eyes open, the more tired and fatigued they will become and will close more rapidly."

3. **Law of Concentrated Attention**

    This law, also put forth by Baudouin,[1] states that repetition lays down pathways in the brain. The communication utilizing these pathways may be either positive or negative, so careful phrasing of communications by the hypnotist is important.
    Attention concentrated on a idea tends to have the idea actualized.[4] One example is the repetitive television jingles and commercials which influence people to buy the advertised product. Another is the repeated practice in acquiring the motor skills to play a musical instrument, ride a bicycle or swim. In hypnosis the use of eye fixation is a typical method of concentrating the subject's attention while the desired behavior is being communicated verbally with repetition.

4. **Law of Association**

    Feelings become connected with ideas and ideas connected with feelings by association. An example is reacting to rock music by feeling more energetic, to blues music by feeling sad, or by associating a new hat with optimism.[3] In the hypnosis process, words and images are used to get the desired associated responses, such as eye closure, muscle catalepsy, or hypermnesia.

References

1. Baudouin, C. *Suggestion and Auto Suggestion*. New York: Dodd Mead, 1922.
2. Coué, E. *How to Practice Suggestion and Autosuggestion*. New York: American Library Service, 1923.
3. Kroger, W.S. *Clinical and Experimental Hypnosis, 2nd Edition*. Phila.: Lippincott, 1977.
4. LeCron, L.M. and Bordeaux, J. *Hypnotism Today*. North Hollywood, Ca.: Wilshire Book Co., 1972.
5. Missildine, W.H. *Your Inner Child of the Past*. New York: Simon and Schuster, 1963.
6. Pierce, F. *Mobilizing the Mid-Brain*. New York: Dutton, 1924.

CHAPTER 11
ETHICAL AND PROFESSIONAL CONSIDERATIONS

Like professionals in other occupations requiring honesty, sensitivity, and a well-developed ethical sense, hypno-investigators are aware of and concerned about professional and ethical issues and related potential problems.

Investigative hypnotists work with volunteer witnesses and victims of crimes, and not with suspects or possible suspects. The exception, in a special situation, would require agreement by both defense and prosecution with both sides stipulating to the results. Whenever possible in these situations, it is desirable to use a non-law enforcement hypnotist to avoid any implication of the abrogating of constitutional rights or the improper or biased conducting of the hypnosis session.

Some of the relevant professional and ethical issues for investigative hypnotists are:

1. **Responsibility**

   The hypno-investigator has the primary responsibility for working with the subject in hypnosis and cannot relegate or relinquish this responsibility to other persons. This includes a responsibility for refusing a hypnosis session when, in his professional judgment, it would be inappropriate or contrary to the subject's interest. In some cases this may involve informing supervisors or administrators as to the advisability of a hypnosis session in the particular case, even though there may be organizational pressure to go ahead with it.

2. **Competence**

   The professional hypno-investigator practices only within his area of competence and declines getting involved outside the scope of his training and experience. This precludes any form of hypnotherapy for those not trained and licensed to practice these techniques.

3. **Moral and Legal Standards**

   The hypno-investigator is bound to abide by the moral and legal standards of the local community in which he practices. This should include an awareness of what constitutes

the accepted standards for investigative and hypnosis procedures.
4. **Misrepresentation**
   The professional practitioner does not misrepresent his credentials, training, experience, or areas of competence.
5. **Public Statements**
   The professional hypno-investigator is careful that statements made to the media, to community groups, or in any public form are factual, accurate, and in good taste.
6. **Confidentiality**
   Information learned from an investigative hypnosis session has the same status as other investigative material. Generally, this information should be kept in confidence with the usual legal and professional exceptions.
7. **Subject Welfare**
   The interests and welfare of the hypnosis subject come first. When there is any conflict between the subject's welfare and the welfare of the hypnotist or the organization, the hypno-investigator, like other professionals, considers the client's welfare primary.[2]
8. **Interprofessional Relations**
   The hypno-investigator should communicate and interact with other professional practitioners on a peer basis. This is based on the assumption that although engaged in different areas of specialization, professional practitioners are equally important in terms of community value.
9. **Publication and Dissemination of Information to the Public**
   It is desirable that hypno-investigators share information with other professionals and with the public. Publication of articles in professional journals, magazines, or interviews and statements to the media, are highly desirable ways of keeping the public informed about this important area of practice. Information presented should be factual and presented in a nonsensational format.
10. **Responsibility Toward The Organization**
    The hypno-investigator often works for a criminal justice agency in some capacity and therefore has responsibilities toward that organization. This includes representing the organization honestly and professionally within the accepted limits of ethical and professional practice.

Education is a lifelong process and hypno-investigators, as do other professionals, need to continue learning and expanding their professional capabilities. Reading relevant articles and books, attending hypnosis workshops, and sharing information with colleagues about cases, problems and legal and technical advances in the field, are all necessary and important activities.

Engaging in research is important, particularly since hypnoinvestigators working in major crime cases have an inside track for gathering data in important real-life situations about the effects of investigative hypnosis. The reporting of research results will enable others to replicate and evaluate the findings.

Because of their desire to maintain high standards of practice in the new specialty of investigative hypnosis, hypnoinvestigators at the Los Angeles Police Department founded the Society for Investigative and Forensic Hypnosis in 1977.[3] It was incorporated as a non-profit organization in California in 1978. In addition to providing a home base for investigative hypnotists, the Society represents the interests and goals of professional practitioners in the applied area of investigative hypnosis and requires its members to adhere to stringent ethical standards. Quoted below is Article IX from the Society's Constitution, titled Standards and Principles of Practice:

In order to achieve unity of purpose, to assure a clear concept of obligations to each other and to the profession, and to provide for the continuing welfare and protection of the general public, all members of the Society have agreed to abide by the following standards and principles of practice.

1. Each member shall recognize the fact his primary responsibility must be to the person who has volunteered for an investigative hypnosis examination, regardless of the circumstances which created the need for the examination.
2. Recognizing that an investigative hypnosis examination cannot be conducted on a person against his will, no member will attempt to conduct an examination when he has reason to believe the examinee has been subjected to coercion or duress. Further, no member shall conduct any examination in violation of any exisiting legislation pertaining to hypnosis. Legal exceptions to this requirement are recognized and may be justified on an individual basis only.
3. No member shall conduct an examination on any person whom he believes to be unfit for a hypnosis interview session.
4. No member shall include in any written report any of his statements purporting to be a medical, legal, or

psychiatric opinion, or which would infringe upon areas under the cognizance of professionals in those fields. This shall not preclude the hypnotist from describing the appearance of behavior of the subject, if this is pertinent to the examination, as long as the hypnotist refrains from offering any diagnosis which he is professionally unqualified to make.
5. A member shall not conduct an examination where he has reason to believe the examination is intended to circumvent or defy the law.
6. A member shall not solicit or accept irregular fees, gratuities or gifts which may be intended to influence his opinion or decision. Further, no member shall set a fee for professional hypnosis services contingent upon the findings or results of such services; nor shall he increase any initial fee as a direct result of his findings during any hypnosis examination.
7. Every investigative hypnosis report shall be a factual, impartial, and objective account of the pertinent information developed during the examination.
8. Information obtained during the course of a hypnosis interview is to be considered "privileged information". The divulging of such information to other than the concerned parties is a serious violation of professional ethics and may subject the examiner to expulsion from the Association.
9. It shall be considered a violation of professional ethics for any member of this Association to deliberately degrade or malign another member of the Association in public, in court, or otherwise. Such conduct may subject the violating hypnotist to censure, investigation and/or expulsion from the Association. It is recognized that occasional differences of opinion regarding techniques and results will occur. In such instances, it shall be clearly stated as a "difference of opinion". Complaints against a member by a member shall be lodged and in writing for review, investigation and necessary action.
10. A member shall not publish or cause to be published any false or misleading advertisments relating to the investigative hypnosis profession.

Any investigative hypnotist who knowingly and deliberately administers examinations in a manner not consistent with the spirit of this document will be considered in violation of the Constitution and Bylaws, thereby subjecting himself to possible censure, investigation, and/or expulsion from the Association.
11. A member shall not conduct an investigative hypnosis examination in which the subject to be examined is suspected of being the perpetrator of the matter under investigation unless prior written agreement has been obtained from the concerned investigating agency and the legal representative of the subject.

Zwerling[5] points out that historically there has been a tendency toward mystification of professional roles. This tendency may increase somewhat when hypnosis is involved as part of the professional's armamentarium. This makes it especially important for the hypnosis professional to educate, demystify, and to have hypnosis understood for what it really is, a natural phenomenon. It is ethically questionable for professionals utilizing hypnosis for psychotherapeutic or other purposes to pass judgment, make public statements, or to criticize investigative hypnosis unless the individual has specific knowledge, training and background in the application of hypnosis to major crime cases.[1]

References
1. *Ethical Standards for Psychologists.* Washington, D.C.: American Psychological Association, 1978.
2. London, P. Ethical Problems in Behavior Control. *Human Behavior and Its Control* (W. Hunt, Ed.). Cambridge, Massachusetts: Schenkman Publishing Company, 1971, 128-133.
3. Reiser, M. *Investigative Hypnosis - A Developing Specialty.* Presented at the California State Psychological Association Convention, Monterey, California, February 11, 1979.
4. Report of the Task Force on the Role of Psychology in the Criminal Justice System. *American Psychologist.* December 1978, 1099-1113.
5. Zwerling, I. *Racism, Elitism, Professionalism.* New York: Jason Aronson Company, 1976.

CHAPTER 12
HYPNOSIS AND THE TRUTH: MACHINES AND DRUGS

Hypnosis is not a truth detection technique. Motivation and cooperation of the subject and a good working relationship with the hypno-investigator are the crucial variables in eliciting accurate information from witnesses and victims of major crimes.

POLYGRAPH

The polygraph is not a lie detector, it merely records physiological outputs of the subject. People are lie detectors and the polygraph operator, like the investigator or the clinician, brings to bear a wide variety of skills and experiences in making determinations of truthfulness or deception.[10]

The field polygraph is only a diagnostic tool which measures physiological functions such as blood pressure, respiration, and galvanic skin response (GSR).[3] The skilled examiner is the key in determining the credibility of the subject and he uses the polygraph as one source in addition to other informational inputs. The polygraph exam includes all behavior from the initial appointment to the final conclusions of the examination. Typically, the polygraph exam consists of three phases.

First Phase

This involves the pretest portion of the examination including the obtaining and evaluating of the case facts. In a controlled test environment the background and history of the subject is reviewed. Rapport is established with the subject and a structured pretest interview is done to elicit clinical and other behavioral manifestations of the subject. Ideally the examiner and the subject jointly develop the series of questions used because the subject should know each and every question he will be asked. Control questions are designed for nervous and anxious subjects. The instrument attachments and procedure are then explained to the subject in detail.

Second Phase

This is the testing phase and is accomplished with the sensors applied to the subject. The instrument is balanced with that subject and baseline measurements are obtained which constitute the subject's norms. The examiner asks the subject the predetermined questions and the subject's responses are noted.

Third Phase

This is the diagnostic portion of the examination. The examiner reviews all available information including physical, clinical, behavioral observations, test records, and interpretations. He numerically quantifies the separate tracings for each question, applies a standard and makes a diagnostic decision. The basic role and responsibility of the examiner is to try to prove the subject truthful.

There is considerable controversy and confusion about the accuracy of polygraph examinations. Essentially, accuracy depends on the qualifications of the examiner making the judgments. According to a recent LEAA study,[13] qualified examiners have shown about ninety percent accuracy. It was felt likely that the more competent examiner can do even better. This rate is highly respectable when compared with the accuracy of annual physical exams to detect fatal illnesses, which averages fifty percent, or mere chance.

There are differences of opinion about ways to beat the polygraph exam and cause diagnostic error. Although possible, it is less likely to occur with a highly competent and knowledgeable examiner. Attempts to beat the polygraph have included ingestion or injection of drugs, prior physical exertion, mental gymnastics including fantasy production, pain infliction during the examination, deliberate muscle movements, the use of hypnosis, or relaxation techniques and other altered states of consciousness. Additional problems may arise when dealing with psychotic or psychopathic personalities.

HYPNOSIS AND THE POLYGRAPH

There have been relatively few replicable studies involving hypnosis and polygraph. Those that have been done are contradictory as to the subject's ability to sufficiently alter physiological responses as to cause inaccuracy.

The polygraph essentially measures autonomic nervous system reactions which are the functions that hypnosis and suggestion also affect. It is possible that post-hypnotic suggestions for amnesia or dissociation can alter polygraph results.

Weinstein and associates researched the effects of hypnosis on polygraph results by creating amnesia for disturbing past experiences in subjects and were able to reduce any negative reactions resulting from them. They concluded that an individual who has committed a crime may repress the experience sufficiently to pass the polygraph test. It was also stated that it was possible for an anxious, guilt-ridden individual who is innocent of any crime to give a false positive on the test.

Germann[4] and Cumley[2] studied this question somewhat earlier and concluded that a subject with amnesia induced by hypnosis or post-hypnotic suggestions will not likely be able to beat the polygraph exam.

Hypnosis has been used effectively to enhance the accuracy of polygraph examinations with guilt-ridden, overly anxious hyperreactors. The subject learns how to remain relaxed at his baseline physiological levels and to respond honestly and accurately to each question asked. One example involved the author's use of hypnosis with a veteran investigator who had been accused of grand theft during the course of an investigation. Although he had reacted strongly during two polygraph examinations, both the examiner and the Internal Affairs investigators had serious questions about the subject's culpability.

Three brief hypnosis sessions enabled the investigator to remain relaxed and to give truthful responses on the next polygraph examination. It was discovered that a repressed early childhood event involving guilt feelings had become associated with the current crime investigation and the original affect was being displaced onto it. The subject passed the third polygraph examination unequivically and a short time later the real suspect was apprehended and the money recovered.

Raskin[9] and Podlesny[8] have extensively reviewed the research literature on polygraph and deception and also have conducted several research studies. They conclude that much more work needs to be done in this area before definitive answers are possible.

VOICE PRINTS

During World War II, Bell Telephone Laboratories conducted

research attempting to identify enemy radio voices. Out of this work grew voice identification using the spectrograph to analyze the sound of spoken words and record the acoustical patterns on dimensions of time, frequency and amplitude. The resulting spectrograms can be used for visual "voice print" comparison. Although not yet admissable in court, voice prints have proved a useful investigative tool. More scientifically based research is necessary, as with the polygraph.[1]

VOICE STRESS ANALYSIS

There has been a recent proliferation of interest in use of instruments called psychological stress evaluators to correlate voice stress factors in vocalizations with truthfulness or deception. There is considerable controversy about the usefulness and accuracy of these instruments and techniques. Among the positive reports are those by Kradz,[6] Worth and Lewis,[15] and Taylor.[11] However, on the negative side, Montgomery[7] reviewed studies on voice stress analyzers and concluded that the ability of voice analyzers to determine truth is questionable. As with the polygraph, it appears that the competence of the examiner and the consequent quality of the evaluation may be primary.

PUPILLOMETRICS

This is a relatively new field of measurement utilizing the change in the size of the pupil of the eye to evaluate sensory, emotional and mental activity.[11] As are the parameters measured by the polygraph and the psychologcal stress evaluator, pupil size changes are also mediated by the sympathetic division of the autonomic nervous system. To date, very little has been done in applying this new area of research to investigative uses.

DRUGS

There are no real truth serums. There are only classes of drugs such as barbiturates, amphetamines, anti-depressants, and tranquilizers which may have sedative effects on individuals. Gottschalk[5] has comprehensively reviewed the use of drugs in interrogaton situations and concludes that individuals may fantasize, confabulate or lie under drugs if they are so motivated. In addition, there are complications in using drugs that involve the issues of coercion, control, and the possibility of adverse toxic and psychophysiologic reactions, including anaphylactic shock.

There is no special power or magic in the use of drugs to elicit information from people, nor is there with hypnosis or routine interview. The key variables remain subject motivation and cooperation, the nature of the relationship to the hypnotist and actual possession by the subject of the information desired. For these reasons, it is generally undesirable for hypno-investigators to utilize drugs in eliciting information from volunteer witnesses or victims.

References

1. Atal, B. Speech analysis and synthesis by linear prediction of the speech wave. *Journal of the Acoustical Society of America,* August 1971, 637-655.
2. Cumley, W.E. Hypnosis and the polygraph. *Police,* November-December, 1959, p. 39.
3. Davis, R.C. Physiological responses as a means of evaluating information. *The Manipulation of Human Behavior* (A. Biderman and H. Zimmer, Eds.). New York: Wiley, 1961, 142-168.
4. Germann, A.C. Hypnosis as related to the scientific detection of deception by polygraph examination: A pilot study. *International Journal of Clinical and Experimental Hypnosis,* 1961, 9, 309-311.
5. Gottschalk, L.A. The use of drugs in interrogation. *Manipulation of Human Behavior* (A. Biderman and H. Zimmer, Eds.). New York: Wiley, 1961, 96-141.
6. Kradz, M.P. *Psychological Stress Evaluator: A Study.* Ellicott City, Maryland: Howard County Police Department, 1971.
7. Montgomery, J. The psychological stress evaluator in truth verification. *Assets Protection,* 1978, 3, No. 1, 6-13.
8. Podlesny, J.A. and Raskin, D.C. Physiological measures and the detection of deception. *Psychological Bulletin,* 1977, 84, No. 4, 782-799.
9. Raskin, D.C., Barland, G.H. and Podlesny, J.A. *Validity and Reliability of Deception,* Mimeo, 1977.
10. Reid, J.E. and Inbau, F.E. *Truth and Deception: The Polygraph Technique.* Baltimore: Williams & Wilkins, 1966.
11. Senders, J.W. *Eye Movements and the Higher Psychological Functions.* Hillside, New Jersey: Erlbaum Associates, 1978.
12. Taylor, L.L. Psychological stress evaluator (PSE). *IACP Police Law Reporter* (no date).
13. Test measures polygraph accuracy. *Law Enforcement Assistance Administration (LEAA) Newsletter,* March 1977, p. 21.
14. Weinstein, M.D., Abrams, S. and Gibbons, D. The validity of the polygraph with hypnotically induced repression and guilt. *American Journal of Psychiatry,* February 1970, 1159-1162.
15. Worth, J.W. and Lewis, B.J. *An Early Validation Study with the Psychological Stress Evaluator (PSE).* Lexington, Virginia: Washington and Lee University, 1972.

CHAPTER 13
HYPNOSIS AND CRIME - SOCIAL AND ANTI-SOCIAL ASPECTS

Hypnosis itself is a benign tool. Like a screwdriver, it can be used as an aid to constructing something or it could be used as a weapon to stab someone. It is the manner of applying the hypnosis process rather than the tool itself which determines whether hypnosis will have a social or antisocial effect. Hammerschlag,[5] Estabrooks,[2] and Watkins[18] concluded that it is possible to misuse suggestion and hypnosis for the purposes of furthering crime. In large part, it depends on the nature of the bond or relationship between the people involved and the consequent amount of influence being exerted. It is interesting to note that most crimes involving the influence of one person on another, such as confidence games, acting-out because of love relationships, or illegally conspiring to gain wealth, do not require the induction of hypnosis. Case reports suggest that hypnosis has rarely been used in crime situations and when it was, tended to involve psychopathic or hysterical personalities.

CASES

These early cases are reported by Hammerschlag:[5]

1. In 1857 a young girl became pregnant as a result of treatment by a therapeutic magnetizer and she had no later memory of it. Experts at that time concluded that impregnation under animal magnetism was possible.

2. In 1858 a 13-year-old girl suffered from a nervous disease. A key question was: Did the girl develop this affliction because of improper treatment, especially magnetic stroking? The court said "yes" and fined the therapist.

3. In 1894 a 36-year-old male named Cyznski was indicted in Munich for "removing her willpower and wickedly abusing Baroness Hedwig von Zedlitz using hypnosis and suggestion". He had married the victim in a fake wedding. Hammerschlag concluded that love, not hypnosis, had overpowered her.

4. A notorious, well-documented criminal case occurred in Heidelburg, Germany in 1934. A woman was defrauded of money by a man posing as a doctor. He had hypnotized her into prostitution, attempts to murder her husband, and also to attempts to kill herself. A prominent psychologist, Dr. Ludwig Mayer, used regression and other techniques to remove the post-hypnotically suggested amnesia. The suspect, Franz Walter, was finally connected to the situation, convicted and sentenced to ten years in prison. Later, medical and psychiatric examinations by reputable experts found no moral defects or predisposition to emotional upsets in the victim.[2]

In 1951 another classic case occurred in Denmark.[14] A man robbed a bank and killed two employees in the process. After he was apprehended, it was discovered that he had been cell mates with a criminal during the Second World War and had been repeatedly hypnotized into an obedient relatonship by the hypnotist who subsequently used the letter "X" as a hypnotic reinforcer to maintain his dominant relationship over the victim. In this situation there was obviously a very close emotional relationship with sexual overtones that has to be considered along with the use of hypnosis as motivating the subject's behavior. This case is reminiscent of some current soap operas on television where all varieties of sexual and aggressive acting-out occur without any necessity of hypnosis.

Whether hypnosis can be used to aid in the commission of a crime has been debated for many years and is still controversial. Erickson,[1] Orne[12] and others tend to think not; however, Kline[6] and Watkins[18] feel that it can. Overall, the weight of the evidence suggest that hypnosis can be used to help motivate a person commit a crime, but the crucial factor seems to be the nature of the relationship between the subject and the hypnotist.

Laboratory-type experiments attempting to clarify this issue are generally equivocal since the subject is usually aware that he will not be permitted to do anything really harmful by the respected experimenter, whether it involves throwing acid, picking up snakes, or using a gun.[9,20]

Estabrooks[2] believed that hypnosis can assist someone in preparing an alibi or in framing an innocent person by inducing delusions in a witness. He felt that murder could be manipulated in certain subjects by use of deception, either by structuring it as an experiment or as a patriotic, idealistic act. It also may depend in part, on the hypnotist's attitude. If the operator is skeptical this usually gets communicated to the subject and will likely result in failure. Some subjects will probably not comply at all while others will obey in order to please the operator and gain approval. When attempting to contravene the subject's normal value system, Estabrooks felt that a lengthy conditioning process would be required. Degree of suggestibility seems to be a crucial variable in influencing the person to comply with this kind of request whether it is done in or out of hypnosis.[13]

An example of the power of suggestion is what typically occurs during normal development. In early childhood much of what is communicated in a forceful, authoritarian way by parents and other authorities is reacted to by the child as if it were hypnotic command. These highly charged messages are inserted into the mind at a subconscious level and may remain relatively untouched and active over many years continuing to exert tremendous influence on the individual's personality, self-concept and value system.

MILITARY AND INTELLIGENCE USES

As incredible as the events in *The Manchurian Candidate* might seem, Estabrooks[2] states that there is some basis in fact for such political, military and intelligence uses of hypnosis. Orne[12] disagrees with this view. The recent release of classified government field studies sheds some light on this question.[11]

Estabrooks believed that a specially selected subject could be given certain vital information and then have amnesia suggested for the hypnosis, as well as post-hypnotic suggestion that no one else will be able to hypnotize the subject except the original operator. He feels it might also be suggested that a subject go into a hypnotic state in certain pre-selected situations and still behave normally with others being unable to detect it. The subject would himself be consciously unaware of his actions and would righteously deny any complicity.

He thinks it is also conceivable to plant in various organizations a subject who has been induced into a multiple personality so that in one conscious role he can sincerely deny any military connection. However, the information he has observed consciously would be retrieved under hypnosis outside of the subject's conscious awareness as part of another personality. Theoretically these individuals would not be detectable by ordinary means such as polygraph or drugs.

The effects of brainwashing[16] as well as manifestations of the Stockholm Syndrome, which is experienced by hostages[4] tend to lend credence to what is possible in humans given sufficient belief, suggestibility, or survival motivation.

Teitelbaum[17] also says that murder, check forgery, gifts by will, false confessions, false alibies, false witnesses, and polygraph distortion are possible with deception and expert applications of suggestion and hypnosis.

SOCIAL USES OF HYPNOSIS

In the criminal justice area hypnosis has been used to elicit key information leading to the solution of major crimes.[13] It has been used in investigations to find misplaced jewelry and important documents and to assist amnesia victims in regaining their memory. It has been useful in assisting law enforcement personnel in learning to relax, in decision-making under stress, and in enhancing the results of polygraph examinations as mentioned in Chapter 12. Hypnosis has been used by both prosecution and defense in preparation of criminal and civil cases and has also been used successfully in the investigation of aircraft accidents to determine causes.[15]

THERAPEUTIC USES

Hypnosis has been used to treat psychosomatic disturbances, traumatic neuroses and sexual dysfunctions. It has also been used as a non-toxic anesthesia in childbirth, surgery, dentistry, and to aid cancer patients in maximizing immune system response.[7] It is useful for ego strengthening purposes in counseling and therapy sessions as well as in more depth-oriented therapy involving hypnoanalysis.[19]

EDUCATIONAL USES

Hypnosis has been used for improving study habits, enhancing learning and concentration,[10] memory improvement, and for optimizing performance on examinations. It has also been used to improve atheletic performance in a variety of sports including golf, tennis, football, basketball, swimming, bowling, and skiing.[3] Hypnosis has been useful in enhancing social skills, dancing, public speaking, and interpersonal ease. It has also been used to tap innate creativity in the areas of art, acting, writing and business, utilizing hetero and self-hypnosis.[8]

References

1. Erickson, M.H. An experimental investigation of the possible anti-social use of hypnosis. *Psychiatry*, 1939, *2*, 391-414.
2. Estabrooks, G.H. *Hypnotism*. New York: Sutton, 1957.
3. Galwey, T. *The Inner Game of Tennis*. New York: Random House, 1964.
4. Hassel, C. The hostage situation: exploring the motivation and the cause. *The Police Chief*, September 1975, 55-58.
5. Hammerschlag, H. *Hypnotism and Crime*. Los Angeles: Wilshire Book Company, 1957.
6. Kline, M.V. The production of antisocial behavior through hypnosis: new clinical data. *International Journal of Clinical and Experimental Hypnosis*, April 1972, 80-94.
7. Kroger, W.S. *Clinical and Experimental Hypnosis, 2nd Edition*. Phila.: Lippincott, 1977.
8. LeCron, L.M. *Self-Hypnotism*. Englewood Cliffs. New Jersey: Prentice-Hall, 1964.
9. Levitt, E., et al. Testing the coercive power of hypnosis: committing objectionable acts. *International Journal of Clinical and Experimental Hypnosis*, January 1975, 59-66.
10. Lozanov, G. *Suggestology and Outlines of Suggestopedy*. New York: Gordon and Breach, 1978.
11. Marks, J. *The Search for the "Manchurian Candidate". The CIA and Mind Control*. New York: Times Books, 1979.
12. Orne, M.T. Can a hypnotized subject be compelled to carry out otherwise unacceptable behavior? *International Journal of Clinical and Experimental Hypnosis*, April 1972, 101-116.
13. Reiser, M. Hypnosis and its uses in law enforcement. *The Police Journal* (British) January 1978, 24-33.
14. Reiter, P. *Antisocial and Criminal Acts and Hypnosis*. Springfield, Illinois: Thomas, 1958.
15. Raginsky, B.B. Hypnotic recall of air crash cause. *International Journal of Clinical and Experimental Hypnosis*, 1969, *17*, 1-19.
16. Schein, E.H. The Chinese indoctrination program for prisoners of war. A study of attempted "brainwashing". *Psychiatry*, 1956, *19*, 152-168.
17. Teitelbaum, M. *Hypnosis Induction Technics*. Springfield, Illinois: Thomas, 1969.
18. Watkins, J.G. Antisocial behavior under hypnosis: possible or impossible? *International Journal of Clinical and Experimental Hypnosis*, April 1972, 95-99.
19. Wolberg, L.R. *Hypnoanalysis*. New York: Grune & Stratton, 1945.
20. Young, P.C. Antisocial uses of hypnosis. *Experimental Hypnosis (L.M. LeCron, Ed.)*. New York: Macmillan, 1952, 403-406.

CHAPTER 14
CRIMINOLOGICAL VERSUS PSYCHOTHERAPEUTIC USES OF HYPNOSIS

Kroger[4] states that hypnosis includes increased susceptibility to suggestion. It involves a super-concentrated state of mind and is actually a part of everyday life as evidenced in our reactions to speech-making, salesmanship, and advertising. Hypnosis, a psychological phenomenon, is a tool that can be used for a wide variety of purposes, constructive or nonconstructive.[1] The specific purpose for and method of application of hypnosis determines its particular specialization.[3] When used to treat psychosomatic symptoms or emotional conflicts, it is being applied as a psychotherapeutic tool.[5] When used by an investigator to elicit crime information from a witness or victim, it is used as an investigative tool.

Although there are some areas of overlap, it is important to delineate the practice and specialization of investigative hypnosis from that of psychotherapeutic hypnosis since both involve different processes, professional training and skill.

Investigative hypnosis has neither intent nor direct application of psychotherapeutic techniques. In criminal cases, for purposes of hypermnesia, hypnosis is specifically a nonpsychotherapeutic tool and the process of working with the subject under hypnosis involves different considerations from those of the health professional working with a patient.

There is sometimes confusion about this point because the hypnotic investigator mostly deals with witnesses and victims who have been traumatized and who are emotionally upset. However, it is important to recognize that investigators routinely deal with the same population of traumatized subjects. The introduction of hypnosis into the investigative transaction doesn't alter that fact. Historically, police have been paid by the the community and are required by law to handle this highly charged emotional area involving distressed witnesses and victims of serious crimes. Erickson[2] has opined that police officers handle more trauma on a day-to-day basis than do most doctors.

In the usual interview situation, investigators commonly encounter emotional reactions since most people have strong feelings about police-related contacts and incidents. The subject's emotional reactions are always present, and the need to deal with them in a professional fashion in no way constitutes psychotherapy. Dentists deal with emotional reactions in their patients every day without extensive training in psychotherapeutic techniques. There is a difference between doing psychotherapy and behaving in a therapeutic manner.

An attitude of sympathetic understanding, the willingness to listen closely to the witness's report, and acceptance of any emotional reactivity, will enable the hypno-investigator to help the subject ventilate, reduce stress and feel relieved. Similar results are obtained when a stressed individual has the opportunity of talking to a good friend or family member and "getting it off his chest".[7]

The issue of possible harm to a subject who agrees to a hypnosis session has been raised by some health professionals who tend to equate all hypnosis uses and applications as requiring psychotherapeutic training. Experience indicates that follow-up with subjects who have participated in investigative hypnosis sessions shows no instance of harm accruing to any subject as a result of the hypnosis session. In fact, there are numerous reports of fewer nightmares, better sleeping patterns, reduced stress and anxiety, and an improvement in the individual's self-esteem.[6] These effects are all therapeutic and result from the subjects opportunity to confront the traumatic stress-related crime event and to deal with it more directly. A likely result is less need for repression and other defenses which might lead to symptoms of distress and an encapsulation of the affect attached to the original incident.

The hypno-investigator should routinely ask the subject about physical or psychological conditions being treated and check with the therapist prior to the hypnosis session. It may also be a good opportunity to educate the therapist or physician about investigative hypnosis so that a more objective, informed judgment can be made.

In special cases the hypno-investigator may feel more comfortable with outside professional consultation. This contingency should be explored and arranged for during the pre-planning phase. These may include some child rape situations, and some involving subjects with a history of severe emotional disturbance. Consultation with a licensed health professional should be considered.

Because investigative hypnosis is a specialty and requires particular training and experience applying hypnosis techniques in crime cases, the typical hypnotherapist is not automatically qualified to work as an investigative hypnotist. When arranging for consultation with a licensed health professional who may have some hypnotherapy training, the hypno-investigator will need to educate the individual in the specific requirements and techniques of investigative hypnosis. Many health professionals experienced in hypnotherapy and desirous of consulting with police agencies in crime cases, have recognized their need for additional training in the criminological area and have arranged for it.

References
1. Conn, J. Is hypnosis really dangerous? *International Journal of Clinical and Experimental Hypnosis,* April 1972, 61-79.
2. Erickson, M.H. Personal Communication. April, 1978.
3. Hilgard, E.R. The domain of hypnosis. *American Psychologist,* November 1973, 972-982.
4. Kroger, W.S. *Clinical and Experimental Hypnosis,* 2nd Edition. Philadelphia: Lippincott, 1977.
5. Reiser, M. A note on the use of hypnosis in a police recruit training problem. *American Journal of Clinical Hypnosis,* July 1973, 65-66.
6. Reiser, M. Hypnosis as a tool in criminal investigation. *The Police Chief,* November 1976, 36-49.
7. Sarbin, T.R. and Coe, W.C. *Hypnosis: A Social Psychological Analysis of Influence Communication.* New York: Holt, Rinehart and Winston, 1972.

CHAPTER 15
EYEWITNESS TESTIMONY

At the turn of the century, Munsterberg[9] pointed out the unreliability of eyewitness testimony and this still remains as a serious problem today.[3,14] There are several pertinent variables involved in eyewitness testimony. They include the perceptive and apperceptive potential of the witness, the person's motivation, the meaningfulness of the event and the affective involvement of the witness.[2] Additional factors are the witness's need to obtain closure by filling in gaps, the need to please and to conform, and the differences between conscious and subconscious perception of significant events.[6,10]

Persons with impaired sensory-motor functions or exaggerated biases and stereotypic tendencies will likely not be as reliable witnesses as less impaired individuals. What is perceived is often a function of preconceptions, fears, anxieties, and unsatisfied underlying needs.

Wells[15] points out that a witness's prior knowledge of the value of an object increased the accuracy of identification of the thief, but that knowledge of the value of the object after the crime did not. His experimental results suggested that the effect of the perceived seriousness on the accuracy of eyewitness identification is mediated by processes that operate during the original perception which include things such as selective attention and encoding.

Normally, witnesses consciously observe only a few distinguishing characteristics of the suspect and they are subject to forgetting and distortion over time. This fallibility of the normal observer has been demonstrated in many tests and experiments over the years with very similar results. A large percentage of these witnesses are unable to accurately describe the suspect.[3]

This situation doesn't necessarily change with the number of witnesses involved since there are numerous instances on record of as many as a dozen witnesses incorrectly identifying a suspect. It is also well known that even trained observers such as police officers commonly make errors of observation and identification. Even the seemingly positive witness may be in error. The good eyewitness may express less confidence in his opinion than witnesses who seem more certain about the identification.[14]

Dorcus[5] observed that the likelihood of a witness accurately recalling information relating to an event appears to be correlated with the emotional involvement of the witness in that event. The greater the personal emotional reactivity, the greater the likelihood of recall of significant details.

Factors contributing to witness errors include:

1. External factors - distance from crime scene; kind of lighting; weather conditions; noise or distractions.

2. Physical factors - wearing corrective lenses; hearing impairments.

3. Emotional factors - fear; anger or revenge; stress.

4. Additudinal factors - biases or prejudices - see what *wants* to see.

Hypnosis is playing a significant role in changing the reliability and accuracy of eyewitness recall in major crime cases.[1] Because corroboration is possible in a large number of instances, hypnosis-elicited information such as suspect descriptions, license numbers, vehicle descriptions, and other key information can provide further investigative leads, and either be verified or discounted.

Levendula[8] experimented with a group of police officers by staging a crime event spontaneously and asking each officer to individually write a crime report on the incident. The police officers were subsequently hypnotized and asked to write a second crime report under hypnosis. The results indicated that the second report tended to be more accurate and contained more details about the suspect than did the original crime report. Since that time there have been hundreds of real life cases tending to confirm these early observations.

Another relatively recent finding is that people are perceiving and recording information consciously and subconsciously at the same time. The inputs perceived and recorded subconsciously are outside the individual's awareness and therefore not available for recall on routine interview. However, under hypnosis this subconscious material may become more accessible and may yield information the subject was not aware of having perceived. Hilgard's[7] work on the "Hidden Observer" phenomenon has validated this dual recording mechanism in laboratory studies and Reiser[12] has also reported on it in the clinical literature. He discusses a case involving an extremely intoxicated witness unable to recall anything of value on routine interview by detectives. Under hypnosis she was able to recall considerable detail of value to the investigators and was able to aid in the construction of a composite drawing, later validated against the photograph of the suspect.

The data collected thus far suggests that addition of hypnosis with a motivated, cooperative witness to a major crime tends to significantly increase the possibility of yielding important information to the case investigators.[4] Although the addition of hypnosis to the investigation armamentarium has worked to increase the amount and accuracy of eyewitness recall, it remains important that, whenever possible, information gained under hypnosis be verified by further investigation.[12]

References

1. Arons, H. *Hypnosis in Criminal Investigation.* Springfield, Illinois: Thomas, 1967.
2. Brown, E., Deffenbacher, K. and Sturgill, W. Memory for faces and the circumstances of encounter. *Journal of Applied Psychology,* 1977, *62,* 311-318.
3. Buckhout, R. Eyewitness testimony. *Scientific American,* December 1974, 23-31.
4. Derrick, C. Interrogation by hypnosis. *The Police Chief,* March 1959, 26-29.
5. Dorcus, R.M. *Hypnosis and Its Therapeutic Applications.* New York: McGraw-Hill, 1956.
6. Gerber, S.R. and Schroeder, O. (Eds.). *Criminal Investigation and Interrogation.* New York: W.H. Anderson Company, 1962.
7. Hilgard, E.R. *Divided Consciousness.* New York: Wiley-Interscience, 1977.
8. Levendula, D. The possible role of hypnosis in criminal investigation. *Criminal Investigation and Interrogation* (S.R. Gerber, Ed.). New York: W.H. Anderson Company, 1962, 335-346.
9. Munsterberg, H. *On The Witness Stand,* 1908.
10. Orne, M.T. The potential uses of hypnosis in interrogation. *The Manipulation of Human Behavior* (A. Biderman & H. Zimmer, Eds.). New York: Wiley, 1961, 159-215.
11. Reiser, M. Hypnosis as an aid in a homicide investigation. *The American Journal of Clinical Hypnosis.* 1974, *17,* 84-87.
12. Reiser, M. *Investigative Hypnosis - A Developing Specialty.* Los Angeles Police Department (Mimeo), 1978.
13. Sobel, N.R. *Eye-Witness Identification: Legal and Practical Problems.* New York: Clark Boardman Company, 1972.
14. Wall, P. *Eye-Witness Identification in Criminal Cases.* Springfield, Illinois: Thomas, 1965.
15. Wells, G.L., Leippe, M.R. and Ostrom, T.M. Crime seriousness as a determinant of accuracy in eyewitness identification. *Journal of Applied Psychology,* 1978, *63,* 3, 345-351.

CHAPTER 16
INTERVIEWING TECHNIQUES AND BODY LANGUAGE

The hypno-investigator should experience and convey confidence in regard to his hypnosis role. Although perceived by the subject as an authority figure with considerable status and prestige, the investigative hypnotist should approach the subject directly and honestly, being himself, maintaining an attitude of equals. The setting and atmosphere should be informal and relaxed with the physical comforts of the subject attended to.[4] This includes issues such as bathroom use, room temperature, choice of chair, and optimal privacy.

Because each hypnosis session needs to be recorded in its entirely, the recording equipment should be operating from the first contact with the subject and should remain on until the session is terminated and the subject has left. Recording should be done openly with the knowledge of the subject and is usually best handled in a casual way and explained as a part of the routine.

The pre-induction discussion should be utilized to increase rapport and establish a good working relationship with the subject. The reasons for the hypnosis session should be clearly stated and a preview of the procedures and questions to be explored under hypnosis should be given.

Positive motivation of the subject is of crucial importance. When indicated, reinforcing statements citing the great value of this service to the community in the prevention of additional crimes may be helpful. It should be mentioned that hypno-investigator and subject have common goals and will be working together to achieve those desired objectives. When resistances are noted during the pre-induction interview, they should be explored with the witness and hopefully resolved. Where resistance in a subject is related to the fear of retaliation or revenge, the hypno-investigator should explain the police protection that may be available and point out that the witness's safety is greatly increased if the suspect is behind bars. This reassurance can be incorporated into an image where the subject is looking through a one-way mirror at the suspect in a locked jail cell, without being seen.

One of the main tasks of the hypno-investigator is to listen with focused attention, allowing the subject to respond as freely and completely as possible. In some instances it is desirable to have the subject give a complete uninterrupted narrative of the crime event before proceeding to question for specifics.

The hypno-investigator has to be neutral, objective and interested only in the truth, whatever it may be. He should carefully avoid undue suggestion, coercion, or leading of the subject in any way. He should use open-ended questions, avoiding references to specific objects or things not previously mentioned by the subject. He also needs to be aware of the time lag for the subject's response in hypnosis and not rush into another question before allowing a response to his previous one.

As much as possible the hypnotist should speak the subject's language. With children, vocabulary and images appropriate to the age and developmental level of the particular child should be employed. With adult subjects, the hypnotist should also be alert to language capabilities and communicate at that level in a professional, nontechnical way.[3] When sexual assaults have been part of a crime situation, the hypno-investigator should reassure the subject that he is not interested in the sexual details of what occurred since they are usually already part of the crime report. The subject should not feel pressured or obligated to review or report on the sexual events unless motivated to do so or unless the information is essential to the case.

In the information-eliciting phase of the hypnosis interview, the investigator should start with what is reassuring by setting the scene in as familiar a way to the subject as possible.[7] After the subject has responded spontaneously in narrative form and has reviewed the crime event overall, the hypno-investigator can begin asking questions of a very general nature such as, "What did you see?", "What happened then?", and "Then what?". When the subject mentions or identifies specific persons or objects, the hypno-investigator can get a bit more specific in questioning: "Describe that person please." "What else do you see about the car?"[11]

The interviewing of a witness or victim in hypnosis does not differ significantly from the usual investigative interview.[10] If anything, the hypno-investigator is more sensitive to the words he chooses in communicating with the subject.[1] He is always cognizant of his responsibility to be nonleading, allowing all of the information to come from the subject. His questions are carefully framed to avoid bias.[3]

It is important that the hypno-investigator maintain a non-judgmental atitude without moralizing or communicating in any way that will increase guilt feelings which may be present in the subject as a result of the crime event.

BODY LANGUAGE

The concept of territoriality is necessary in understanding issues of social order. Each group of mammals marks off a territory to keep its group members in and aliens out. Man has his fixed territories, from homes to favorite chairs to keys to the executive washroom.

Kinesic behavior wasn't generally noted until the 1950's and the dominance behaviors of man not studied until the 1960's because of denial and scientists' concern with the spoken language. Studies in sociology, anthropology, and ethology, now clearly indicate that man employs all of the locational, territorial, pecking order and bonding behaviors that are typical of the higher apes.[12]

Dr. Edward Hall of Northwestern University has discussed proxemics, a theory of zones and territories, and how people handle them. He describes four distinct zones for most people.[5]

1. Intimate Distance - From actual contact to six to 18-inches away. Violation of this zone can be seen in elevator behavior where people will stand rigidly observing individual privacy.

2. Personal Distance - Close is approximately one-and-one-half to two feet and far is two-and-one-half to four feet. Moving in too close to an acquaintance is considered being pushy.

3. Social Distance - Close is four to seven feet, the distance at which we usually transact personal business, such as a wife talking to a repairman. Far is from seven to 12 feet, which is exemplified by the boss talking to an employee across a large desk.

4. Public Distance - Close is 12 to 25 feet, such as at informal gatherings. Far is 25 feet or more, such as at political speeches and stage performances.

The need for sensitivity about these zones and respective distances is exemplified in the interaction between the lion tamer and the lions. Very careful attention is paid to the degree of intrusiveness.[9]

There are also cultural differences that need to be considered. The body is considered sacred to an American. To an Arab the violation of body is considered relatively insignificant, but the violation of the ego by insult is considered a major problem.

The typical American has a two-foot bubble of privacy around him, which corresponds to arm length. Intrusion into this body space is very serious when permission is not given. The act of speaking to a stranger in a large metropolitan area will usually get a startle reaction and defensive posture.[8]

Common body language signs an individual may utilize when his private territory is invaded include preliminary tension signals such as rocking, leg swinging, or tapping. Stronger signals consist of closed eyes, pulling down of the chin, and hunching of shoulders. If early signals are ignored he will likely move away. Studies of violent individuals suggest they have a more extended body territory and hyper-react with aggressiveness when their space is invaded.[13]

People have learned over time to hide their real feelings and can to some degree control facial displays; however, eye movements and expressions are hard to mask.[6]

The hypno-investigator can sometimes detect signs of resistance from the subject's body language. Crossed arms or legs, clenched fists, restlessness, and voluntary finger movements rather than reflex ideomotor responses are a few common cues.[14]

The investigative hypnosis session involves considerable closeness and psychological intimacy; however, the old knee-to-knee, hand-holding of the strokers and magnetizers of Mesmer's time are not desirable. Special attention needs to be paid to problems of touching during the hypnosis procedure and implicit permission should be gotten from the subject, prior to physical contact.

References

1. Barbara, D.A. *Your Speech Reveals Your Personality.* Springfield, Illinois: Thomas, 1958.
2. Beier, E.G. and Valens, E.G. *People-Reading.* Stein and Day, 1975.
3. Bernstein, L., Bernstein, R.S., and Dana, R.H. *Interviewing: A Guide for Health Professionals.* New York: Appelton-Century Crofts, 1974.
4. Bingham, W.V. and Moore, B.V. *How to Interview.* New York: Harper, 1959.
5. Birdwhistell, R.L. *Kinesics and Context.* Philadelphia: University of Pennsylvania Press, 1970.
6. Ekman, P. and Friesen, M.V. *Unmasking the Face.* Englewood Cliffs, New Jersey: Prentice-Hall, 1975.
7. Erickson, M.H. Personal Communication.
8. Fast, J. *Body Language.* New York: Pocket Books, 1971.

9. Goffman, E. *Interaction Ritual.* Garden City, New York: Anchor Books, 1967.
10. Kahn, R.L. *The Dynamics of Interviewing: Theory, Techniques and Cases.* New York: Wiley, 1957.
11. Royal, R.F. and Schutt, S.R. *The Gentle Art of Interviewing.* Englewood Cliffs, New Jersey: Prentice-Hall, 1976.
12. Scheflen, A.E. *Body Language and Social Order.* Englewood Cliffs, New Jersey: Prentice-Hall, 1972.
13. Scheflen, A.E. *How Behavior Means.* Garden City, New York: Anchor Books, 1974.
14. Spiegel, J.P. and Machotka, P. *Messages of the Body.* New York: The Free Press, 1974.

CHAPTER 17
ROLE OF THE COMPOSITE ARTIST

The experienced composite artist has a potentially important role to play in investigative hypnosis. Ideally, the artist is trained in investigative hypnosis and participates in the hypnosis session, interacting with the subject to elicit accurate physical descriptors and structural facial details. The artist's skills allow them to be translated into an accurate representation of the witness's revivified mental image of the suspect. The police artist must be aware of the anatomical probabilities of described physical and facial features and be able to predict, within normal limits, what facial details and proportions are likely to go together and which are not.[1] This knowledge is especially important when working with subjects who may have some underlying motivation to distort or to fabricate.[4]

Many law enforcement agencies do not have the services of a composite artist and instead make use of one of the several commercial composite kits available. These devices, including the Identi-Kit,[3] the Multiple Image Maker and Identification Compositor, and the Photo-Fit, are systems currently on the market utilizing overlays, film strips, or multiple choice approaches. Although using slightly different approaches, they all attempt to assemble the suspect's face using an array of parts the witness may select from.[2]

It is the author's opinion that these kits can be very useful in arriving at an approximation of a suspect's facial appearance. However, the kits have some inherent limitations. They lack the flexibility, creativity and perceptiveness of the composite artist who is able to gradually upgrade the drawing in very subtle ways until it closely matches the subject's recalled mental picture.

The police artist may work in black and white or in color, depending on what reproduction equipment is available for distributing the finished drawings to field personnel. Currently, experimental works is being done at the Los Angeles Police Department by composite artist, Fernando Ponce, using three-dimensional graphics. Similar to sculpture techniques, the artist fashions from plasticene material a face having depth and texture as well as specific facial features. This enables increased possibilities for description and recognition purposes.

Agency size usually is a determining factor in whether a police artist is available in-house or whether outside artists are utilized on a part-time basis, such as a newspaper artist asked to volunteer services in a particular case. The large law enforcement agency with a heavy case load of major crimes will find the in-house artist's work invaluable in the identification and concomitant prevention of further crimes by the rapid apprehension of that suspect.

At the Los Angeles Police Department, the police artist who has been trained in investigative hypnosis is present during the entire investigative hypnosis session. The hypno-investigator works with the subject to the point of getting a narrative description of the suspect, usually during the TV technique (described in Chapter 31), and the artist begins his preliminary or upgraded drawing.

At an appropriate point in the session the hypno-investigator will indicate to the subject that the police artist would now like to ask specific questions about the suspect's features in order to construct a more accurate composite drawing. When the preliminary drawing is done as far as is possible, the hypno-investigator and the police artist then together work with the subject.

They have the subject remain in hypnosis, but with eyes open examine the police artist's drawing and compare it with the accurate and vivid image of the suspect that the subject has kept in mind from the TV documentary film. In a process involving eyes open and closed comparisons between mental image and drawing as it is being modified, the subject aids the composite artist in drawing a face that eventually will look as much like the suspect as possible.

Corroboration of composite drawing details done under hypnosis with those done nonhypnotically, at the Los Angeles Police Department and at other criminal justice agencies, indicates the likelihood of getting increased accurate detail under hypnosis. This requires a motivated, cooperative witness.

In some cases, witnesses in the hypnosis process have expressed some frustration about the difficulty of translating into words the recalled mental image of the suspect. In a few cases, the subject with some training and facility in drawing or art has been able to directly draw an accurate rendition of the suspect's face, acting as an artist as well as being the subject under hypnosis. However, most subjects lack the necessary training and skills and would find it very difficult. For the majority of cases, the presence of a police artist is most desirable. If that isn't possible, one of the kits may be adequate.

References
1. Allen, A.L. *Personal Descriptions.* London: Butterworth and Company, 1950.
2. Allison, H.C. *Personal Identification.* Boston: Holbrook Press, 1973.
3. Owen, C. Identi-kit enters its second decade, ever growing at home and abroad. *Fingerprint and Identification,* November, 1970, 11-17.
4. Ringel, W.E. *Identification and Police Line-Ups.* Jamaica, New York: Gould Publications, 1968.

CHAPTER 18
ADDITIONAL INDUCTION TECHNIQUES, DIRECT AND INDIRECT

Teitelbaum[12] classifies hypnosis approaches to the subject into four basic categories: The relaxation approach; the catalystic approach; the permissive approach; and the authoritarian approach.

A variety of relaxation approaches are usually used in so-called indirect methods of induction where the word "hypnosis" is avoided and terminology suggesting relaxation and comfort are used instead. The operator utilizes physiological parameters such as breathing, muscle relaxation and includes suggestions of mental quiet and relaxation of the total organism. This reduces the possibility of resistance arising with subjects who are sensitive to the word "sleep".

The catalystic approach involves the use of rapid techniques. Word cues or acts precipitate the subject into a hypnotic state as a form of conditioned reflex.

The permissive approach minimizes anxieties by communicating to the subject that all hypnosis is self-hypnosis and that the subject is in complete control at all times during the hypnosis procedure.

In the authoritarian approach, the operator openly dominates and "takes control" of the subject who is lead to believe that he must and will behave as the hypnotist commands.

Although each of these approaches may be appropriate in a specific situation, the combined relaxation and permissive approaches are recommended for the majority of subjects of hypno-investigators.[1,10,11,13]

DIRECT INDUCTION TECHNIQUES

Eyes Opening and Closing Technique

The subject is asked to close the eyes on odd numbers and

open them on even numbers. The operator then begins counting; on one, the subject's eyes should be closed. On the count of two the subject will open his eyes, and close them again on three. The operator continues to count slowly, gradually increasing the time spent on the odd numbers with the eyes remaining closed. The operator intersperses suggestions of eye fatigue and heaviness, with increasing difficulty in opening the eyes on even numbers. It is suggested that shortly it will be so difficult to open the eyes on even numbers that they will instead remain closed and that will be fine. When the subject's eyes remain closed during the count of several odd and even numbers, the operator should then suggest that as the count continues, each number spoken will enable subject to go deeper into hypnosis and become even more relaxed.

Sacerdote's Sculpture Technique

The operator asks the subject to raise the non-dominant hand in a relaxed pose to eye level and to pay close attention to what can be observed about the subject's own hand. The operator then begins to describe the hand as if it were a piece of sculpture pointing out the smoothness, the symmetry, the shape of the fingers and fingernails, the texture of the surface, smooth flowing lines, in a slow soothing tone of voice. There should be frequent lengthly pauses between descriptions with the instruction that as the subject pays attention to this hand, more and more about the hand will become obvious and can be appreciated by the subject and as it becomes obvious and appreciated the subject may relax and think about a favorite picture or painting or sculpture and as this happens the subject's eyes may close and the subject may feel more relaxed and comfortable. Suggestions can then be given that the hand will slowly lower to the subject's lap and as it reaches the lap the subject's eyes will be closed, if not already shut and the subject will go into a deep state of relaxation.[9]

Imagery Techniques

Kroger and Fezler[8] describe numerous imagery techniques that can be used for hypnotic induction and deepening. The subject is asked to close his eyes and relax, to begin breathing more deeply and regularly, to relax with each breath that is taken. The hypnotist then describes a scene that the subject is asked to imagine. The scene should be relaxing and agreeable to the subject. It can be a beach scene, a mountain scene, a country scene, a desert scene, a swimming pool scene, ad infinitum. The operator utilizes in his description as many of the sensory modalities as possible. In describing a beach scene, he could talk about the clean smell of the sea air, the fresh taste of the salt upon the lips, the pleasant relaxing warmth of the sun on the body, the satisfying tension of the leg muscles as one walks through the sand, the feeling of feet and toes sinking into the sand, and the soothing sound of the surf as the waves come in, one after the other. There is also the endless reassuring movement of the ocean under the blue sky, the white fleecy clouds and the seagulls flying lazily in the air.

Nonverbal Technique (Written)

This induction technique is written out on a card or sheet of paper and handed to the subject. It may be suitable for deaf or hearing impaired subjects and for those who have difficulty maintaining concentration.

"As you read the instructions on this card *slowly* and *carefully,* your eyes will gradually become very *tired* and your eyelids will become *very, very heavy.* But you will be able to read to the end of this card and follow these instructions which will be helpful to you.

"Breathe in *deeply,* and exhale *slowly,* and begin relaxing all of the muscles in your body, large and small, from the top of your head to the tips of your toes. With each breath you take, you are *breathing in relaxation,* and *exhaling tension.* It's *relaxation in, tension out.*

"But no matter how deeply you relax, whenever I touch your *right shoulder,* your eyes will open and you will become fully *consciously and normally alert.* Whenever I touch your left shoulder, your eyes will close and you will go back into a *deep state of relaxation and hypnosis.*

"Whenever I touch your *forehead,* you will *remain deeply relaxed and in hypnosis,* your *eyes will open* and you will be able to read and follow any additional instructions written or signaled to you.

"With each word you are reading and with each breath you are taking, your *eyes* are becoming *more and more tired,* and your *eyelids* are becoming *heavier and heavier.* Very soon you will feel more and more like closing your eyes and drifting into a deep, pleasant state of relaxation, physically, mentally and spiritually.

"When you finish reading the suggestions on this card, your

eyelids will close and remain tightly closed as if glued shut, and you will continue to relax more easily and deeply.

"Do you have any questions so far? You can let me know by shaking your head. If you do, write your question on this paper near you. If not, just continue reading and following the written instructions.

"Very soon, you will come to the end of these instructions. When you finish reading the last word, focus your very tired, drowsy eyes on the black dot and silently and slowly count from 1 to 20.

"With *each count* you make, and with *each breath* you take, you *eyelids* will get *heavier and heavier.* You will feel very *drowsy* and will want to *close* them by the time you count to 15. You will then be in a *very relaxed, very drowsy state.* With each number you count past 15, you will *go deeper relaxed*, into a *deep, deep,* pleasant hypnotic state.

"Very good. When you finish reading this sentence, focus your tired, drowsy eyes on the black dot and begin counting silently to 20."

Erickson's Naturalistic Techniques

This is a slightly modified induction technique that is characteristic of the naturalistic approach.[3]

"I would like to have you take a comfortable position in your chair with your legs uncrossd, your feet flat on the floor, and your elbows at the sides of your chest and with your hands on your thighs, but without your thumbs touched each other. Look about the room and pick some small spot to look at steadily. Don't move a single muscle in your body, just keep looking at that spot. Don't even speak. Just listen. In that way, you will keep your ears in the same position and you will hear me more clearly. As you look at that spot and continue to look at that spot, there will occur within you a number of changes.

"You probably have not realized it but already the rhythm of your breathing has changed. It is slower, it is comfortable, and it is a good rhythm. I can see your pulse in the temple (or neck) and I can tell you that your heart has slowed down a little bit and that means that your blood pressure has lowered to meet the resting condition of your body.

"Now I would like to explain something to you. When you first went to school and learned to recognize numbers and letters, you didn't know at that time that you were learning those numbers and letters for all the rest of your life. You learned what a 'three' looked like and what a 'six' looked like and what a 'nine' looked like. You formed a mental picture of those numbers and you formed the mental visual picture to stay with you all the rest of your life. You learned to form a mental visual picture of each letter of the alphabet without thinking about the fact that you would keep that visual image all the rest of your life. In looking at that spot that you have chosen, you have already formed a visual mental picture of it so you can now close your eyes and just look at the mental visual picture that you have formed of it.

"As I talk to you, you can keep right on looking mentally at that mental picture. As I talk to you, if you want to, you can hear any sounds that you wish: a sonic boom, the cars on the street, the noise in the next room, but actually, the only important thing for you right now is the sound of my voice and the meaning of what I say to you, so you don't really need to give attention to anything else unless you have a particular interest in the sonic boom, or the cars on the street, or the birds outside.

"Now I am going to discuss your problems and I will do it in this way. I will sketch it in general and I want you to realize that I am going to ask of you only the things that are actually possible for you to do. There are many things that we can do of which we are unaware. We can attend a lecture and because the lecturer is interesting and stimulating, we don't even notice the passage of time and are just interested in what he is saying. But if we attended a lecture where the lecturer was dull, boring and tiresome, one would feel the hardness of the seat of the chair, and yet it is the same chair in which you could sit and listen to an interesting lecturer and never feel all the discomforts and distress of not moving and the hardness of the seat, but with the good lecturer, you don't even hear anything except his voice. Now you are here to listen to me. You are here to do certain things. In your lifetime of experience, you have felt things and you have not felt some things that you could have felt if you had paid attention to them. You have had much experience in forgetting things that would seem upon ordinary thinking to be unforgetable.

"For example, you are introduced to somebody and you reply, "I am very pleased to meet you, Mr. Jones," and two seconds later, you are thinking to yourself, "What on earth is his name?"

You have forgotten just as fast as you heard it. In other words, you can do any of the things that I will ask of you. You know how to move. You can lower your blood pressure, but you don't know how you do that. You can slow down your heartbeat, but you don't know how you do that. You can alter the rhythm of your breathing, but you don't know how you do that; but all of the things I ask you to do, every one of them, will be within the range of your experience, so just listen carefully, knowing that I will ask of you only those things that I know you can do.

"First of all, I want you to enjoy feeling very comfortable. In fact, you can enjoy yourself so much that you can let your unconscious mind listen to me while your conscious mind can sleep or busy itself with thoughts about things far removed from this office, because many of the things that I want to assist you in accomplishing are governed by your unconscious mind, and so now continue as you are, at ease, in comfort, and at the proper time I will give you all the directions necessary for you to remember what is important to remember."

The following is another variation on the Ericksonian technique:

Instructions: Have subject sit comfortably in a chair. Point to any object suitable for eye fixation.

"Now just look right at this. Don't move, and don't talk. Take a deep breath, let it out slowly. The *only* thing that's important to you is what I'm saying to you. And when next I say "Now," just close your eyes...Now close your eyes, and keep them closed until I ask you to open them. And as I speak to you...your heart rate...changes, your respiration rate...changes, your blood pressure...changes, your temperature...changes. And I'm going to remind you of the time when you first learned how to write. Just let your mind drift back to that time...You're sitting hunched over that scratchy brown paper, with the light blue lines. Big spaces between the lines, separated by broken blue lines. You're squeezing onto that thick old pencil very tightly. And you wonder 'Does the "m" have one hump, or two. Or is it the "n" that has two humps?' 'And where do I make the line and the circle for the "d," the "p," the "b"?' 'Is the "w" an upside-down "m"?' 'Is the "e" the one that's the short loop, or is it the "l"?' 'Which way does the hump face for the "b"?' I know it's different drom the "d".'

"And now, just let your mind drift again...To a very pleasant and happy time in your life. It can be a scene from the present, the recent or distant past. It doesn't really matter. Just so long as it's a time when you were very very happy and carefree. Just let all the details of that scene come very clearly to you. The time of the year...Who was there...What the weather was like ...the temperature...Notice the colors...Any sounds and smells. And now tell me, how old are you in this scene? And what's taking place?

"Now in order to deepen the hypnosis, just count to yourself silently, slowly and mentally from one to twenty. And feel more and more comfortable and deeper into the hypnosis with each count. Go ahead. Next, I'm going to ask you to come out of the hypnosis...from the neck up. Your body will remain completely in hypnosis, but you'll be completely awake and alert from the neck up. Just count to yourself silently, slowly and mentally from 'A' to 'E', and on 'E' your eyes will open, and you'll be out of the hypnosis from the neck up, but your body will remain deeply in the hypnosis. Go ahead and count from 'A' to 'E'. (Allow subject time for self-observation, and ask) How does it feel to have your body in hypnosis?

"Now you know what it feels like to be in hypnosis. Close your eyes and return fully and completely into the hypnosis. Now come completely out of the hypnosis, just go ahead and count once again to 'E', silently, mentally and slowly. Take your time, there's no rush at all. And on 'E' your eyes will open and you'll be completely out of the hypnosis."

Indirect Techniques

Erickson and others have also developed several indirect hypnosis techniques.[5,6,7]

Rehearsal Technique

This technique may be useful for very anxious subjects or those who are skeptical or who have resistances based on fear or apprehension. It is suggested to the subject that it would be very instructive to rehearse the hypnosis technique before actually doing it formally. The subject is asked to comply with all of the suggestions even though it is just a rehearsal and to go through the motions as if the subject were actually participating in a real hypnosis induction session. This technique allows the subject to retain the feeling of being in control and yet gradually experiencing the induction process, which has a desensitizing effect. Quite frequently the "rehearsal" subject will go into a good state of hypnosis and relaxation without needing a second, formal induction process.

Observation Technique

This is a variation on the rehearsal technique except that the intended hypnotic subject is asked to watch someone else being hypnotized and to observe very closely all of the reactions and manifestations of the subject as the hypnosis procedure occurs. This has the effect of conditioning the observer who often will also respond to hypnotic suggestions directed at the primary subject. Erickson utilizes subtle voice cues, eye contact, and covert suggestions to the observer during this technique.

Pantomime Techniques

Erickson[4] describes techniques using sign language, touching cues, and other gestures in working with deaf, speech-impaired persons, and others who have difficulty with the usual verbalized instrutions.

References

1. *A Syllabus on Hypnosis and a Handbook of Therapeutic Suggestions.* Des Plaines, Illinois: American Society of Clinical Hypnosis, 1973.
2. Crasilneck, H.B. and Hall, J.A. *Clinical Hypnosis. Principles and Applications.* New York: Grune & Stratton, 1975.
3. Erickson, M.H. Naturalistic techniques of hypnosis. *American Journal of Clinical Hypnosis,* 1958, 1, 3-9.
4. Erickson, M.H. Pantomime techniques in hypnosis and the implications. *American Journal of Clinical Hypnosis,* 1964, 7, 64-70.
5. Erickson, M.H. and Rossi, E.L. and Rossi, S. *Hypnotic Realities. The Induction of Clinical Hypnosis and Forms of Indirect Suggestion.* New York: Irvington Press, 1976.
6. Evans, F.J. An experimental indirect technique for the induction of hypnosis without awareness. *International Journal of Clinical and Experimental Hypnosis,* 1967, 15, 72.
7. Haley, J. (Ed.). *Advanced Techniques of Hypnosis and Therapy. Selected Papers of Milton H. Erickson.* New York: Grune & Stratton, 1967.
8. Kroger, W.S. and Fezler, W.D. *Hypnosis and Behavior Modification: Imagery Conditioning.* Philadephia: Lippincott, 1976.
9. Sacerdote, P. Some individualized psychotherapeutic techniques. *International Journal of Clinical and Experimental Hypnosis,* 1970, 18, 160-180.
10. Spiegel, H. and Spiegel, D. *Trance and Treatment.* New York: Basic Books, 1978.
11. Spiegel, H. An eye-roll test for hypnotizability. *American Journal of Clinical Hypnosis,* 1972, 15, 25-28.
12. Teitelbaum, M. *Hypnosis Technics.* Springfield, Illinois: Thomas, 1969.
13. Weitzenhoffer, A.M. *General Techniques of Hypnotism.* New York: Grune and Stratton, 1957.

CHAPTER 19
TRANCE DEPTH PHENOMENA

Hypnotic ability appears to be a normally distributed trait. Depth potential varies from person to person and within the same person at different times. Although certain hypnotic behaviors tend to occur more frequently at particular levels of hypnosis, research studies reveal that there is no direct correlation with hypnotic phenomena and the depth of hypnosis.[1,8] Most subjects appear to have an optimal level of hypnosis which remains fairly constant and practice may help an individual achieve this depth.[4]

There are a large number of depth classification scales and criteria.[2,5,6,10] Most of these have been used in research studies in attempting to increase specificity of hypnotic behavior in trance states; however, these scales really measure only the amount of suggestibility the subject evidences in the hypnotic state using behavioral indices. These scales are reviewed in some detail by Weitzenhoffer[8] and Hilgard.[3]

One of the oldest and most mentioned scales of hypnotic depth is the Davis-Husband Scale of Hypnotic Susceptibility.[1,4] It divides hypnosis into five depth categories which in turn are subdivided by a number of hypnotic responses at each level. A simplified version of this scale which can be used by the hypno-investigator more easily is the shortened three-depth version as follows:

Light Trance
1. Relaxation
2. Eye closure
3. Slowing of muscular activities
4. Ability to perform simple post-hypnotic suggestions

Medium Trance
5. Glove anesthesia
6. Partial amnesia
7. Catalepsy of entire skeletal musculature

Deep or Somnambulistic Trance

8. Ability to open eyes without affecting trance
9. Posthypnotic anesthesia
10. Bizarre posthypnotic suggestions
11. Positive hallucinations
12. Negative hallucinations
13. Subjective feeling of detachment

A more detailed scoring system for depth of hypnosis used for research purposes is the Lecron-Bordeaux Scale as follows:[4]

LECRON-BORDEAUX SCORING SYSTEM FOR INDICATING DEPTH OF HYPNOSIS

Depth	Score	Symptoms and Phenomena Exhibited
Insusceptible...	0....	Subject fails to react in any way.
Hypnoidal......	1....	Physical relaxation.
	2....	Drowsiness apparent.
	3....	Fluttering of eyelids.
	4....	Closing of eyes.
	5....	Mental relaxation, partial lethargy of mind.
	6....	Heaviness of limbs.
Light trance....	7....	Catalepsy of eyes.
	8....	Partial limb catalepsy.
	9....	Inhibition of small muscle groups.
	10....	Slower and deeper breathing, slower pulse.
	11....	Strong lassitude (disinclination to move, think or act).
	12....	Twitching of mouth or jaw during induction.
	13....	Rapport between subject and operator.
	14....	Simple posthypnotic suggestions heeded.
	15....	Involuntary start or eye twitch on awakening.
	16....	Personality changes.
	17....	Feeling of heaviness throughout entire body.
	18....	Partial feeling of detachment.
Medium Trance.........	19....	Recognition of trance (difficult to describe but definitely felt).

TRANCE DEPTH PHENOMENA

Depth	Score	Exhibited
	20....	Complete muscular inhibition (kinesthetic delusions).
	21....	Partial amnesia.
	22....	Glove anesthesia.
	23....	Tactile illusions.
	24....	Gustatory illusions.
	25....	Olfactory illusions.
	26....	Hyperacuity to atmospheric conditions.
	27....	Complete catalepsy of limbs or body.
Deep or Somnambulistic Trance.........	28....	Ability to open eyes without affecting trance.
	29....	Fixed stare when eyes are open; pupillary dilation.
	30....	Somnambulism
	31....	Complete amnesia.
	32....	Systematized posthypnotic amnesias.
	33....	Complete anesthesia.
	34....	Posthypnotic anesthesia.
	35....	Bizarre posthypnotic suggestions heeded.
	36....	Uncontrolled movements of eyeballs, eye coordination lost.
	37....	Sensation of lightness, floating, swinging, of being bloated or swollen, detached feeling.
	38....	Rigidity and lag in muscular movements and reactions.
	39....	Fading and increase in cycles of the sound of operator's voice (like radio station fading in and out).
	40....	Control of organic body functions (heartbeat, blood pressure, digestions).
	41....	Recall of lost memories (hypermnesia).
	42....	Age regression.
	43....	Positive visual hallucinations; posthypnotic.
	44....	Negative visual hallucinations; posthypnotic.

Depth	Score	Exhibited
	45	Positive auditory hallucinations; posthypnotic.
	46	Negative auditory hallucinations; posthypnotic.
	47	Stimulation of dreams (in trance or posthypnotic in natural sleep).
	48	Hyperaesthesias.
	49	Color sensations experienced.
Plenary Trance	50	Stuporous condition in which all spontaneous activity is inhibited. Somnambulism can be developed to that effect.

Yardstick of Hypnosis

Probably the best measure of hypnotic depth, which usually fluctuates during the hypnosis process, is the subject's report. LeCron[4] recommends the yardstick approach in having the subject estimate his own depth of hypnosis.

In this technique, it is explained to the subject that in his present state of hypnosis he is somewhere on the yardstick of hypnosis from zero to 36. The numbers on the yardstick from zero to 12 represent a light state, from 13 to 24 a medium state, and from 25 to 36, a deep state of hypnosis. On signal, the subject's inner mind will indicate where on the yardstick of hypnosis he is at that moment. The subject can be asked to verbalize the number that pops into mind from the subconscious or to give a finger signal indicating the digit on the yardstick.

Because verbalizing requires the engaging of higher cortical centers and therefore a possible lightening of the hypnotic state, it may be more accurate to utilize an ideomotor finger signal which allows the subject to respond at a reflex level and remain relatively close to the part of the sine wave of hypnotic depth he is experiencing at that moment. The subject's response will ordinarily give an accurate indication of hypnotic depth.[7]

Percentage of the Population Able to Reach Various Depths

- 5% - refractory cases (do not seem able to go into trance)
- 95% - light trance
- 55% - medium trance
- 20% - deep trance

There are a variety of statistical estimates given for suggestibility among normal adults, but the above percentages seem fairly representative.

The subject of investigative hypnosis need only achieve a light to medium state in order to experience enhanced recall and to elicit crime details of significance to the case investigator. A very deep or somnambulistic state may be counterproductive because of the lethargy and difficulty in verbal response the subject experiences at that level. Subjects in a light hypnotic state may experience some of the variables usually associated with deep hypnosis and vice versa. Hypnotic behavior is ideosyncratic and varies with individuals rather than being only a function of hypnotic depth. The expectations that the hypno-investigator establishes with the subject prior to hypnosis, as well as during the hypnosis process, are highly important regarding the degree of success the subject achieves with the recall tasks.

In those instances where the subject is refractory and apparently unable or unwilling to go into hypnosis, waking suggestions and/or ideomotor responses may be utilized, including the pendulum, in order to retrieve information and to further evaluate the subject's cooperativeness and hypnotizability.

References

1. Ehrenreich, G.A. The influence of unconscious factors on hypnotizability. *Clinical Correlates of Experimental Hypnosis* (M.V. Kline, Ed.). Springfield, Illinois: Thomas, 1963, 136-151.
2. Frankel, F.H. *Hypnosis. Trance as a Coping Mechanism.* New York: Plenum Medical Book Company, 1976.
3. Hilgard, E.R. *Hypnotic Susceptibility.* New York: Harcourt, Brace & World, 1965.
4. LeCron, L. and Bordeaux, J. *Hypnotism Today.* New York: Grune & Stratton, 1949.
5. Shor, R.E. Three dimensions of hypnotic depth. *The Nature of Hypnosis* (R.E. Shor and M.T. Orne, Eds.). New York: Holt, Rinehart and Winston, 1965, 306-321.
6. Shor, R.E. and Orne, E.C. *Harvard Group Scale of Hypnotic Susceptibility.* Palo Alto, California: Consulting Psychologists Press, 1962.
7. Tart, C.T. Quick and convenient assessment of hypnotic depth: Self-report scales. *American Journal of Clinical Hypnosis,* 1978, *21,* 186-207.
8. Von Dedenroth, T.E.A. Trance depth: An independent variable in therapeutic results. *American Journal of Clinical Hypnosis,* 1962, *4,* 174.
9. Weitzenhoffer, A.M. *General Techniques of Hypnotism.* New York: Grune & Stratton, 1957.
10. Weitzenhoffer, A.M. and Hilgard, E.R. *Standard Hypnotic Susceptibility Scale.* Palo Alto, California: Consulting Psychologists Press, 1959.

CHAPTER 20
VICTIMOLOGY AND TRAUMATIC REACTIONS

Crisis states result from stress overloads that are sudden, arbitrary and unpredictable. They can be precipitated by accidents, natural disasters, or crime.[6] Being victimized by violent crime is one of the most stressful events one can experience. The shock and injury to the individual's ego lead to a state of crisis involving emotional flux, disequilibrium and the potential for either increased disturbance or improved functioning. The outcome of the crime victim's state of crisis and coping abilities will often hinge on how it is handled by those interveners from the criminal justice system.[7]

Rape is one of the most traumatic crimes against the person because it involves a forcible intrusion into the most private body space, with aggressive and violent intent. The victim of rape suffers extreme psychological insult and commonly goes through what has been described as the rape trauma syndrome.[3] The effects of rape have immediate and long term consequences.

The first phase is the acute one which involves considerable disorganization in the victim's life style. Physical symptoms become apparent and there is a predominant feeling of fear. Victims express a wide range of feelings after the assault which include, humiliation, embarrassment, anger, revenge and self-blame.

The second phase, which begins about two to three weeks after the assault, involves reorganization of the victim's life style. Physical activities are altered and nightmares and phobias are frequent during this time. The victim may want to change residence or telephone number and contact family members not usually seen on a regular basis. Early dreams and nightmares involve violent acts during which the dreamer doesn't act. Over time, a second type of dream occurs involving the fighting-off of an assailant, thus mastering the situation.

Victims of traumatic situations may develop a variety of phobias. Fear of being indoors, outdoors, of being alone, of crowds, of being approached from behind, and sexual fears have all been reported as common. There is a heightened sense of helplessness, intensification of conflicts, a tendency to devalue one's self as a person, and difficulty in maintaining trusting relationships with men.[9]

Two types of responses in rape victims have been described.[2,5] They are the expressed style, in which the victim is overtly physically upset and emotional, and the controlled style, in which denial and reaction-formation defenses seem to be the most used. In addition, there are feelings of shock and disbelief, particularly during the early phase.

Some victims of crime or of other traumatic events exhibit a delayed reaction. These individuals may seem in control and calm at the time of the event, but several weeks later come apart emotionally and likely need professional help, which may include hospitalization.

Bard[1] points out that it does not matter what body orifice is violated. From the victim's point of view they are symbolically the same in that forceful access has been made into the individuals most private self. If the investigative focus is on the sexual rather than on the hostile, aggressive aspects of the attack, it has a tendency to discount the traumatic nature of the experience on the victim.

There are special considerations in regard to child victims who may be confused, frightened and physically injured.[4] It is important to have some understanding of the developmental level of that age child, particularly of the verbal capabilities. One should use appropriate vocabulary and images in a kindly supportive way.[12]

The hypno-investigator should be relaxed and informal during the prehypnosis session. The establishment of rapport can be aided by asking about the child's interests such as pets, school, neighborhood, family, friends, and by allowing the child to ask questions as well. A preview of the session should be given and the ground rules established as to areas to be covered and areas to be avoided.

In a hypnosis session with an eight-year-old female rape victim, the author asked the subject if she would like to imagine the rapist in a carnival-type game of throwing baseballs to "hit the target and dunk the man". The child gave the rapist three imaginary dunks, but refused to allow him to remain in the barrel to drown. In this way she was able to gain a sense of mastery over a previously helpless and traumatic encounter.

Rape victims should be seen for investigative hypnosis in the absence of friends or family members because of the potential for inhibited responsiveness and precipitating feelings of guilt or shame. With child victims it is usually acceptable that a parent sit immediately outside the room in which the hypnosis session is being conducted and be available to the child on call.

Victims and witnesses of a major crime may cry or have other emotional reactions during the hypnosis session just as they would if they were being interviewed without hypnosis.[10] The fact that the reactions occur in a state of hypnosis does not make them uniquely different from nonhypnotic reactions. Emotional reactivity can include crying, laughter, anger, fear, trembling. spasms, paleness, nausea, and feelings of warmth or cold.

The number of severe emotional reactions during investigative hypnosis appears to be relatively small and are handled readily by the usual techniques of reassurance, deepening the hypnotic state, and supporting the subject's ventilation in order to provide relief. Weitzenhoffer[13] reports that he has observed emotional reactions in less than one percent of many hundreds of cases.

An empathic, accepting approach is most appropriate to the subject's emotional reaction. The person should be permitted to ventilate sufficiently without being criticized or stifled by the operator. Handing the subject a kleenex accompanied by soothing comment is usually very effective.

The hypnotist should always respond to affective reactions of the subject acceptingly, treating them as normal expectable reactions. In most cases the subject should remain in hypnosis until the reaction has subsided. This allows continued control over the situation and reduces the possibility of further anxiety and trauma to the individual.

Subjects who have volunteered for investigative hypnosis sessions have reported subsequent feelings of relief, improved functioning, sounder sleep, fewer nightmares, better appetite, and less guilt and anxiety about the crime event. Allowing the victim of a traumatic crime to confront the situation and to deal with it in a constructive supportive environment is often very helpful to that individual.[8,11]

References

1. Bard, M. and Ellison, K. Crisis intervention and investigation of forcible rape. *The Police Chief,* May 1974, 68-73.
2. Burgess, A.W. and Holstrom, L.L. *Rape: Victims of Crisis.* Bowie, Maryland: Robert J. Brady Co., 1974.
3. Burgess, A.W. and Holstom, L.L. Rape trauma syndrome. *American Journal*

of Psychiatry. September 1974, 981-986.
4. Burgess, A.W. and Holstrom, L.L. Sexual trauma of children and adolescents. *Nursing Clinics of North America*, September 1975, 551-563.
5. Burgess, A.W. and Holstrom, L.L. Coping behavior of the rape victim. *American Journal of Psychiatry*, April 1976, 413-418.
6. Krystal, H. (Ed.). *Massive Psychic Trauma*. New York: International Universities Press, 1968.
7. Lazarus, R.S. *Psychological Stress and the Coping Process*. New York: McGraw Hill, 1966.
8. London, P. and McDevitt, R. Effects of hypnotic susceptibility and training in response to stress. *Mental Health Digest*, May 1971, 39-43.
9. Notman, M.T. and Nadelson, C.C. The rape victim: psychodynamic considerations. *American Journal of Psychiatry*, April 1976, 408-412.
10. Schultz, L.G. (Ed.). *Rape Victimology*. Springfield, Illinois: Thomas, 1975.
11. Spector, G.A. and Claiborn, W.L. *Crisis Intervention*. New York: Behavioral Publications, 1973.
12. Stevens, D. and Berliner, L. *Special Techniques for Child Witnesses*. Seattle, Washington: Harborview Medical Center (Mimeo).
13. Weitzenhoffer, A.M. *General Techniques of Hypnotism*. New York: Grune & Stratton, 1957.

CHAPTER 21
TRANSFERENCE AND COUNTERTRANSFERENCE REACTIONS

Transference is the development of an emotional attitude on the part of the subject toward the hypnotist in the form of either a positive affectional reaction or a hostile negative reaction. The attitude in either case is derived and "transferred" from early parent and childhood relationships.[4]

Countertransference is the emotional attitude the hypnotist reacts with, based on his own early child relationships and conflicts.

Transference is an every day phenomenon which occurs in a wide variety of situations. Usually it involves responses to people in authority such as doctors, dentists, bosses, police officers, or people in maternal-sexual roles such a waitresses, nurses, or secretaries. Transferences are usually more intense in intimate and close relationships such as in therapy and in love.[5]

Transference is present to some degree prior to the preinduction phase with the establishment of an imaginal relationship between the subject and the hypnotist. It continues and may intensify during the hypnosis session and may affect the outcome of suggestions and responses by the subject. A mild positive transference is desirable in establishing the working alliance between subject and hypnotist. A negative transference will hinder the feeling of rapport and likely reduce the information yield.

Transference resistances are interferences that should be noted by the hypnotist, focused on, and resolved in order to reestablish a good working relationship with the subject.

The personality of the hypnotist and the particular approach to men and women subjects can greatly influence the kind of transference tendencies elicited and therefore the subject's responsiveness. Transference may increase or decrease suggestibility depending on the compliance and dependency needs of the subject, particularly in reaction to authority figures. The use of command or authoritarian approaches as opposed to permissive ones and the question of which may elicit more responsiveness has much to do with the subject's reactions to early paternal and maternal influences as reflected in the transferred feelings toward the hypnotist.[3]

Watkins[10] points out that subjects in experimental situations are more hypnotizable than are patients in hypnotherapy because the transference resistances are seldom mobilized in the nontherapeutic setting. He also emphasizes the importance of motivation in obtaining a positive transference, minimal resistance, and positive responsiveness on the part of the subject. Weitzenhoffer[11] also agrees that the subject's reactions to hypnosis induction are variable. Whether the subject is defiant, compulsive or compliant depends on his attitudes toward early authority figures and the character structure which developed from those interactions.

The countertransference reactions of the hypnotist need to be examined and understood in order to work effectively with the witness or victim. These reactions typically include erotic, hostile, or anxiety feelings toward the subject. Working with the victims of rape or other sexual crimes requires special sensitivity and awareness of possible intensified transference and countertransference reactions.[6]

Erickson[1] points out that one should never try to correct the subject's behavior, alter it, or force a response. Accepting and utilizing the subject's responses in order to optimize trance behaviors result in more effective hypnosis. Although a subject may originally volunteer for a hypnosis session and later show resistance indicative of ambivalence, the hypnotist can recognize the phenomenon and use it to their mutual benefit.

The hypnotic subject is a functioning personality who is aware of what is going on and should be treated with the same courtesy and considerations given to a witness or victim in the waking state.[8] An essential difference is that the hypnotized subject is relaxed and able to sit quietly for relatively long periods of time without feeling upset. The nonhypnotized subject, in contrast, may feel deserted or neglected should the interviewer not respond immediately and continuously.

Although Watkins[9] says that the true science of hypnotizing should be based on a deep and intimate knowledge of the person's personality structure, transference needs, ego defenses, and the mix of these factors, he is referring to psychotherapy rather than investigative hypnosis. Certainly the hypno-investigator needs to be aware of transference and countertransference phenomena and possibilities. However, as pointed out earlier, he will be less likely to encounter very strong reactions with his motivated, cooperative volunteer subjects than will the psychotherapist.

It should be kept in mind that transference needs may fluctuate during the hypnosis session and will affect the depth of hypnosis in certain situations.[7] It is possible that a subject will be most responsive initially to a permissive approach and then as the trance state deepens, become more responsive to authoritative types of communication.

The hypno-investigator should recognize that he has encountered and dealt with transference and countertransference reactions in his every day nonhypnotic work with witnesses and is not suddenly discovering completely new phenomena. Hopefully, as an investigative hypnotist, he will be able to deal with them more sensitively and effectively.

References

1. Erickson, M.H. Deep hypnosis and its induction. *Advanced Techniques of Hypnosis and Therapy* (J. Haley, Ed.). New York: Grune & Stratton, 1967, 7-31.
2. Frankel, F.H. *Hypnosis: Trance as a Coping Mechanism.* New York: Plenum Medical Books Company, 1976.
3. Gill, M.M. and Brenman, M. *Hypnosis and Related States: Psychoanalytic Studies in Regression.* New York: International Universities Press, 1959.
4. Kline, M.V. *Psychodynamics and Hypnosis.* Springfield, Illinois: Thomas, 1967.
5. Kline, M.V. *Freud and Hypnosis: The Interaction of Psychodynamics and Hypnosis.* New York: Julian Press, 1958.
6. Menninger, K., et al. *The Vital Balance.* New York: The Viking Press, 1962.
7. Shor, R.E. Three dimensions of hypnotic depth. *International Journal of Clinical and Experimental Hypnosis,* 1962, *10,* 23-38.
8. Spiegel, H. and Spiegel, D. *Trance and Treatment.* New York: Basic Books, 1978.
9. Watkins, J.G. Trance and transference. *Journal of Clinical and Experimental Hypnosis,* 1954, *2,* 284-290.
10. Watkins, J.G. Transference aspects of the hypnotic relatonship. *Clinical Correlations of Experimental Hypnosis.* (M.V. Kline, Ed.). Springfield, Illinois: Thomas, 1963, 5-24.
11. Weitzenhoffer, A.M. *General Techniques of Hypnotism.* New York: Grune & Stratton, 1957.

CHAPTER 22
WAKING, HYPNOTIC AND POSTHYPNOTIC SUGGESTIONS

Waking suggestions are those given to a subject in a nonhypnotic state. Hypnotic suggestions are made during hypnosis to take place while the subject is in the hypnotic state. This includes most of the induction and deepening suggestions given. Posthypnotic suggestions are made during hypnosis to be carried out by the subject after termination of the hypnotic state.[2]

Weitzenhoffer[15] and Van Pelt[14] point out that there is no essential difference objectively between waking and hypnotic suggestion except the increased amount of suggestibility. The lighter the hypnotic state the more like waking suggestion the instructions will be. Waking suggestions usually require much repetition whereas in the hypnotic state one statement may be sufficient. With some subjects anything the hypnotist says in their presence is taken as direct suggestion. For this reason, the hypnotist should always be sure that the subject understands when a suggestion is being directed at him and when it is not.

Salzberg[12] researched the differences among waking, hypnotic and posthypnotic suggestions and found that both hypnotic and posthypnotic suggestions led to better performance whereas waking suggestion led to poorer performance. He also found that the subjects' performance tended to improve with hypnosis or posthypnotic suggestions as the tasks became more complex. Dhanens[3] found improved recall with motivated hypnosis subjects and contextual material.

"Mary, you are a good girl." "Would you mind standing up for a second?" If given to a nonhypnotized subject, these are examples of waking suggestions. There are hundreds of other common examples of waking suggestion that include commercials suggesting that viewers buy certain products, magazine and newspaper ads, political speeches and religious sermons. Recent work by Lozanov[11] involving the use of waking suggestions for learning and educational purposes, which he calls suggestology, has validated the tremendous effect of suggestion, with or without formal hypnosis. Others[1,7,16] have also considered this issue.

One can view the variety of altered states of consciousness as a continuum from full conscious alertness at one end, to hypnoidal states, deeper hypnotic states, and states of sleep and unconsciousness at the other end. The hypnoidal state is considered a precursor of hypnosis and is induced by nonformalistic techniques. The fixing of one's attention, physical inhibition and eye fatigue lead to some dissociation which produces a hypnoidal effect, a kind of reverie state. In this state the attention span fluctuates, critical thinking is reduced and there is a tendency to increased suggestibility. Examples of hypnoidal states include absorption while watching a movie, highway hypnosis, losing one's boundaries while reading an interesting novel, or being in pain.[8]

Hypnotic subjects will sometimes distort or elaborate a suggestion that is given. This is usually related to the subject's understanding of what is said, the degree of rapport and motivations, attitudes, values, expectancies, and personality. These elaborations sometimes help the subject to maintain psychological stability and a sense of being in control of the situation. The hypnotist should take the subject's needs into consideration when making suggestions since the more these needs are satisfied, the more likely the subject will be to carry out the suggestion effectively.[10]

Although there is some correlation with the subjects ability to carry out posthypnotic suggestions and the depth of hypnosis, there are exceptions and variations.[9] Some subjects can carry out simple posthypnotic suggestions in a very light or medium state of hypnosis depending on motivation and absence of resistances. Generally, posthypnotic suggestions tend to be more effective if amnesia for them is suggested by the hypnotist.[17] The suggested amnesia makes it less likely that conscious censorship factors and resistances will later interfere with the carrying out of the suggestion. However, posthypnotic suggestions can still be useful and effective even if amnesia is not involved.[13]

Weitzenhoffer[15] recommends allowing the subject to remain quiet for about five minutes after giving the posthypnotic suggestions, telling the subject to relax very deeply and that when the hypnotist begins counting, the subject will wake up slowly. "At the count of three you will be wide awake and will have no memory of what I have said to you while you were hypnotized, but the suggestions will nevertheless be very effective."

The hypno-investigator should keep in mind that it is not unusual for a subject to fail to carry out a particular suggestion. This is likely either due to resistance factors, to poor phrasing of the suggestion, or some misunderstaning of it on the part of the subject. The easiest, most direct way of finding out the reasons for difficulty is to ask the subject what his feelings and reactions are to the suggestions given.

Generally, posthypnotic suggestions tend to lose their effectiveness over time. However, simple suggestions given to a deeply hypnotized subject can last months or years, while a difficult task which is resisted or given to a subject in a light to medium state may not remain activated for very long. Repetition is usually required for reinforcement purposes in order to maintain the force of a posthypnotic suggestion over time. For maximum effectiveness, posthypnotic suggestions should be worded as specifically as possible, repeated several times, and the relayed back by the subject to make sure the suggestions have been comprehended clearly and accurately.

LeCron[10] points out that posthypnotic suggestions initiate a time-limited form of compulsive behavior even though the idea may be recognized as a suggestion by the subject. If amnesia for the suggestion is made, the subject will later rationalize carrying out the suggestion, particularly if it is felt to be somewhat silly or out of character.

Erickson[4] says, "The hypnotized subject, instructed to execute some act posthypnotically, invariably develops spontaneously a hypnotic trance. This trance is of brief duration, occurs in direct relation to the performance of the posthypnotic act, and apparently constitutes an essential part of the process of response to and execution of the posthypnotic command..."

It is good procedure for hypno-investigators to use waking suggestions in the pre-induction phase of the session while giving the subject a preview of what will be required, the techniques to be used, and of how the subject may feel in the hypnotized state. These waking suggestions may effectuate the hypnotic suggestions given during induction and deepening and may also tend to reduce resistances.

Posthypnotic suggestions can be very effective for future rapid induction purposes on cue, or future resolution of confusion and resistance, in enabling recall of presently repressed memories, and in coming to terms with the traumatic event experienced by the victim or witness.

The hypno-investigator should remember to remove any posthypnotic suggestions not intended to remain after the hypnosis session is terminated since suggestions of this type left inadvertently, may cause the subject some discomfort.[5]

Some of the typical hypnotic suggestions given to witnesses are those used in upgrading a composite drawing being constructed by the police artist. After the original rough drawing has been done with the hypnotic subject's eyes closed, the instruction is given that on signal the subject will remain deeply relaxed and in hypnosis but able to open the eyes, look at the preliminary drawing and compare it with the mental image of the suspect that will remain vividly and accurately in mind. The subject will be able to make suggestions to the police artist to allow the drawing to be made more accurate. It may even be a look-alike for the suspect.

A standard posthypnotic suggestion given to a witness is that after the session, some additional information may drift up into consciousness, perhaps in hours, days, or weeks. Should that occur, the subject may call the case investigator and relay the recalled information. This procedure has frequently led to additional useful information being recalled after the sesson proper.

An interesting example of the use of posthypnotic suggestion involved the case of an elderly lady who had misplaced some valuable jewelry and despite intensive searching was unable to find it. Because of certain resistances she was unable to recall adequately during the hypnosis session. The hypno-investigator suggested, posthypnotically, that on returning home, each time the phone would ring, her recall would get increasingly better and at some point in time, the ringing of the telephone would jog her memory of where the jewelry was placed. Some days later, the subject was awakened from a deep sleep by the ringing of the telephone. She went directly to the bookshelf behind which she had hidden the jewelry and recovered it.

It is important to keep in mind that expectancy set and how suggestions are worded are crucial in terms of the response that is likely to result.[6] Sometimes merely changing a few words or giving a new cue can bring about a useful response from the subject.

References

1. Barber, T.X., Spanos, N.P. and Chaves, J.F. *Hypnosis, Imagination and Human Potentialities.* New York: Pergamon Press, 1974.
2. Cheek, D.B. and LeCron, L.M. *Clinical Hypnotherapy.* New York: Grune & Stratton, 1968.
3. Dhanens, T.P. and Lundy, R.M. Hypnotic and waking suggestions and

recall. *International Journal of Clinical and Experimental Hypnosis,* 1975, *23,* 68-78.
4. Erickson, M.H. and Erickson, E.M. Concerning the nature and character of post-hypnotic behavior. *Modern Hypnosis* (L. Kuhn and S. Russo, Eds.). North Hollywood, California: Wilshire Book Company, 1974, 105-142.
5. Estabrooks, G.H. *Hypnotism.* New York: Dutton, 1957.
6. Fisher, S. The role of expectancy in the performance of post-hypnotic behavior. *The Nature of Hypnosis* (R.E. Shore and M.T. Orne, Eds.). New York: Holt, Rinehart & Winston, 1965, 80-88.
7. Furneaux, W.D. Hypnotic susceptibility as a function of waking susceptibility. *Experimental Hypnosis* (L.M. LeCron, Ed.). Secaucus, New Jersey: Citadel Press, 1972, 115-136.
8. Hilgard, E.R. and Hilgard, J.R. *Hypnosis in the Relief of Pain.* Los Altos, California: William Kaufman, Inc., 1975.
9. Hilgard, E.R. *The Experience of Hypnosis.* New York: Harcourt, Brace & World, 1965.
10. LeCron, L.M. and Bordeaux, J. *Hypnotism Today.* North Hollywood, California: Wilshire Book Company, 1972.
11. Lozanov, G. *Suggestology and Outlines of Suggestopedy.* New York: Gordon & Breach, 1978.
12. Salzberg, H.C. The effects of hypnotic, post-hypnotic and waking suggestion on performance using tasks varied in complexity. *Clinical Correlates of Experimental Hypnosis* (M.V. Kline, Ed.). Springfield, Illinois: Thomas, 1963, 227-234.
13. Teitelbaum, M. *Hypnosis Induction Technics.* Springfield, Illinois: Thomas, 1969.
14. Van Pelt, S.J. *Hypnotic Suggestion.* New York: Philosophical Library, 1956.
15. Weitzenhoffer, A.M. *Hypnotism: An Objective Study in Suggestibility.* New York: Wiley, 1953.
16. Wells, W.R. Experiments in waking hypnosis. *Modern Hypnosis* (L. Kuhn and S. Russo, Eds.). North Hollywood, California, Wilshire Book Company, 1974, 45-55.
17. Wolberg, L.R. *Hypnosis. Is It For You?* New York: Harcourt, Brace, Jovanovich, 1972.

CHAPTER 23
MEMORY, AMNESIA AND TIME DISTORTION

Neurophysiologists seem to agree that memory is a function of biochemical changes in the brain and that bits of information are stored in individual brain cells subject to recall upon electrochemical activation.[1,9,10,18]

More recently, Pribram has proposed a new theory of memory involving the hologram. He tries to explain why traces of the same memory may be shown to exist in more than one part of the brain and how the distribution occurs. He theorizes that information is stored in the brain following holographic principles. A holograph is a scene recorded on a photographic plate in the form of a complex pattern that seems meaningless; however, when the pattern is illuminated by a proper light, the original image is reconstructed. "What makes the hologram unique as a storage device is that every element in the original image is distributed over the entire photographic plate. The hypothesis is attractive because remembering or recollecting literally implies a reconstructive process — the assembly of dismembered mnemonic events."[12]

Whether one uses the cybernetic model[8,11] or the holographic one, it appears that investigative hypnosis is an effective tool for achieving hypermnesia, or heightened memory, in the motivated subject.[14]

Reports by Hilgard,[7] Cheek,[3] and Reiser[14] indicate that retrieval potential is significantly influenced by original perceptions and encoding. Research in laboratory settings, with anesthetized "unconscious" surgery patients, and with a heavily intoxicated witness to a homicide, reveals that perceptual recording occurs at two levels simultaneously. Information is perceived at both conscious and subconscious levels though the subject is unaware of the subliminal perceptions. Under hypnosis this information may be retrieved as originally viewed by what Hilgard calls the "hidden observer."[6]

Some early work by Dorcus[5] reveals that three out of four crime-related cases yielded information of value to the police although the memories recalled were fragmentary. Dorcus believed that hypnosis was of value in helping the subject overcome some emotional blocking associated with the original experience, thus enhancing recall.

Experiments on memory are thought to have started formally with Hermann Ebbinghaus around 1885 using verbal learning techniques under standard laboratory conditions. This approach continued for the next 80 years. Beginning about 1965, with the emphasis on cognitive learning psychology, new approaches and theories about memory have appeared which no longer emphasize verbal learning.[6]

Some of the complex conceptual problems studied by memory theorists have included the nature of attending, how materials are organized, coding of information, rehearsal strategies, and how short term memory is related to long term memory. It appears that some material can be processed in parallel into both short and long term memory simultaneously rather than being processed sequentially. To date, however, there are no completely validated and accepted processes in regard to memory function. This work is ongoing and most of it remains to be done. Hypno-investigators working with subjects to achieve hypermnesia can make a significant contribution to this knowledge.

Several different kinds of memory have been identified:[6]

Episodic (redintegrative) - these involve autobiographic past events that are associated with particular cues. Souvenirs are common cues, such as the lock of hair that helps vividly recall a particular person or occasion.

Semantic memory - the recall of something previously learned such as a poem or song and doesn't require remembering when or in what context the original learning occurred.

Recognition - what is seen has been perceived before, such as a familiar picture, place or face.

There appear to be significant differences between memory involving verbal and imagery systems.[16] Imagery seems to be the vehicle utilized when information is presented and stored simultaneously by both conscious and subconscious systems, whereas verbal systems seem to be used for storing information sequentially over time.[1]

Amnesia

The detective and the hypno-investigator most often work

with witnesses and victims who have been severely traumatized by crime events. Most of these individuals are within the normal range of mental and emotional health, and commonly utilize the defense mechanisms of repression and dissociation in order to ward off the emotionally disturbing memories.[3]

Repression and amnesia are similar in that they both involve intact memories which have been perceived, stored and can be retrieved under certain circumstances. Amnesia is the more neutral term whereas repression implies an avoidance of unpleasant or anxiety producing events.[15] However, both amnesia and repression are considered "disorders" of memory.

Amnesias can result from organic or functional disturbances. They can be classified as retrograde when the forgetting involves something that occurred prior to the onset of the amnesia, or anterograde when the subject is unable to remember something that occurred after the amnesia has become manifest. Amnesias represent a problem of memory retrieval rather than initial storage. It also implies a temporary rather than permanent forgetting since the memory is recoverable. Post-traumatic amnesia is common after head injuries. Witnesses may gradually recover brain functions affected and often can do well with hypnotic recall.

The temporary forgetting associated with hypnosis can be labeled either spontaneous amnesia or suggested amnesia. Posthypnotic amnesia was first described by Puységur and described in his 1784 book. He named this state "artificial somnabulism" because he thought it resembled sleepwalking and this term still remains as a description of the very highly hypnotizable individual.

The variety of partial or total amnesias for information that may occur during or after the hypnotic session depend largely on the stated or implied suggestions given by the hypnotist.[17] Posthypnotic suggestion is not necessary for spontaneous amnesia to occur. The specific mechanisms of hypnotic amnesia have not yet been explained satisfactorily.

The imagery selected by the hypnotist is very important in removing the amnesia for the repressed information. Suggesting that the subject imagine unlocking the trunk of memory, or opening the filing cabinet of subconscious memory and retrieving the right folder containing the information in question, may aid in reversing the amnesia. However, recall can be partial or complete depending on the nature of the subject's repressive forces, ego strength, and the need for defenses against recall.[13]

Experimental hypnosis is still in its infancy. Much work remains to be done in the areas of memory and amnesia, attending, and parallel processing of perceptions.

Time Distortion

Cooper and Erickson[4] describe the ability of a subject to distort his sense of time while in a hypnotic state. Subjectively, time can be speeded up, slowed down, and even stopped by the hypnotic subject, when suggested.

Time distortion techniques can be extremely useful in investigative hypnosis when crime events have involved many hours, but where the time available for hypnotic sessions is very limited. Time condensation can be used with the witness. It can be suggested that although the crime event may originally have occurred over ten or twelve hours, reviewing all of the relevant and significant details seen, heard and experienced, will take only 15 minutes of real time on the clock. In hypnosis, it may seem to the subject as if ten or twelve hours have again transpired. In this way the subject's unconscious is able to focus on significant details and behaviors as structured by the hypno-investigator. It is important to mention the various kinds of significant information to be recalled during the time distortion experience. This may include information about a vehicle, suspects, street names, license plates, clothing, conversation, or weapons.

In addition to condensing long crime events into a shorter time frame, time distortion suggestions can be used to expand time when the original events occurred very rapidly. With a hit-and-run accident situation, which can occur in split seconds, it is possible to expand the time using a slow motion or freeze frame approach so that what is perceived in the revivification process occurs much more slowly, with greater attention to detail possible. This technique has yielded useful vehicle, suspect, license and other valuable information.

While the subject views the crime event on the imaginary television screen during the TV technique, the hypno-investigator, as desired, can suggest that the film will go into slow motion, stop completely or reverse. The subject can also be told that when the camera zooms in on the suspect's face, the frame will freeze and although there was originally only a short time to look at the suspect, there will now be all the time in the world to look at the close-up on TV and to describe every feature very vividly, and accurately.

References

1. Baddeley, A.D. *The Psychology of Memory.* New York: Basic Books, 1976.
2. Brunn, J.T. Retrograde amnesia in a murder suspect. *American Journal of Clinical Hypnosis,* 1968, *12,* 209-213.
3. Cheek, D.B. and LeCron, L.M. *Clinical Hypnotherapy.* New York: Grune & Stratton, 1968.
4. Cooper, L.F. and Erickson, M.H. Time distortion in hypnosis. *Experimental Hypnosis* (L.M. LeCron, Ed.). New York: Macmillan, 1952.
5. Dorcus, R.M. Recall under hypnosis of amenestic events. *International Journal of Clinical and Experimental Hypnosis,* 1960, 7, 57-61.
6. Hilgard, E. *Divided Consciousness.* New York: Wiley Interscience, 1977.
7. Hilgard, E.R. *The Experience of Hypnosis.* New York: Harcourt, Brace & World, 1965.
8. Maltz, M. *Psychocybernetics.* New York: Prentice-Hall, 1960.
9. McCleary, R.A. and Moore, R. *Subcortical Mechanisms of Behavior.* New York: Basic Books, 1965.
10. Penfield, W. Memory mechanisms. *Archives of Neurology and Psychiatry.* 1952. *67,* 178-198.
11. Penfield, W. *The Mystery of the Mind.* Princeton, New Jersey: Princeton University Press, 1975.
12. Pribram, K.H. The neurophysiology of remembering. *Scientific American,* January 1969, 73-86.
13. Reiff, R. and Scheerer, M. *Memory and Hypnotic Age Regression.* New York: International Universities Press, 1970.
14. Reiser, M. Hypnosis as an aid in a homicide investigation. *American Journal of Clinical Hypnosis.* October 1974, 84-87.
15. Schachtel, E.G. On memory and childhood amnesia. *A Study of Interpersonal Relations* (P. Mullahy, Ed.). New York: Hermitage, 1949.
16. Singer, J.L. and Pope, K.S. *The Power of Human Imagination.* New York: Plenum Press, 1978.
17. Spiegel, H. and Spiegel, D. *Trance and Treatment.* New York: Basic Books, 1978.
18. Wallach, H. *On Perception.* New York: Quadrangle Books, 1976.

CHAPTER 24
DIFFICULT SUBJECTS AND RAPID TECHNIQUES

The refractory subject may be one of those few people considered to be nonhypnotizable. However, it is more probable that the difficult subject manifests resistances for conscious or unconscious reasons. Many of the common resistances emanate from the myths and misinformation about hypnosis, such as the fear of being controlled, of losing control, of telling secrets, of failing, or the need to feel superior to the hypnotist.[8] An overly casual attitude and apparent lack of feeling about being hypnotized is usually also a sign of resistance in a naive subject.

Like patients in psychotherapy, volunteer witnesses and victims of major crimes are consciously motivated. They want to help the police to apprehend the criminal. However, unconscious fears of retaliation or of humiliation about testifying in court can lead to unconscious resistances if not confronted and handled constructively.

Some apparently willing and motivated subjects enter hypnosis fairly easily but may laugh and come out of hypnosis. Others may appear comfortable but open their eyes, complain about room temperature, or about the hardness of the chair. Other subjects may remain in hypnosis exhibiting an anxious expression, perspiration, or rapid breathing.[1] If these signs are noted by the hypno-investigator, they should be inquired about before proceeding, otherwise the subject may feel resentful and develop increased resistance because of the hypnotist's insensitivity.

Occasionally, resistant behavior may be related to fear of a flashback. In a highly motivated group of professional men and women learning about hypnosis, Cheek found approximately 10 percent who showed a distress reaction because the hypnotic state reminded the subject of some experience associated with loss of consciousness, fear, or great physical stress. He describes the case of a physician who became apprehensive about inducing hypnosis in people. Finger signals revealed that as a child he had a tonsillectomy performed in a doctor's office. However, his parents had not told him he would be operated on and he had been forcibly "put to sleep with ether". Hypnosis unconsciously reminded him of this childhood trauma.[1]

One way of dealing with resistances is to word suggestions in order to utilize the subject's actual behavior to reinforce the suggestions. An example might be telling the subject that one of his hands might do something. Perhaps it will push down or maybe it will move upward, or perhaps it might do nothing at all. The subject is also told that he might feel a tingling in his hands, or a sensation of warmth, or a sense of heaviness or lightness, but certainly something will happen. Perhaps what he will feel will be a twitching of the muscles of the hands or the fingers, maybe the middle finger would move, or the little finger, or perhaps the whole hand. As many responses to the suggestion as possible are mentioned to the subject without indicating which particular ones will be experienced. If the subject continues to show resistance, he is told that this is very constructive and that he is being most cooperative.

The hypnotist should not attempt to correct the subject's behavior or to force him into a response. As Erickson[3] indicates, accepting and utilizing the subject's responses, whatever they are, will further the trance behavior and make the hypnosis more effective.

There are specific hypnosis techniques which may be utilized with difficult or resistant subjects that have proved effective:

Fractionation Technique

The fractionation technique can be very effective in inducing a deep trance state and may succeed when other induction methods have failed.[4,9] It is also useful for handling subjects who doubt that they have been hypnotized. Essentially, this technique involves hypnotizing and waking the subject repeatedly in fairly rapid succession. Each rehypnotization makes the subject a bit more suggestible and deepens the hypnotic state. Just prior to dehypnotizing the subject, he is told that in a moment he will be awakened but when touched on the shoulder will immediately close his eyes and go back into an even deeper state of hypnosis than before. A touch on one shoulder can be the awakening signal and a touch on the opposite shoulder the signal for rehypnotization. The rapid succession of hypnotization and awakening, with suggestions of deepening and increased relaxation each time, allows many hypnosis "sessions" to be condensed into one, giving the subject repeated hypnosis experiences in a brief period of time and conditioning for increased depth.

Visualization Technique

The subject is asked to pick an incident from a movie, television or a football game and to try to recall it in exact detail and keep it in mind. The subject is also told that his right arm will rise when he visualizes a clear mental picture of the chosen scene. If nothing happens, the subject is urged to concentrate even more and is given suggestions for hand levitation. As the hand begins to move, the subject is told to keep the image in mind and pay attention to nothing else. Additional suggestions for deepening are given at this point and the hypnotist assists in the levitation by raising the arm in front of the subject. The hypnotist indicates that the arm will move toward the subject, and when the hand touches the face, will go into a deep state of hypnosis, continuing to keep the image clearly in mind.[10]

Confusion Technique

Suggestions are given to the subject which are too complex and difficult for him to handle and the impossibility of following the confusing directions ultimately forces the subject into hypnosis as an escape. The hypnotist makes contradictory statements in a way that convinces the subject that something very meaningful and precise is being communicated. However, the subject doesn't have sufficient time to recognize the illogical nature of the suggestions. Erickson firmly suggests levitaton of the right hand while maintaining the left hand immobile. He immediately follows this by suggestions of levitation of the left hand and immobility of the right hand, then immobility of both hands, followed by suggestions that one hand is lifting while the other hand is pressing down. The suggestions are then reversed. It is important that these suggestions are given quickly, consistently, and confidently.[3]

A simpler variation on the confusion technique is described by LeCron.[6] The subject is asked to slowly count backward aloud from 100 and to pay a minimum of attention to what the hypnotist is saying while counting. After the subject has begun counting, the hypnotist begins giving suggestions of relaxation, heaviness, and eye closure. He mentions that before the subject reaches zero he will deeply hypnotized. As the subject continues counting backward, arm levitation is suggested and as the subject becomes confused, the hypnotist tells him that he will lose track of his count before he has mentioned ten more numbers. This technique can be made even more difficult for mathematically inclined subjects by having them count backwards by three's or seven's.

Mechanical Aids

Although mechanical devices such as flashing lights, synchronizers, spirals, and other gadgets are generally not desirable for investigative hypnosis, in special situations, a mechanical aid might be useful.

With resistant subjects who are mechanically trained or oriented, it may be useful to utilize a galvanic skin response (GSR) device to enable the subject to get feedback based on the electrical potential of the skin. As the subject relaxes, the audible tone decreases and will convince the skeptical subject that he is indeed responding physiologically and will act as a reinforcer for further hypnotic suggestions. The pendulum may also be used as an aid and is discussed in Chaper 30.

Rapid Techniques

For investigative hypnosis purposes, it is generally desirable to use a slower induction technique which enables the subject to relax and to establish a relationship with the hypno-investigator. However, in special circumstances such as the witness being injured or hospitalized, or being a trained hypnotic subject, rapid techniques can be utilized effectively without compromising the potential information yield from the subject.[11] When rapid techniques are used with unsuspecting subjects, there is the possibility of resentment and resistance resulting because of the feeling of having been manipulated, surprised or taken advantage of. The slower techniques with accompanying explanations and previews tend to avoid this kind of reaction. Rapid induction techniques involve misdirection of attention and the element of surprise.[5]

The Watch Technique

A wrist watch or a finger is held in front of and slightly above the subject's eye level and he is instructed to focus his attention on it.[7] The watch or finger is slowly moved downward and closer to the subject's face and as the subject's eyes follow the object downward, the eyelids begin closing. As the watch is moved down, out of the line of sight of the subject with the eyelids almost closed, the subject is unobtrusively squeezed on the neck or the shoulder while simultaneously the instruction to relax and go into deep hypnosis is forcefully given. The subject, not expecting the physical pressure because of being distracted by watching the object, will go into hypnosis since the forceful command has bypassed his conscious censorship and is accepted subconsciously.

The Tension and Relaxation Technique

The subject is asked to close his eyes and press his feet firmly down on the floor as if trying to push them through the floor. He is then told to press his hands tightly on the sides of the chair as hard as he can and to grip the chair tighter and tighter with his hands. "You are building up tension in your hands and arms. I am sure you will agree that the opposite of tension is relaxation, therefore, the more tension you build up in your arms and legs, the more you will relax." When the subject shows signs of strain the hypnotist says, "Now, because your arms are so tense they will relax more than they ordinarily do. You will also feel so good to relax your legs; your whole body is going to relax deeper and deeper relaxed." If necessary, other parts of the body can be utilized in a similar fashion until hypnosis is achieved.[5]

Pressure Points

Most people have heard about nerve centers and pressure points. In this technique, the hypnotist takes advantage of some of the mythology and uses a technical-sounding explanation of the deep relaxation and hypnosis that will result when certain nerves are pressed. He then presses lightly on the lower part of the subject's head at the same time pressing with his forefinger and thumb on the subject's forehead just above the nose. The pressure is equally maintained on both areas while the hypnotist says, "You feel yourself sinking deeper and deeper and becoming more and more relaxed." When the subject's eyes droop and his head slumps forward, the pressure above the nose is relaxed at the same time the pressure at the back of the head is increased, so the subject's head comes forward even more. Suggestions of increased relaxation and limpness are given at the same time.[5]

References
1. Cheek, D.B. and LeCron, L.M. *Clinical Hypnotherapy.* New York: Grune & Stratton, 1968.

2. Ellen, A. *The Intimate Casebook of a Hypnotist.* New York: New American Library, 1968.
3. Erickson, M.H. The confusion technique in hypnosis. *American Journal of Clinical Hypnosis,* 1964, 6, 183-207.
4. Fross, G.H. *Handbook of Hypnotic Techniques.* South Orange, New Jersey: Power Publishers, 1974.
5. Kroger, W.S. *Clinical and Experimental Hypnosis, 2nd Edition.* Philadelphia: Lippincott, 1977.
6. LeCron, L.M. *Experimental Hypnosis.* Secaucus, New Jersey: Citadel Press, 1972.
7. Leitner, K. *Scientific Hypnotism for Professionals.* New York: Stravon, 1953.
8. Magonet, P. *Practical Hypnotism.* North Hollywood, California: Wilshire Book Company, 1957.
9. Teitelbaum, M. *Hypnosis Induction Technics.* Springfield, Illinois: Thomas, 1969.
10. Weitzenhoffer, A.M. *General Techniques of Hypnotism.* New York: Grune & Stratton, 1957.
11. Whitlow, J.E. A rapid method for the induction of hypnosis. *Experimental Hypnosis* (L.M. LeCron, Ed.). Secaucus, New Jersey: Citadel Press, 1972, 58-63.

CHAPTER 25
SELF-HYPNOSIS

Self-hypnosis can be useful for purposes of relaxation and stress management. Additionally, the hypno-investigator often finds that self-hypnosis enables him to become more attuned to working with a subject in a sensitive, empathic way.

There are differences of opinion about the difficulty in learning self-hypnosis without being hypnotized by someone else previously. Apparently it is possible to learn self-hypnosis without hetero-hypnosis as a prerequisite. However, it is likely more economical of time and effort to work with an experienced hypnotist in learning self-hypnosis techniques.

Self-hypnosis can be useful in achieving more effective study approaches, in reducing examination anxiety, in overcoming bad habits, in dealing with stress, and in changing attitudes, values and motivation.[2,3] Like any other skill, self-hypnosis requires practice in order to become more adept at it.

There are a variety of self-hypnosis approaches and techniques.[1,5,6] It is often very helpful to make a tape recording of an induction that can be used for practice and reinforcement purposes. The recording should be done in a slow, low tone of voice, and can be listened to either lying down or sitting in a chair.

LeCron[4] suggests the following self-hypnosis talk:

"Now that you are comfortable, you will listen closely to my voice and will follow all the suggestions given. This will teach you how to enter hypnosis and to produce it yourself. Your eyes are now closed. Take another deep breath, hold it a few seconds and let it out.

"The more you can relax, the deeper you will be able to go into hypnosis. Let all your muscles go as loose and limp as possible. To do this, start with your right leg. Tighten the muscles, first making the leg rigid, then let it relax, from your toes up to your hip. Then tighten the muscles of the left leg. Let that leg relax from the toes up to the hip.

"Let the stomach and abdominal area relax, then your chest

and breathing muscles. The muscles of your back can loosen — the shoulders and neck muscles relaxing. Often we have tension in this area, but all these muscles loosen. Now your arms from the shoulders right down to your fingertips. Even your facial muscles will relax. Relaxation is so pleasant and comfortable. Let go completely and enjoy the relaxation. All tension seems to drain away and you soon find a listlessness creeping over you, with a sense of comfort and well-being.

"As you relax more and more, you will slip deeper and deeper into hypnosis. Your arms and legs may develop a feeling of heaviness or instead you may find your whole body feeling very light as though you are floating on a soft cloud.

"Now imagine that you are standing at the top of an escalator, such as those in some stores. See the steps moving down in front of you and see the railings. I'm going to count from ten to zero. As I start to count, imagine you are stepping on the escalator, standing there with your hands on the railing while the steps move down in front of you, taking you with them. If you prefer you can imagine a staircase or an elevator instead. If you have any difficulty visualizing the escalator or staircase or elevator, just the count itself will take you deeper and deeper.

"(Slowly) ten - now you step on and start going down. Nine - eight - seven - six. Going deeper and deeper with each count. Five - four - three. Still deeper. Two - one - and zero. Now you step off at the bottom and will continue to go deeper still with each breath you take. Deeper and deeper with each breath. You are so relaxed and so comfortable. Let go still more. Notice your breathing. Probably it is now slower and you are breathing more from the bottom of your lungs, abdominal breathing.

"In a moment you will notice that your hand and arm are beginning to lose any feeling of heaviness and are becoming light. If you are right-handed, it will be your right arm, if left-handed, it will be the left.

"The arm is getting lighter and lighter. It will begin to lift. Perhaps just the fingers will move first, or the whole hand will start to float up. It will float up towards your face, as though your face were a magnet pulling it up until the fingers touch your face some place. Let's see where that will be. The arm begins to bend at the elbow. It is floating upward. If it has not started of its own accord, lift it voluntarily a few inches to give it a start. It will continue to go up of its own accord with no further effort. It floats on up towards your face, higher and higher.

"The higher your hand goes, the deeper you will go; the deeper you go, the higher the hand will go. Lifting, lifting, floating up higher and higher, going higher and higher. Now, if it has touched your face, let your hand go down to any comfortable position. If it has not touched yet, it can continue to float up until it does touch. You can forget about the arm while I tell you how you can put yourself into hypnosis whenever you may wish to do so.

"You will use much the same method being used now. When you have made yourself comfortable you will merely close your eyes and drift into hypnosis. But in your first three or four practice sessions it would help you if you would light a candle and when you have made yourself comfortable and look at the flickering flame for two or three minutes, then close your eyes.

"Then you will think to yourself the phrase, 'Now I am going into hypnosis.' Then repeat to yourself the words, 'relax now' three times, saying them very slowly. As you do this you will slip off into hypnosis. You say nothing aloud, you merely think these words. When you have done this, take another deep breath to help you relax more and go through the relaxation just as you have done before. Tell your muscles to relax as I have done.

"When you have finally relaxed your arms, imagine the escalator, elevator, or staircase. Now you should count backwards from ten to zero, including the zero. Count slowly. In the first four practice sessions, repeat the count three times, as though going down different levels. With practice you need only count once.

"Whenever you are ready to awaken all you need to do is think to yourself, 'Now I am going to wake up.' Then slowly count to three and you will be wide awake. You will always awaken refreshed, relaxed and feeling fine.

"While you are in hypnosis if something should happen so you should awaken, you will do so instantly and spontaneously — something such as the phone ringing or a real emergency like a fire. You will awaken instantly and be wide awake and fully alert. Actually, this would happen without such a suggestion being necessary, for your subconscious mind always protects you.

"Now I will count to three and you will be wide awake. If convenient, you should then go through this formula for self-hypnosis and put yourself back in. You will remember the formula and go through it exactly as given. Now awaken as I count. One. Coming awake now. Two - almost awake. Three - now you are wide awake. Wide awake."

References
1. Adams, P. *The New Self-Hypnosis.* North Hollywood, California: Wilshire

Book Company, 1978.
2. Caprio, F.S. and Berger, J.R. *Helping Yourself With Self-Hypnosis.* Englewood Cliffs, New Jersey: Prentice-Hall, 1963.
3. Duckworth, J. *How to Use Auto-Suggestion Effectively.* North Hollywood, California: Wilshire Book Company, 1972.
4. LeCron, L.M *Self-Hypnotism.* Englewood Cliffs, New Jersey: Prentice-Hall, 1964.
5. Sparks, L. *Self-Hypnosis.* North Hollywood, California: Wilshire Book Company, 1973.
6. Weitzenhoffer, A.M. *General Techniques of Hypnotism.* New York: Grune & Stratton, 1957.

CHAPTER 26
HYPNOSIS WITH CHILDREN AND ELDERLY PERSONS

It is generally agreed that children make the best hypnotic subjects. There is a decline in hypnotic susceptibility with increasing age after pre-adolescent years and an abrupt decline in hypnotizability after middle age.[12] Recent studies indicate that hypnotic susceptibility is related to the capacity for imaginative involvement and that children generally can enter hypnotic states more easily than adults.[9] Children even younger than previously thought are capable of spontaneous hypnotic behaviors.[13]

The child may slip in and out of hypnosis so rapidly and easily that the inexperienced hypnotist may question whether the subject is actually hypnotized. Unlike adults, children may squirm, scratch or open their eyes while remaining deeply hypnotized. These are considered normal behaviors in children but are indications of resistance in adults.[8]

The child's responsiveness is largely dependent on the nature of the rapport established with the hypnotist. The preinduction discussion, which explores the child's environment and interests, is very useful in establishing a positive relationship and in determining language and vocabularly capabilities.[5]

LaScola[8] recommends the "Lullaby Technique" as the initial induction procedure with children. This involves suggesting that the child close his eyes and letting the whole body just go limp like a bowl of cooked spaghetti when the hypnotist snaps his fingers. Deepening can be accomplished by suggesting a walk down a flight of stairs, counting down from ten and suggesting going deeper with each count.

Because of the ease with which the child goes into deep hypnosis it usually isn't necessary to spend much time with specific deepening approaches. Some continued talk of becoming drowsy and sleepy and yet able to hear everything that is said, will usually be sufficient. It can then be suggested that the child look at a magic TV set and watch a repeat of a favorite cartoon or program. The entire program can be seen in a minute or less. Most young children are "hypnotized" by television and will readily accept this "magical" implementation of their wishes and fantasies.

Another useful approach with young children is the "Sleepy Fingers Technique." The hypnotist places the child's index and little fingers of one hand on the arm of the chair and raises the two middle fingers so they are not touching the chair. The child is then told that he and the hypnotist can play "Let's pretend." The two fingers resting on the chair arm (the hypnotist touches them to reinforce the suggestion) have gone to bed and are very comfortable and relaxed as they sleep. The hypnotist then suggests that the two raised fingers, which the child is instructed to focus on, are getting so tired and sleepy having to stay up like that. They would really like to be with the other two fingers in that warm, comfortable, secure bed. And as the child watches them, the fingers still up are getting more and more tired and sleepy and slowly begin moving down toward the bed to join the other two fingers. As they drift down, the child's eyes will get more heavy and sleepy and will close. Then the child can keep the eyes closed, remaining very relaxed, safe and secure, pretending that all of the fingers are now in bed, asleep and dreamy.[1]

Little research has been done in regard to the hypnotizability of elderly subjects. A recent study by Berg and Melin[2] found that there were no significant differences in hypnotizability between sexes or between age groups. However, there was a marked decline in people 85 years or older. It is possible that difficulties with concentration and attention may be involved in addition to other biochemical, arteriosclerotic variables of old age. However, it should be noted that there are elderly people who are physiologically and psychologically quite young and intact who would make good hypnotic subjects. There are also people of younger ages who appear to be old beyond their years, who have difficulty with concentration and do not make good hypnotic subjects. Each person should be evaluated individually as to the potential for being a good hypnotic subject. Age factors may well be secondary to motivational and relationship variables in the hypnotic situation.[4]

In recent years, the author had the opportunity of working with several female rape victims, all over the age of 80. In those cases, hypermnesia seemed almost impossible because of the difficulty the subjects exhibited in listening to instructions, in following suggestions and in staying on one topic for more than a second or two.[3] In contrast, the author has had good results

CHAPTER 27
LEGAL ASPECTS OF HYPNOSIS

Hypnosis has had two main applications legally.[2] One is its use as an analytical tool to determine the state of mind of a suspect or defendent at the time a crime was committed. This application of hypnosis is highly problematical because it involves issues such as the constitutional right against self-incrimination and the self-serving motivation of the subject with the possiblity of creating a more convincing alibi under hypnosis.

The second main use of hypnosis legally is as an investigative tool for the refreshment of witness memory[14]. In this application, hypnosis is used only with volunteer witnesses and/or victims of crimes where the issues of self-incrimination, questionable motivation and self-serving memories are not usually a problem. McCormick points out that the law already recognizes hypnosis as a useful investigative tool.[10]

Many courts have liberally defined what may be used to refresh memory.[3,13,18] A leader in this area has been the United States Court of Appeals for the Ninth Circuit which has stated, "It is quite immaterial by what means the memory is quickened; it may be a song, a face, or a newspaper article, or a writing of some character. It is sufficient that by some mental operation, however mysterious, the memory is stimulated to recall the event, for when set in motion it functions quite independently of the actuating cause." [Jewett V. United States, 15F.2d 955, 956 (Ninth CIR. 1926)][7]

Cases Involving Hypnosis As An Analytical Tool
People V. Ebanks, 117 CAL. 652 (8-23-1897)
Joseph Ebanks was convicted of murder. A defense expert witness, a hypnotist, said he had hypnotized the defendent who had denied his guilt under hypnosis. The court refused to allow the hypnotist to testify, stating, "The law of the United States does not recognize hypnotism. It would be an illegal defense

with young subjects, particularly between the ages of 7 and 14, who were victims of rape and witnesses to family homicides. In all of these cases, careful attention had to be given to the typical anxieties about retaliation and to the reduction of guilt feelings.[16]

The issue of whether aged people have memory difficulty because of faulty acquisition or retrieval problems is still unclear.[6]. Kimmel[7] reports several recent studies which have concluded that age-related decline in memory is a problem of retrieval rather than a problem of acquisition. In measuring young subjects against older ones, very little difference in recall was found when cues were given to both groups. However, when no cues were used, the younger subjects had better recall than did the older ones.[10,11] The marked decline in short-term memory seems to suggest learning deficiencies with advancing age as an additional problem.

References

1. *A Syllabus on Hypnosis and a Handbook of Therapeutic Suggestions.* Des Plaines, Illinois: American Society of Clinical Hypnosis, 1973.
2. Berg. S. and Melin, E. Hypnotic susceptibility in old age. Some data from residential homes for old people. *International Journal of Clinical and Experimental Hypnosis,* 1975, *23,* 184-189.
3. Botwinick, J. *Cognitive Processes in Maturity and Old Age.* New York: Springer, 1967.
4. Hilgard, J.R. *Personality and Hypnosis: A Study of Imaginative Involvement.* Chicago: University of Chicago Press, 1970.
5. Jersild, A.T. *Child Psychology.* Englewood Cliffs, New Jersey: Prentice-Hall, 1960.
6. Johnson, L.K. *Memory Loss With Age: A Storage or Retrieval Problem?* Presented at the Gerontological Society, San Juan, Puerto Rico, December 1972.
7. Kimmel, D.C. *Adulthood and Aging.* New York: Wiley, 1974.
8. LaScola, R. Hypnosis with children. *Clinical Hypnotherapy* (D.B. Cheek and L.M. LeCron, Eds.). New York: Grune & Stratton, 1968, 201-211.
9. London, P. *The Childrens' Hypnotic Susceptibility Scale.* Palo Alto, California: Consulting Psychologists Press, 1962.
10. London, P. and Cooper, L.M. Norms of hypnotic susceptibility in children. *Developmental Psychology,* 1969, *1,* 113-124.
11. Moore, R. and Lauer, L. Hypnotic susceptibility in middle childhood. *International Journal of Clinical and Experimental Hypnosis,* 1963, *11,* 167-174.
12. Morgan, A.H. and Hilgard, E.R. Age differences in susceptibility to hypnosis. *International Journal of Clinical and Experimental Hypnosis,* 1973, *21,* 78-85.
13. Olness, K. and Gardner, G.G. Some guidelines for uses of hypnotherapy in pediatrics. *Pediatrics,* 1978, *62,* 228-233.
14. Stone, L.J. and Church, J. *Childhood and Adolescence.* New York: Random House, 1957.

and I cannot admit it." The California Supreme Court later affirmed the trial court's decision not to allow the witness' testimony.

Cornell V. Superior Court of San Diego County, 52 CAL. 2d 99, 338 P. 2d 447 (5-5-59)

The attorney for a murder defendent petitioned the California Supreme Court for mandamus to require the trial court and the sheriff to allow his client to be examined by a hypnotist in order to aid in his recall of events on the night of the murder. While noting that the evidence developed under hypnosis might not be admissible at trial, the California Supreme Court reversed the trial court and held that the accused's right to counsel included the right to be examined under hypnosis to assist in preparing his defense. The sheriff was ordered to provide appropriate quarters for the hypnosis session to be done.

People V. Marsh, 170 Ca. 2d 284 (5-8-59)

Marsh's defense against a conviction for escape from Chino State Prison was that his act was not voluntary, but caused by hypnotic suggestion given him by another inmate. A court-appointed expert witness, a psychiatrist, testified that a suggestion of the type claimed by the defendent would not cause him to escape. On appeal, the California Supreme Court held that "A person can testify as an expert in his field when, because of his profession, or special knowledge, skill or experience not common to men in general, he is able to form an opinion when men in general would be left in doubt." The conviction was affirmed.

People V. Busch, 56 Ca. 2d 868 (11-22-61)

Convicted of three counts of murder and one count of assault with intent to commit murder, Busch was sentenced to death. On automatic appeal to the California Supreme Court, the trial court's decision was upheld, to exclude a doctor's testimony involving the use of hypnosis with Busch as an analytical tool. The Supreme Court said, "In laying a foundation for the introduction of opinion evidence of the state of mind of a person based upon the use of a technique not recognized by the Courts as sufficiently reliable to form the basis for such an opinion, at the very least, some showing of its successful use in the examination of others than the defendent for the same purpose, either by the witness or by other experts in the field, would appear to be required." Also, "A proper foundation was not established as to the reliability of an analytical tool still seeking recognition in the field of psychiatry, or as to the qualifications of this particular witness to give an opinion on the state of mind of the accused..."

State V. Nebb, No. 39, 450, Ohio C.P., Franklin County, May 28, 1962 (unreported)

By stipulation, with the jury excused, the defendent in a homicide case, Nebb, testified while in a hypnotic trance in the courtroom. As a result of his testimony, the prosecution was persuaded that the defendant was telling the truth about the events surrounding the murder and subsequently reduced the charges against him. The court indicated that testimony given under hypnosis would have to be excluded if it tended to incriminate the witness. (See Leyra V. Denno, 347 U.S. 556 (1954)).

People V. Modesto, 59 CAL. 2d 722, 382 P. 2d 33 (6-4-63)

Modesto was convicted of the murder of two sisters and sentenced to death. It was automatically appealed to the California Supreme Court which held the trial court erred in excluding a psychiatrist's explanation of using hypnotic techniques in a psychiatric examination to determine the defendant's intent. It said the trial court had not properly exercised its discretion regarding admission or exclusion of evidence when it excluded, outright, tape recordings made of the hypnosis session, though the hypnotist was an expert psychiatrist and the defense had offered to prove that hypnosis was an accepted analytical tool. The court said the proper procedure would have been to weigh the probative value of the tapes against the risk that the jury might improperly consider them as independent proof of the facts contained therein.

Regina V. Pitt, 68 D.L.R. 2d at 516.66W.W.R. at 403 (1967, Canada)

The defendant, in an attempt murder case, had amnesia for the crime situation and was permitted to be hypnotized in court with the jury present. He was given a posthypnotic suggestion by the hypnotist for hypermnesia on awakening. No questioning was done during the hypnosis session proper. The defendant testified posthypnotically with improved recall. The court said it would be unfair to deny the accused the right to accepted psychiatric procedures.

Jones V. State, 542 P. 2d 1316 (Okla. Crim. App. 1975)
In this case the appellate court held that hypnosis is inadmissible to establish the truth of an accused's assertions.

Hypnosis As An Investigative Tool

The following cases involve the use of hypnosis as an investigative tool for the refreshment of witness memory:

Harding V. State, 5 Md. App. 230, 246A. 2d 302, Cert. denied 395 U.S. 949 (1968)
A girl was shot and raped and couldn't recall the crime. She remembered under hypnosis and the trial court said the evidence was admissable. The Maryland Court of Special Appeals affirmed the conviction over the defendant's objections to the use of hypnosis to restore the victim's recall of the crime. The defense objected to the hypnotist's testimony on the basis of his qualifications because he did not graduate from any school of hypnotism. The appeals court said that the admission of expert testimony is primarily a matter for the trial judge to decide. It indicated that formal training is unnecessary as long as the record demonstrates that he is possessed "of any knowledge or information which would elevate his opinion above the level of conjecture or personal reaction." The court emphasized the professional expertise of the psychologist who had conducted the hypnosis session and who laid a solid foundation for the testimony. In addition, there was additional evidence to corroborate the witness' testimony. "Modern medical science recognizes that hypnosis can aid in recall, though fantasy may be mingled with fact."

State V. Jorgensen, 49 Pac. 2d 312 (Oregon App., 1971)
In this murder case, a prosecution witness' poor memory was restored by the use of drugs and hypnosis. The court held that hypnosis is allowed as long as adequate cross examination is possible by the defense.

People V. Peters, 4 Crim. 5996, March, 1974
In this unreported case, a police officer was ambushed by the newly-elected president of a motorcycle club. Hypnosis was used to enhance the officer's recall of the events. Though the court didn't directly answer on the question of hypnosis, it gave some pertinent dicta: (1) California law does not preclude hypnosis as to state of mind. (2) The evidence would have been ad-

missible if a proper foundation had been laid. (3) The value of hypnosis as a tool of discovery was acknowledged by *Cornell*. (4) The possibility of misuse of hypnosis by the prosecution exists because of increased suggestibility. (5) It precluded blanket approval, indicating that cross examination was needed to overcome any objections.

Wyller V. Fairchild-Hiller Corporation, 503 F. 2d 506 (Ninth Circuit, 9-13-74)

In this civil case, four years after a helicopter crash at Ketchikan, Alaska, in which two persons were killed, hypnosis was used with Wyller, a surviving passenger, to improve his limited recall of the events surrounding the accident. Monetary awards were made by the trial court to the plaintiff, and the helicopter manufacturer appealed citing that, 1. Wyller's testimony was rendered inherently untrustworthy by his having undergone hypnosis, 2. That the district court erred in admitting testimony from Wyller and the hypnotist concerning the content of tape recordings made while Wyller was in a hypnotic state, 3. That the court should not have permitted the hypnotist's testimony as the the reliability of statements made by the hypnotized Wyller, and 4. That the court erred in failing to give the jury a cautionary instruction regarding Wyller's testimony insofar as it consisted of information recalled by means of hypnosis.

The appellate court affirmed the trial courts finding. It stated, "We cannot accept Fairchild's argument that Wyller's testimony was rendered inherently untrustworthy by his having undergone hypnosis. Wyller testified from his present recollection, refreshed by the treatment. His credibility and the weight to be given such testimony were for the jury to determine. Fairchild was entitled to, and did, challenge the reliability of both the remembered facts and the hypnosis procedure itself by extensive and thorough cross examination of Wyller and the hypnotist. Under the circumstances we perceive no abusive discretion by the district court."

Kline V. Ford Motor Company, 523 F. 2d 1067 (9-22-75)

Because of severe head injuries and amnesia following a one-car accident, the witness remembered nothing about the event. Her memory was then revived under hypnosis, resulting in full recall of events leading to the accident. The trial court excluded the witness's testimony to events recalled after hypnosis and sustained Ford's objection that she was not competent as a witness to testify to facts recalled under hypnosis. The appellate court found the ruling erroneous.

"Competence refers to the condition of the witness at the time he or she is called to testify. Jacqueline (witness) was fully capable of expressing herself and understanding her duty as a witness to tell the truth (e.g., CAL. EVID. CODE Sections 405,701 and annexed comment (West, 1966); B. Witkin *Cal. Evidence* (2d ed. 2966) Section 768 at 716). She was present and personally saw and heard the occurrences at the time of the accident. She was testifying about her present recollection of events that she had witnessed. That her present memory depends on refreshment claimed to have been induced under hypnosis goes to the credibility of her testimony not to her competence as a witness. Although the evidence by which recollection was refreshed is unusual, in legal effect her situation is not different from that of a witness who claims that his recollection of an event that he could not earlier remember was revived when he thereafter read a particular document. (Wyller V. Fairchild-Hiller Corp.). Here, as in Wyller, we cannot accept defendant's argument that plaintiff's testimony was rendered inherently untrustworthy by her having undergone hypnosis. Plaintiff testified from her present recollection, refreshed by the treatment. Her credibility and the weight to be given to such testimony were for the jury to determine."

People V. John Quaglino, 109524 (Superior Court, Santa Barbara County, 1976). Quaglino V. California, 77-1288 (October 30, 1978)

The Ford car that struck and killed Dyanne Quaglino had been registered to a Richard W. Bellmore. It was found shortly after the accident behind the apartment complex where Quaglino lived. Quaglino told authorities he had been in bed with his girlfriend at the time of his wife's death. The car had been sold to "Bellmore" by a car dealer named Jensen. When Jensen was first shown a picture of Quaglino, he said it "Struck a bell" but could not be more specific. After being hypnotized, a week later, by a Santa Barbara psychiatrist, Jensen picked Quaglino's picture from a stack of seven photographs as being the "Richard Bellmore" to whom he had sold the car.

Jensen subsequently picked Quaglino out of a line-up and identified him in a preliminary hearing. Psychiatrists testified on both sides. Defense psychiatrists did not disapprove of the concept of memory enhancement by hypnosis, but did object to its use in this case because of prior police contact coupled with undue suggestions on their part as to the killer's identity. The first two trials resulted in hung juries, the third resulted in a conviction. The hypnosis evidence remained the same in all three cases.

On appeal, the California Court of Appeals concluded that hypnosis was "a valid and reliable technique for improving recollection." The California Supreme Court and the U.S. Supreme Court refused to hear the case and let the conviction stand.

State V. McQueen, 244 S.E. 2d 414 (June 6, 1978)

The defendant, McQueen, was convicted in Superior Court of two first degree murder offenses and he appealed. The North Carolina Supreme Court affirmed, holding that the fact that a state witness had been hypnotized prior to trial did not render her testimony inadmissible.

"The witness testified that, following the events in question, she endeavored to block them from her memory and her recollection of them became uncertain, but, thereafter, prior to the trial, she was hypnotized at her request, and, as a result, as of the time of her testimony, she clearly remembered what she had seen and heard at the time of the events to which her testimony relates. According to her testimony, her memory of these events was refreshed by the hypnotic procedure which she underwent sometime prior to the trial. The fact that the memory of a witness concerning events, distant in time, has been refreshed, prior to trial, as by the reading of documents or by conversation with another, does not render the witness incompetent to testify concerning his or her present recollection. The credibility of such testimony, in view of prior uncertainty on the part of the witness, is a matter for the jury's consideration. So it is when the witness has, in the meantime, undergone some psychiatric or other medical treatment by which memory is said to have been refreshed or restored. So it is when the intervening experience has been hypnosis."

United States V. Adams, 581 F. 2d 183 (June 14, 1978)

The Ninth Circuit Court of Appeals affirmed the conviction of two defendants on charges of conspiracy to assault with intent to rob, robbery, and murder, in a post office robbery situation. For the first time in a *criminal* case, the Court admitted eyewitness testimony refreshed under hypnosis, in spite of the fact that there were questions about the hypnosis methods used in this case. These questions involved an uncertified hypnotist conducting the session, and no record being made of the identity of those present, the questions asked, or the responses given.

The Court said, "Although we do not approve of the hypnosis methods used here, Adams did not object to the adequacy of the foundation laid for the receipt of the testimony. Rather he attempted to exclude all in-court testimony of Morin on the grounds that no testimony from witnesses who had been hypnotized could be reliable, and that the use of testimony of a witness who has been hypnotized would deny the defendant his Sixth Amendment right to confrontation and his right to call witnesses on his own behalf. The predicate for both constitutional arguments is that the in-court testimony of a witness who had earlier been subject to hypnosis is unreliable as a matter of law rendering the witness legally incompetent to testify. We rejected that premise in Kline V. Ford Motor Company, Inc., supra, and we see no reason for a different result in the context of a criminal case."

Teitlebaum[16] also recommends that the test of general reliability in regard to hypnosis be discarded and that the courts concern themselves on a case-by-case basis as to whether in each particular case a proper foundation is established for its admission and that proper procedures be used in the court room to insure that the jury has all the facts and can make up its own mind.

HYPNOSIS LEGISLATION

Legislation involving the investigative uses of hypnosis is a rarity. One of the first state laws which addresses itself to investigative hypnosis is H.B. 3125 enacted in the state of Oregon in June, 1977. Local civil liberties groups in Salem, hostile to investigative hypnosis had attempted to quickly push through a bill completely proscribing the use of hypnosis by criminal justice personnel. However, the legislation finally passed actually recognizes investigative hypnosis and sets some guidelines for its use. The bill reads as follows:

H.B. 3125 (Oregon)

Section I. If either prosecution or defense in any criminal proceeding in the state of Oregon intends to offer the testimony of any person, including the defendant, who has been subjected to hypnosis, mesmerism or any other form of the exertion of will power or the power of suggestion which is intended to or results in a state of trance, sleep or entire or partial unconsciousness relating to the subject matter of the proposed testimony, performed by any person, it shall be a condition of the use of such testimony that the entire procedure be recorded either on videotape or any mechanical recording device. The unabridged videotape or mechanical recording shall be made available to the other party or parties in accordance with ORS 135.805 - 135.990.

Section II. (1) No person employed or engaged in any capacity by or on behalf of any state or local law enforcement agency shall use upon another person any form of hypnotism, mesmerism, or any other form of the exertion of will power or the power of suggestion which is intended to or results in a state of trance, sleep or entire or partial unconsiousness without first explaining to the intended subject that:

(a) He is free to refuse to be subject to the processes delineated in this Section;

(b) There is a risk of psychological side effects resulting from the processes;

(c) If he agrees to be subject to such processes, it is possible that the process will reveal emotions or information of which he is not consciously aware and which he may wish to keep private, and;

(d) He may request that the process be conducted by a licensed medical doctor or a licensed psychologist at no cost to himself.

(2) In the event that the prospective subject refuses to consent, none of the processes delineated in Subsection (1) of this Section shall be used upon that person.

Section III. No evidence secured in violation of Section I or II of this Act shall be admissible in any criminal proceeding in this State.

In the future it is likely that other state legislatures will consider legislation recognizing and affecting the applications of investigative hypnosis. Because of the proprietary interests of various groups, it is important that lawmakers have the facts from all concerned parties, including the people, before laws are passed. It is in society's interest to have qualified law enforcement personnel continue to utilize hypnosis as an effective investigative tool.[1,7]

References
1. Arons, H. *Hypnosis in Criminal Investigation.* Springfield, Illinois: Thomas, 1967.

2. Bryan, W.J. *Legal Aspects of Hypnosis.* Springfield, Illinois: Thomas, 1962.
3. Dilloff, N.J. The admissibility of hypnotically influenced testimony. *Ohio Northern University Law Review,* 1977, *IV,* 1-23.
4. Hanley, F.W. Hypnosis in the court room. *Canadian Psychiatric Association Journal,* 1969, *14,* 351-354.
5. *Harding V. State of Maryland.* 246A. 2d 302 (Oct. 9, 1968).
6. H.B. 3125. Oregon Legislature, June 1977.
7. Johnson, A. Hypnosis and the law: A meeting of the minds. *Prosecutor's Brief,* March-April 1978, 34-36.
8. *Kline V. Ford Motor Co., Inc.,* 523 F. 2d 1067 (1975).
9. Kroger, W.S. *Clinical and Experimental Hypnosis: 2nd Edition.* Philadelphia: Lippincott, 1977.
10. McCormick, C.T. *Handbook of the Law of Evidence, 2nd Edition.* St. Paul, Minnesota: West Publishing Company, 1972.
11. *People V. Peters.* 4th Crim. 5996, 1974.
12. *Regina V. Pitt.* 68 D.L.R. 2d at 516.66 W.W. R at 403 (1967).
13. Romanoff, R.A. A survey of case law (what the judges think of hypnosis). *Hypnosis Quarterly* 1977, *20,* 1-8.
14. Schafer, D.W. and Rubio, R. Hypnosis to aid the recall of witnesses. *International Journal of Clinical and Experimental Hypnosis,* 1978, *26,* 81-91.
15. *State of North Carolina V. Roger Lee McQueen.* No. 92. Supreme Court of North Carolina, June 6, 1978.
16. Teitelbaum, M. *Hypnosis Induction Technics.* Springfield, Illnois: Thomas, 1969.
17. *United States V. Adams.* 581 F. 2nd 193 (1978), 581 *Federal Reporter, 2nd Series.*
18. *Virginia Researcher.* Charlottesville, Virginia, March 1975.
19. *Wyller V. Fairchild-Hiller Corporation.* 503 F. 2d 506 (1974).

CHAPTER 28
EXPERT WITNESS CONSIDERATIONS

An expert witness is a person who has special knowledge, skill, experience, training or education sufficient to qualify him as an expert on the subject to which his testimony relates. The expert may be a person skilled in some art, trade, science, or profession who has knowledge of matters not within the knowledge of men of average education, learning and experience and who may assist the jury in arriving at a verdict by giving an opinion on a state of fact shown by the evidence and based upon his special knowledge.[4]

Even though the witness has not had any personal experience he may still be qualified to testify as an expert on a subject which he can show familiarity with as a result of study, reading and education. It isn't necessary that the expert have a complete knowledge of the subject if the issue he is testifying about is one on which he has the special knowledge required.[11]

Before expert testimony is allowed in a case, it has to be demonstrated that the witness has the required knowledge, skill or experience not known to the common man. Opposing counsel may stipulate or accept the witness as an expert without testimony about his background or he may cross-examine in detail on *voir dire.*

The investigative hypnosis expert should come to court with a prepared list of his qualifications. This list should include the following:

1. Formal Education: College, post-graduate work, majors, honors, special seminars or tutorials, degrees earned.

2. Police and Investigator Training: Pertinent schools, courses and seminars.

3. Hypnosis Training: Formal and informal including the number of hours, subjects covered, instructor's qualifications, text books used, number of subjects hypnotized, etc.

4, Professional Certificates and Diplomas: Basic police training, investigative training, and investigative hypnosis training.

5. Academic Appointments and Teaching Experience: Both

police and non-police areas.

6. Research Participation and Experience: Survey and applied studies.
7. Offices Held and Memberships in Professional Societies and Organizations: Police, Investigative, Hypnosis.
8. Experience as an Investigator and as a Hypnotist: Include number of subjects hypnotized, number of cases worked on, number of cases observed or assisted in.
9. List of Own Publications: Reports, and professional papers written.
10. Professional Books, Journals and Articles read on Hypnosis, Particularly Investigative Hypnosis.
11. Professional Consultants Worked with and Their Qualifications.
12. Agencies Consulted with in Regard to Investigative Hypnosis.
13. Previous Court Qualifications and Experience as an Expert Witness.

Some of the typical questions asked in qualifying as an expert are:

How long have you been a police officer?
How long have you been using hypnosis?
How long have you been using hypnosis in criminal investigations?
How many persons have you hypnotized?
How many hypnosis sessions have you participated in for the purpose of enhancing recall?
What training have you received in the area of investigative hypnosis?

The expert witness should be calm, professional and dignified in testifying, maintaining an attitude of objectivity and lack of bias. Answers should be confined to facts whenever possible and opinions given when requested. Opinions should include not only the conclusion but the means at arriving at the conclusion and should be given in plain language that the jury can understand.[7] Although the investigative hypnosis expert should be familiar with the terminology used in hypnosis, he should avoid technical terms whenever possible and explain the terms when they need to be used.[9]

It is desirable to avoid quoting text books or articles as authority since many may contain inconsistencies which opposing council can use to discredit the expert's testimony. Hypothetical questions posed should be answered within the limits of the expert's knowledge and experience. If questions about neurology or unconsious psychic processes are asked, the police expert would likely answer that these questions are outside the area of his expertise since he is not a psychiatrist or neurologist.[1]

The expert should avoid exaggerating or embellishing because this will likely be used against him on cross-examination. On cross-examination counsel may try to show a lack of qualification, inconsistent statements, bias, error in observed facts, error in assumed facts or error in expert opinion.[7]

The investigative hypnosis expert should carefully review the tape of the hypnosis session prior to going to court and be very familiar with details of the complete session, including methods of induction, deepening, estimations of depth of hypnosis of the subject, questions asked and information elicited under hypnosis.[6] The expert should be prepared to explain the reasons for procedures used during the hypnosis session and to refute attacks based on issues raised by opposing experts.[3] Many of these issues were reviewed in the previous chapter. Though the expert may disagree with opinions of other experts in the field, a professional stance should be maintained in relationship to them without demeaning or belittling.[6,8]

The expert's testimony may not involve his participation as the investigative hypnotist in the particular case. The key issue may concern itself with showing that the hypnosis session was conducted in an atmosphere of fairness and that no suggestions were made to the witness to unduly influence the nature of his response.[2]

Following is an excerpt from the preliminary hearing in a Federal Court homicide case in which the defense counsel's expert witness tried unsuccessfully to impeach the key prosecution witness's testimony on the basis of tainting as a result of having undergone hypnosis for the purposes of recall *(United States V. Adams.* 581 F. 2d 193 (1978));

Defense counsel: This is a motion regarding the hypnotism of three eyewitnesses to the robbery and murder, which are counts three and four of the indictment in this case.

The essence of the motion is that by hypnotizing those witnesses the government has essentially rendered them incompetent, because once they have been hypnotized it becomes impossible for them to extricate what they have lived through under hypnosis from what they witnessed during the crime itself.

The Court: And what do you propose to offer to support that contention?

Defense Counsel: I propose to offer, first, the testimony of the doctor, the dentist who hypnotized these people at the request of the postal inspectors, to lay a foundation for what happened to these witnesses, whether or not they were successfully hypnotized.

Very briefly, what they went through under hypnosis, how many times they were hypnotized, that type of thing.

I then intend to offer the testimony of Dr. Bernard Newton (sic), who is a psychologist who specializes in clinical psychology, using hypnotism, to offer his opinion on the validity of the techniques used, the effect of hypnosis upon witnesses, particular eye witnesses.

Those are the two I intend to offer. It may become necessary, depending on the testimony of Dr. Carnow, the government's hypnotist, to briefly put on one or two of the witnesses themselves, but I don't think that will be necessary.

The Court: What support do you have for the proposition that a witness having been subjected to hypnosis thereby is rendered incompetent as a witness?

Defense Counsel: Well I anticipate...

The Court: Scientific proof that this occurs...

Defense Counsel: Yes, opinion by an expert. Opinion by an expert, yes, sir.

The Court: In order to take the opinion of a scientific expert that this is what happens, it is necessary in every case, then, to explore in detail what happened to this particular witness and then make an individualized judgment that this particular witness, in view of all these circumstances, has become incompetent to testify?

Defense Counsel: Well, it would be my position that any witness who has been hypnotized is not a competent witness thereafter, but there are factors which may aggravate the degree to which that witnesses recollection of the event is contaminated by what happened by his experience under hypnosis, and I believe those aggravating factors are present in this case.

That is why the testimony of the hypnotist is important.

The Court: If you take the general position that any witness who has been hypnotized thereby becomes incompetent to testify...do you have any authority to support that position? That is a very broad position..

Defense Counsel: Yes, sir, it is. I think the testimony of the expert...

The Court: No. Authority, legal authority.

Defense Counsel: I have cited in my memorandum the cases I have been able to find on the subject. There are two Ninth Circuit civil cases in which witnesses who were hypnotized were allowed to testify.

The Court: That is contrary authority.

Defense Counsel: Yes, sir.

The Court: Even in a civil case.

Defense Counsel: Yes, sir.

The Court: Yes.

Defense Counsel: But the court, in making and arriving at that determination, made factual statments which my expert will indicate are incorrect, scientifically unfounded.

So that at this hearing there will be a...

The Court: Do you think we can derive a rule of law that affects all cases based upon the opinion of one expert that a witness' mental capacity has become so tainted or so adversely affected by being subjected to hypnosis that the witness is automatically disqualified from testifying? That is what you are asking this Court to do?

Defense Counsel: I am only asking this Court to rule upon the facts in this case that I will develop.

Obviously, that ruling may have implications beyond this case, but I would not ask the court to make a per se ruling.

I would ask an opportunity to develop the particular facts and circumstances of this case and have Dr. Newton testify about those particular facts and circumstances.

The Court: Thank you. Let me ask, is the government prepared to offer contrary expert testimony?

Prosecutor: No, sir, the government is not.

The government's position is that this is not an expert issue. It is a legal issue and it is one that has been decided in this circuit, to the effect that whether a person has undergone hypnosis does render him incompetent, but that fact may go to the weight of his testimony.

The following is an excerpt from the transcript of the landmark case *Harding V. State of Maryland* (246a. 2d 302, October 9, 1968). The psychologist who performed hypnosis with the key witness is being questioned by counsel:

Q. I direct your attention to October 12, 1966, and I ask you on that date did you have occasion to contact one Mildred Hortense Coley?

A. Yes.

Q. And under what circumstances did you meet Miss Coley and where was it?

A. The state police called me and asked me if I would come over there, or they told me they had an individual who had been the victim of some criminal act and that she was having a difficult time or could not recall the events that occurred or circumstances under which these events occurred, and asked me if I would come over there and give any assistance I could.

Q. And upon your arrival what did you do?

A. Upon my arrival I was familiarized with more details of the situation and I met the young lady and explained to her what I was going to do to help her get her memory back, whatever memory she may have lost as a result of trauma of the incident.

Q. You say you were filled in on the background by the police and you informed her what you intended to do and the purpose of it. Then what mechanics did you utilize in order to effect what you were about to do?

A. I used a thumb tack, the sort that has a shiny head. There's a blank wall and I just pinned the thumb tack in and asked her to concentrate, focus her eyes on the thumb tack and listen to my voice and the voice might make her simply just relax, relax, relax, you are getting very tired; very monotonous and repetitive manner.

Q. In this manner were you able to put her into some sort of trance state?

A. She was under hypnosis.

Q. What happened as a result of what you did?

A. Well she went into a reduced state of consciousness.

Q. And what did you do?

A. Then I recalled the date in question and simply asked her to tell me everything that happened.

Q. Was she able to tell you?

A. Yes. She was able to relate everything that occurred.

Q. You put her into this state of reduced consciousness and she told you her story. Then what did you do?

A. Then she got into the state of reduced, then I — then two of the state troopers came in. I asked two state troopers to come in.

Q. Do you know who they were?

A. I believe Sgt. Greffen and I believe Trooper George.

Q. What participation did they take in what you were doing?

A. I just wanted them simply as witnesses since they were interested in it, and I was disinterested. I believe they recorded everything that she said.

Q. They recorded it, you say?
A. I believe so. Tape recorder; I'm not sure.
Q. Then what did you do?
A. Well, after I was finished I gave her the suggestion that when she would awaken she would relate that which she had related under the state of reduced consciousness.
Q. You say you gave her a suggestion. What do you mean by that?
A. I simply told her that when she would awaken she would recount the same thing that she recounted under the state of reduced consciousness.
Q. Was she able to do that?
A. Yes.
Q. And was her ability to recall the result of your suggestion that she would?
A. I don't understand the question.
Q. You say you suggested that she could recall what she had told you while under hypnosis?
A. Right.
Q. And that after this suggestion she was awakened?
A. Uh-huh.
Q. And then she recalled what she had said while under hypnosis?
A. Yes, in its entirety.
Q. Then she recalled this the second time after you awakened her, when she was still under hypnosis?
A. No.
Q. Was this recollection a result of the suggestion you made to her?
A. Yes, in that it was in a situation that provided her to want to do so.
Q. You said your questioning took the form — you reminded her, brought her attention to the time you were discussing. What form did the questioning take thereafter?
A. Here is how I started out. I told her I'm going to ask you to tell me everything that happened, or I recall something, I don't recall, tell me everything that happened on June 26, whatever it was, and she went on and recounted, and as her — I would occasionally say, and tell me what else, what else happened, and this is essentially the form of the questioning.
Q. At any time during your hypnosis of her did you suggest any answers to any questions?
A. No, I never do.
Q. Did you relate any stories that you thought would be

likely?
A. No.
Q. Did the policeman participate in any way by suggesting any answers to her?
A. No. I never permit this. Usually when I put the person under hypnosis I usually give instructions the person will not hear any other voice or sound except mine, so no other external source can go through to her, since she can't hear.
Q. Is the information that results from such a session as you describe reliable or unreliable?
A. In this situation I would say that it was reliable.
Q. Why would you say that?
A. Because there was certain information that was provided by the police to me later and there were also self-corroborative statements she made. Also, her recall afterwards was essentially the same.
Q. If she had been falsifying under hypnosis, would her later recall have been the same?
A. Might not have been. Also, if she wanted to falsify she could have falsified before I induced hypnosis.
Q. You stated in one of your previous answers you felt in this instance the information you received from the subject was reliable. Why would this instance be more reliable than any other one you might have referred to?
A. For the one reason this was something that she would have no reason to withhold, say, in a completely conscious state, since there was no threat to her vital interest to withhold this information. If she wanted to lie, she certainly could have given a statement without any difficulty, which she was unable to do. Secondly, there was some corroborative material within her statement that would indicate some of the things occurred, not occurred, but some of the things she had seen, she could have only seen if she had been there.
Q. Unable to do? Could it have been the fact that she was unwilling to do it?
A. No. If she would have been unwilling to do it, it would probably have been impossible to even hypnotize her.

Trooper George's testimony confirmed that given by the psychologist as to what occurred when he was present and in addition showed that Mildred Coley was hypnotized for approximately 45 minutes. No witness testified as to what she said during or after the hypnosis.

The trial judge gave a precautionary instruction to the jury as follows:

"You have heard, during this trial, that a portion of the testimony of the prosecuting witness, Mrs. Coley, was recalled by her as a result of her being placed under hypnosis. The phenomenon, known as hypnosis has been explained to you during the trial. I advise you to weigh this testimony carefully. Do not place any greater weight on this portion of Mrs. Coley's testimony than on any other testimony that you have heard during this trial. Remember, you are the judges of the weight and the believability of all of the evidence in this case."

References

1. Arons, H. *Hypnosis in Criminal Investigation.* Springfield, Illinois: Thomas, 1967.
2. Derrick, C. Interrogation by hypnosis. *Police Chief,* March 1959, 26-29.
3. Field, P.B. and Dworkin, S.F. Strategies of hypnotic interrogation. *Journal of Psychology,* 1967, *67,* 47-58.
4. Fricke, C.W. *California Criminal Evidence, 9th Edition.* Los Angeles, California: Legal Book Corp., 1978.
5. Hanley, F.W. Hypnosis in the court room. *Canadian Psychiatric Association Journal,* 1969, *14,* 351-354.
6. Hypno-induced statements: safeguards for admissibility. *Law and the Social Order,* 1970, 99-120.
7. Petersen, R.D. *The Police Officer in Court.* Springfield, Illinois: Thomas, 1975.
8. Scott, E.M. Hypnosis in the courtroom. *American Journal of Clinical Hypnosis,* 1977, *19,* 163-165.
9. Teitelbaum, M. *Hypnosis Induction Technics.* Springfield, Illinois: Thomas, 1965.
10. Tierney, K. *Courtroom Testimony.* New York: Funk & Wagnalls, 1970.
11. Walls, H.J. *Expert Witness.* London: John Long, 1972.

CHAPTER 29
AGE REGRESSION AND AUTOMATIC WRITING

There are several forms of age regression. One is a relatively complete form of regression called revivification in which the subject, in a deep state of hypnosis, appears to regress back to and behave as if again actually at the previous age.[5] This behavior can include revivifying the earlier forms of voice, handwriting, language usuage and handedness.[11]

The second type of regression is the *partial* form. In this state the subject is aware of his present situation and environment and retains the hypnotist's identity. The subject may understand recalled childhood events from his adult viewpoint and reflect on these early occurrences. Partial regression is possible with only a light state of hypnosis required.[6]

The third form of regression, a variation on the partial type, is the one most commonly used in investigative hypnosis. The subject, rather than asked to re-experience or relive the orginal event, is structured to watch it as an observer and to review what is happening. This changes the role of the subject from participant to observer and creates objectivity and distance from the original traumatic event. Although some emotion may be re-experienced by the subject in the observer role, who reviews the original crime as if on television, the affect usually will have less intensity than if revivified with the subject in the participant role.

In special crime situations, more direct age regression may be desirable and there are several useful techniques in assisting the subject to go back in time. The hypnotist can use the time machine or time tunnel concept, the magic carpet of time on which the subject floats backward in time to the desired date, the time train which goes backward in time with a stop at each station representing an appropriate interval, watching the hands of a clock move backward to reverse time, turning back the pages in a book of time, or tearing off the pages of a calendar back to the date desired.

The more complete the regression, the greater the likelihood of eliciting emotional or affective reactions which may have no relationship to the crime information desired. Repressed childhood events and memories may become reactivated inadvertently if a complete age regression is suggested.[8] Since most investigative hypnosis sessions with witnesses or victims involve crimes of relatively recent occurrence, the regressions involved will not likely get into emotionally disturbing or painful repressed memories from childhood.[9]

Age regression is related to hypermnesia in that partial regression techniques are used as an aid in the recall of memories.[10] Some subjects experience vivid age regression although for most, the adult observing ego is present, resulting in partial rather than a full dissociation by the subject.[3]

Some normal ego contact remains during regression situations and this Hilgard attributes to a "hidden observer" which permits the subject to remain in contact with the hypnotist regardless of the age regressed to. He also points out that some of the experimental-theoretical issues in regard to age regression may not be relevant when the goal is a pragmatic one,[4] as in remembering a crime event.

Automatic Writing

This technique can be useful in eliciting repressed information in certain situations by bypassing the subject's conscious cortical levels.

One drawback is that it may take the subject quite a long time to learn how to write freely and spontaneously with this technique. However, with this approach, the subconscious mind can freely bring out any information it wishes to.

The subject should be in a medium to deep state of hypnosis and should be told that his writing hand and arm, from fingertips all the way up to the shoulder, will develop a mind of its own and on signal will feel separate and dissociated from the rest of the body. The hypnotist should lightly stroke the subject's hand and arm to reinforce this suggestion. The subject should be seated at a desk or have a clipboard and pad available for writing. The hypnotist should place a soft pencil or ball point pen in an upright position between the thumb and forefinger of the subject's writing hand. Additional suggestions for arm independence, separateness and dissociation are given to the subject along with the suggestion that, on signal, the hand will begin writing by itself, freely and spontaneously. The information it writes will be relevant to the crime in question and may consist of license plate data, or any other visually depictable material. It may include such diverse items as designs on the suspect's t-shirt, or the logo on a bumper sticker. The subject doing automatic writing may respond slowly or rapidly, run words together, or write or print unintelligibly. However, suggestions can be given that, shortly, with eyes open in hypnosis, the subject will be able to look at his production, understand and interpret it for the hypno-investigator. This will sometimes enable scribbles to be rendered intelligible by the subject's subconscious knowledge.[1,7]

References

1. Cheek, D.B. and LeCron, L.M. *Clinical Hypnotherapy.* New York: Grune & Stratton, 1968.
2. Edmonston, W.E. Hypnotic age-regression: An evaluation of role-taking theory. *American Journal of Clinical Hypnosis,* 1962, 5, 3-7.
3. Hilgard, E.R. *The Experience of Hypnosis.* New York: Harcourt, Brace and World, 1968.
4. Hilgard, E.R. *Divided Consciousness.* New York: Wiley Interscience, 1977.
5. Kline, M.V. Hypnotic regression: a neuro-psychological theory of age regression and progression. *Clinical Correlates of Experimental Hypnosis* (M.V. Kline, Ed.). Springfield, Illinois: Thomas, 1963, 452-462.
6. LeCron, L.M. A study of age regression under hypnosis. *Experimental Hypnosis* (L.M. LeCron, Ed.). Secaucus, New Jersey: The Citadel Press, 1972, 155-174.
7. Mühl, A.M. Automatic writing and hypnosis. *Experimental Hypnosis* (L.M. LeCron, Ed.). Secaucus, New Jersey: The Citadel Press, 1972, 426-438.
8. Orne, M.T. The mechanisms of hypnotic age regression. *Journal of Abnormal and Social Psychology,* 1951, 46, 213-225.
9. Reiff, R. and Scheerer, M. *Memory and Hypnotic Age Regression.* New York: International Universities Press, 1959.
10. Walker, N.S., Garrett, J.B. and Wallace, B. Restoration of eidetic imagery via hypnotic age regression. *Journal of Abnormal Psychology,* 1976, 85, 335-337.
11. Young, P.C. Hypnotic regression - fact or artifact? *Modern Hypnosis* (L. Kuhn and S. Russo, Eds.). North Hollywood, California: Wilshire Book Company, 1974, 56-63.

CHAPTER 30
IDEOMOTOR AND IDEOSENSORY TECHNIQUES

Ideomotor activities involve the involuntary capacity of muscles to respond almost instantaneously to thoughts, feelings and ideas.[2] These reflex responses are related to survival needs and are part of everyday, normal experience. Subcortical mechanisms are involved in involuntary responses such as blinking, breathing, heartbeat and are mediated autonomically. Reflex responses can be conditioned and brought under the subject's voluntary control. Biofeedback training programs enable individuals to produce increased alpha brain waves, or to reduce galvanic skin response. In hypnosis the subject can learn to produce reflex responses which activate fingers to yield information from subconscious levels of awareness.[3]

The pendulum, which can be made from a piece of string and a weight, is an excellent tool to capitalize on ideomotor responses of the subject either in or out of hypnosis.[5] There are four basic pendulum movements possible: clockwise, counterclockwise, in and out away from the subject, or back and forth across the subject. Each of these movements can be assigned a meaning. One direction can mean "yes", another direction "no", the third "I don't know", and the fourth "I don't want to answer". These responses allow questions to be answered directly from the subconscious mind by reflex via the autonomic nervous system to the musculature of the body as reflected in the micro-tremors which activate the pendulum in a particular direction.

The subject is told what the four possible pendulum movements are and asked to establish his own replies. He holds the pendulum with the dominant hand, hanging between the index finger and thumb, with the elbow resting on a solid surface. The hypnotist requests the subject's subconscious mind to select one of the four movements to represent the "yes" response. The subject is also told the harder he tries to keep the pendulum still, the more it will swing in a definite direction. He is to keep his eyes on the ball of the pendulum and watch as it moves in a wider and wider arc.

When the subject has established a response for each of the four possible movements, he can then be asked questions which can be answered subconsciously by one of the replies. In situations where it is desirable not to have the subject know what his response is to a particular question, the procedure can be done with the subject's eyes closed. Hypnosis is not required for this purpose. This will tend to minimize any resistances and tendencies toward conscious control of the pendulum movement.[1] Because the pendulum doesn't require hypnosis, it can be used with subjects who are unable to make use of a standard hypnosis approach.

Ideomotor finger signaling is also an extremely useful technique in investigative hypnosis. The subject, in hypnosis, is told that each time the index finger of his dominant hand is touched by the hypnotist, it will automatically raise up. The hypnotist then touches the index finger about five times and then indicates that whenever the finger is touched or whenever the answer to a question is honestly and accurately "yes" the finger will also raise up by itself automatically. The hypnotist then alternates touching the index finger and saying "yes" in completing the conditioning of the index finger as a "yes" response. In similar fashion, the middle finger of the subject's right hand is conditioned as a "no" response. The subject's little finger is then conditioned as an "I don't know response" in the same way. The subject can then be asked questions that can be answered by "yes" or "no" about license numbers, names, whether the objects, faces or events of the crime were originally perceived and are now subject to recall.

Because there is sometimes a discrepancy between a license number that has been verbalized by a hypnotized subject and the letters and digits elicited by ideomotor finger signaling, it is preferable to check out this information both ways. Because ideomotor signaling involves the inihibition of higher cortical levels, resulting in a reflex movement, it is likely that the finger signal will be more reliable than the verbalized information.

In eliciting license plate information under hypnosis with ideomotor signaling, the hypno-investigator can start by asking the subject if the license plate was perceived at all initially in relationship to the crime situation. If the "yes" finger responds, the questioning can continue by eliciting the colors on the license plate, the state of origin and other identifiers such as renewal sticker or state motto. The subject can then be asked if there are six or more characters on the license plate and, by the finger responses, determine how many there are. The subject may be asked if the first character on the license plate is a letter of the alphabet. If the answer is "no" the next question can verify it as a number. The subject is then instructed to indicate by a "yes" response when the appropriate license plate character is mentioned by the hypno-investigator. The hypnotist then slowly, allowing lag time, gives numbers from one through zero, or letters of the alphabet from A to Z, and notes the ideomotor response. This procedure is followed for each of the individual characters on the license plate until all the information is elicited. It should then be rechecked.

If the "yes" and "no" fingers rise simultaneously, it suggests that either the subject did not perceive that particular item or that he has some confusion because of the way the question was phrased. It is not unusual that a witness does not register all of the letters or digits on a license plate, but still be able to recall enough information to be of help to the investigators. The kidnapping of a busload of school children in Chowchilla, California was an example. Under hypnosis the bus driver was able to recall all but one digit of the suspect's van license plate, which helped the FBI investigators in that case.

Ideosensory Techniques

Ideosensory activity involves the ability of the subject to develop sensory images which utilize one or more of the senses. Common examples involve day dreaming, fantasies, and illusions.[3]

Ideosensory techniques are very useful in investigative hypnosis and can be used to assist the subject to relax and to restructure the original crime situation, enhancing the possibility of recall. It is desirable to use as many ideosensory modalities as possible to increase the recall effect. Imagery involving sight, hearing, muscle movement, touch, smell, and taste, can be suggested which increases the likelihood of the subject's access to repressed information.

The subject may be asked to visualize his favorite place or vacation spot which can be at the beach, the mountains, the desert, the country, the snow, on a sailboat, or any other place or situation of extreme relaxation and satisfaction.

A typical example of the use of ideosensory images is the beach scene:[4]

"Imagine yourself walking along the beach on a warm summer day. The sun is high over head and you can feel the warmth of the sun on your skin. You look up at the blue sky and the white fleecy clouds and you see a few seagulls wheeling around making their cawing sounds. As you walk on the beach, you feel your feet sinking into the warm sand which pushes up between your toes. You take a deep breath and smell the fresh salt air and as you lick your lips you can taste the clean salt spray from the nearby waves. You look out at the ocean and you see the light blue waves tumbling onto the shore and you hear the noise as the last wave breaks on the beach. As you look out at the ocean which is calm, deep and endless, you feel yourself getting more and more relaxed, realizing that you too are a part of nature's design. And as you continue to smell the fresh salt air and be aware of the whitecaps, the summer sun, the blue sky, the white fleecy clouds, and feel the pleasant heat on your skin, you feel like melted butter, and become more and more relaxed, feeling secure, pleasant, and at one with nature."

Ideosensory images are very effective as part of the induction and deepening technique. They can help the subject to more easily visualize the suggested television documentary when the information retrieval portion of the session is reached.

References
1. Cheek, D.B. and LeCron, L.M. *Clinical Hypnotherapy.* New York: Grune & Stratton, 1968.
2. Hilgard, E.R. *The Experience of Hypnosis.* New York: Harcourt, Brace and World, 1968.
3. Kroger, W.S. *Clinical and Experimental Hypnosis, 2nd Edition.* Philadelphia: Lippincott, 1977.
4. Kroger, W.S. and Fezler, W.D. *Hypnosis and Behavior Modification: Imagery Conditioning.* Philadelphia: Lippincott, 1976.
5. LeCron, L.M. *Self-Hypnotism.* New York: Prentice-Hall, 1964.

CHAPTER 31
T.V. AND OTHER RETRIEVAL TECHNIQUES

After an optimal state of hypnosis is achieved, the hypno-investigator indicates that the subject, in imagination, will be watching a special documentary film on television from a safe, secure and comfortable place.[4] This special documentary can be speeded up, slowed down, stopped, reversed, with close-ups possible on any person, object or thing in the film. The sound can be turned up high so that anything that is said, even a whisper, can be heard very clearly. This will be a documentary film of the incident in question and will depict accurately and vividly everything of significance and importance the subject perceived and experienced in relationship to that crime event. And even though what occurred was very traumatic, the subject watching the TV documentary will be able to remain calm and relaxed, feeling detached from what is happening on the television set. The subject will be observing it as a reporter, covering an event to be written up accurately for a news story.

The following is from a recent case report:[3]

"When asked if she watched television, she nodded in the affirmative. To subsequent questions she verbalized that she usually sat in a favorite rocking chair, that her television set was a color set and that it took a few moments to warm up. She was asked to visualize herself sitting in her favorite rocking chair about to watch television and that she was going to see a very special program. This special program would be a TV movie which would slow down, stop and give close-ups on scenes or people, thus enabling her to see more clearly certain things in this movie. However, whatever she viewed, she would remain relaxed and detached because she would know she was watching a special television program produced by the network and therefore would be able to see things clearly and easily. She was then asked to visualize herself turning the TV set on and then returning to her rocking chair to wait for the set to light up. It was reiterated during this wait that this film was documentary which would capture in detail everything that had happened on the preceding December 17 from about midnight to about 2:00 a.m. It was suggested that the TV screen was now bright and she could see the movie clearly and to begin describing it.

"Slowly, she began talking in a very low voice, saying they (meaning her friend and her) had been talking, dancing and acting silly. However, their activities were not too clear to her. Then someone was at the door and a man came in. At this point, it was suggested to her that the film would stop and that there would be a close-up giving sharp details of the man who had come in. She described him as tall and thin and in his early 20's. It was suggested that the camera would zoom in on his face for a more detailed close-up allowing her to clearly see his features. She described the shape of his face, nose and nostrils, ethnic origin, hair style including sideburns, lips, size of head, mustache, beard and clothing worn. At one point during the description, she commented that she couldn't see if the suspect had a mustache because she had had too much to drink. It was repeated that she could see him clearly because these details were automatically registered in her subconscious mind. More description followed.

"It was suggested that the film would go into a slow motion sequence beginning with the suspect's knocking at the door, which would allow her to hear what had happened in detail at that point. She indicated that nothing was said after the knock, that the man was let in silently because her friend acted as if he knew the person although she had never seen him before. Then her friend came out of the kitchen with a gun in his back pocket and went outside on the steps with the visitor. She heard shots, felt scared and upset, turned the lights out and called the police.

At this point, with the witness' approval, the investigators and artist present were invited to ask questions. A zoom-in, close-up of the suspect's face was suggested. She elaborated on facial features, hair style, whiskers and absence of glasses. The investigators felt they had now exhausted the possible information and it was decided to terminate the hypnotic interview. The witness was told that she was now turning off the television set, sitting back in her rocking chair, feeling relaxed and comfortable. It was suggested that she could or not remember what she saw on the film as she chose; whatever was comfortable for her. She would awaken and become alert, feeling very relaxed and rested and that residual conflict over the traumatic event or the interview situation would gradually get resolved. A slow count to the letter "E" was initiated, interspersed with suggestions of feeling refreshed and relaxed upon awakening. It was also mentioned that she might recall something more later on, and if so, she would feel free to call the investigators with this information. She became alert on the count of the letter "E", laughed and said she felt very good. Additional conversation revealed a diminution in her original anxiety and upset...

"The police artist present during the interview indicated that he had gotten sufficient details to enable him to draw a composite picture of the suspect. Subsequently, it was learned that the suspect was identified in a police line-up and that he was 'a dead ringer' for the composite drawing."

It is desirable to structure the subject to report what is happening on the television documentary in the present tense, third person. For example, "The man is grabbing Jane", rather than, "The man grabbed me". However, if after several reinforcements for present tense and third person the subject continues to respond in the first person, past-tense, it's not desirable to persist with the restructuring. The information retrieved in this way, although from a less regressed and dissociated state, may be no less valuable to the investigators (See transcript in Chapter 39).

OTHER RETRIEVAL TECHNIQUES

Induced Dream

Suggesting that the witness have a dream, on signal, about the crime event in question is useful as a preview device before retrieval techniques are used for recall of specific crime details. The subject is instructed to have the dream about the crime even remaining calm and relaxed. Although the dream will take only two minutes on the clock, it will seem much longer in hypnosis and be all the time necessary to complete the dream. It will allow the subconscious mind to review all of the perceptions and events and to make them more available for later recall.

The induced dream may have the effect of loosening up the repressed material, having the subject become familiar with it subconsciously and therefore less anxiety producing and of also structuring the subject for improved later recall.[5]

Blackboard Technique

For recall of information which can be written or printed such as names, numbers, places or dates, the blackboard technique may be effective. In hypnosis, it is suggested that the subject imagine a large blackboard covered with a soft velvet cover obstructing the view of what is written on the blackboard in large white block letters. The subject is told that on signal the velvet cover will be pulled away and some interesting and important information printed on the blackboard will suddenly become visible to the subject. The hypnotist begins counting to five and just before the final number is reached, adds that when the cover is removed, what is written on the blackboard will be the license number, or name, or other desired information for that particular crime event. As the last number is given, the fingers are snapped near the subject's ear as a distractive, reinforcing cue. The subject is then asked to verbalize what is seen written on the blackboard.

Time Door to Memory Room

As a final deepening technique and lead-in to information retrieval, the hypnotized subject may be structured to go down to the basement of a building on an escalator, elevator or stairs, whichever is comfortable. Upon arrival in the basement, the subject walks down the corridor and approaches a large ornate door, which is the door of time, allowing access to any point in the past, in the memory room. The hypnotist describes in some detail the opening of the door and entrance to the memory room where memories become more easily accessible. In the memory room, time distortion can be utilized to expand time, contract time, to project into future or go back into past situations.

With highly traumatized witnesses or victims, it is desirable after the crime details are elicited to use future projection. The subject visualizes himself in the future, functioning well, feeling healthy and strong, and having constructively dealt with the traumatic nature of the crime event. He is asked to see himself sleeping more soundly, having good appetite, having pleasant dreams, and feeling more in control of himself and his environment.

Another technique in the memory room is to have the subject approach the filing cabinets of memory. Each cabinet represents a particular year, and each drawer in the filing cabinet containing the folders of exact memories by month and day. The subject can be structured to go to the particular filing cabinet for the year desired, pull out the drawer having the folder for the exact month and date in question, and look in the folder to recover the exact memories as recorded on the transcripts made from the memory tapes. The tapes themselves may also be played if desired.

A variation on the filing cabinets of memory technique is the trunk of memories in which keepsakes and nostalgic items are stored. With certain individuals and in specific situations, the trunk of memory may have more impact than the filing cabinet concept.

Head Pressure Technique[2]

With subjects who have difficulty with other techniques but seem to respond well to laying on of hands and have a good working alliance with the hypno-investigator, this technique may be useful. The subject is told that the hypnotist will press with his hands against the sides of the subject's head and maintain the pressure while counting slowly. With each count, things become less tight and when the pressure is released, the information desired will suddenly pop into mind.

Ericksonian Approach[1]

"Feel rested and comfortable and leave behind, but available upon request, practically everything of importance, knowing but not knowing that it is available upon request. Now, you are sitting there rested and wide awake, ready for discussion of what little there is (the hypnotist then talks in general terms about the environment involving the crime in question and some of the observable features available to the subject). Well, now perhaps matters will become available..."

References
1. Haley, J. *Advanced Techniques of Hypnosis and Therapy. Selected Papers of Milton H. Erickson.* New York: Grune & Stratton, 1967.
2. Kroger, W.S. *Clinical and Experimental Hypnosis, 2nd Edition.* Philadelphia: Lippincott, 1977.
3. Reiser, M. Hypnosis as an aid in a homicide investigation. *Journal of Police Science and Administration,* 1974, *17,* 84-87.
4. Reiser, M. Hypnosis as a tool in criminal investigation. *The Police Chief,* November 1976, 38-40.
5. Weitzenhoffer, A.M. *General Techniques of Hypnotism.* New York: Grune & Stratton, 1957.

CHAPTER 32

WITNESS IDENTIFICATION PROCEDURES — LINE-UPS AND PHOTOGRAPHS

Identifications of suspects by witnesses are covered by formal rules of evidence that had been adopted by all trial courts.[2]

A witness is competent to testify, that is, legally fit or qualified, when the facts in question are within his personal knowledge or have been perceived by his senses. Those usually considered incompetent to testify include idiots, psychotics and young children who are not capable of understanding the requirements of an oath. A witness' credibility may be supported or attacked on the facts, motives and character.[3]

Wall[5] points out that the normal human fallibilities of perception and memory are the two principal causes of erroneous identification. The second major identification problem is the power of suggestion. This may involve a purposeful or unwitting attempt to improperly suggest an identification to a witness. The original identification of the suspect is extremely important and may be either corporeal, seeing the suspect in the flesh, by photographic or other representation of the suspect.

Line-Ups

The dangers of a one-suspect show-up as opposed to a properly conducted line-up have been discussed in detail.[2,4,5]

The line-up must be conducted in a fair, objective manner, which means that the witness' attention not be directly or indirectly pointed toward a particular person among those shown in the line-up. Rules of evidence have been developed in order to maximize the likelihood of fairness in regard to the compositon of a line-up, how many persons are in it, what they look like, what they wear, who they are, are important issues in ensuring lack of bias. Generally, members of a line-up should resemble each other in appearance and dress as closely as possible and no comment should be made to the witness as to whether the actual suspect may or may not be present among those being viewed.

The witness should be shown a physical or photo line-up first. If the witness is confused or can't decide, hypnosis should then be used to refresh memory, including post-hypnotic suggestions of improved recall. The witness should then look at the line-up or photographs again. Viewing both times should be in the normally alert state to avoid the charge of having recall only while hypnotized rather than having present memory refreshed.

Photographs

Wall[5] characterizes the use of photographs as one of the most valuable tools of law enforcement for identification purposes. He indicates the same need for caution and fairness using photographs as with in-person identifications. One of the usual requirements is that a series of photographs be shown to the witness rather than just one picture, because of the strongly suggestive influences involved. He cautions against showing a photograph to a witness after an in-person identification has already been made since this may tend to have some reinforcing effect on the original identification which might not otherwise have occurred.

Discussing use of photographs for witness identification purposes, Ringel[4] quotes from the United States Supreme Court Decision in Simmons V. United States (36 1.w. 4227, 31868):

"Despite the hazards of initial identification by photograph, this procedure has been used widely and effectively in criminal law enforcement, from the standpoint both of apprehending offenders and of sparing innocent suspects the ignominy of arrest by allowing eye witnesses to exonerate them through scrutiny of photograph. The danger that use of the technique may result in convictions based on this identification may be substantially lessened by a course of cross-examination and trial which exposes to the jury the method's potention for error. We are unwilling to prohibit its employment, either in the exercise of our supervisory power or, still less, as a matter of constitutional requirement. Instead we hold that each case must be considered on its own facts, and that convictions based on eye witness identification at trial following a pre-trial identification by photograph will be set aside on the ground only if the photographic identification was so impermissibly suggestive as to give rise to a very substantial likelihood of irreparable misidentification. . ."

A more recent U.S. Supreme Court Case involving photo identification is of interest (Manson V. Braithwaite, 75-871, 61578). In this case, an undercover Connecticut State Police officer purchased heroin from a man in an apartment. At the time, the officer was two feet away from the suspect and talked to him for two or three minutes during the transaction. Later the undercover officer described the suspect to a second officer who suspected from the description that the seller was Brathwaite. He obtained a photograph of Brathwaite and two days later the undercover officer identified the photograph as the person who had sold him the narcotics. Brathwaite was convicted.

On appeal, the U.S. Court of Appeals for the Second Circuit reversed the conviction saying that the photograph should not have been admitted as evidence because it was unduly suggestive of guilt when shown to the undercover officer. However, the U.S. Supreme Court, in a majority opinion, said the Appeals Court was wrong, even though it agreed that the photo identification was unduly suggestive. Justice Blackmun held that,"Surely, we cannot say that under all circumstances of this case there is a 'very substantial likelihood of irreparable misidentification'. Short of that point such evidence is for the jury to weigh." Blackmum listed some factors to be taken into consideration in assessing the reliability of a witness's identification of the suspect: The opportunity that a witness had to see the suspect, the witness's degree of attention, the degree of certainty of the identification, and the time between the crime and the identification.

Because the typical process involved in investigative hypnosis leads to a description and/or a composite drawing or Identi-kit version of the suspect prior to apprehension, there should be minimal difficulty with witness identification procedures.[1] However, the problems and cautions discussed above are relevant during and after the apprehension of suspects using hypnosis as they are routinely in non-hypnosis cases.

References
1. Allen, A.L. *Personal Descriptions.* London: Butterworth & Co., 1950.
2. Allison, H.C. *Personal Identification.* Boston: Holbrook Press, 1973.
3. Petersen, D.R. *The Police Officer in Court.* Springfield, Illinois: Thomas, 1975.
4. Ringel, W.E. *Identification and Police Line-Ups.* Jamaica, N.Y.: Gould Publications, 1968.
5. Wall, P.M. *Eye-Witness Identification in Criminal Cases.* Springfield, Illinois: Thomas, 1965.

CHAPTER 33
OFFICE PROCEDURES

The investigative hypnotist needs to decide on an appropriate location in advance of the hypnosis session, either a police facility, the subject's home or apartment, or perhaps a hotel room, depending on the situation and circumstances of the case. The appointment should be reconfirmed with the subject just prior to the hypnosis session to ensure that there has not been a change of mind or the development of other problems or interferences. It can be suggested to female subjects that they wear slacks in order to be comfortable during the hypnosis session.

Some basic physical considerations for the hypnosis session include scheduling a quiet room if possible where there will likely be few distractions or noises. If this isn't feasible, the background noise can be incorporated into the hypnosis deepening process. Phones that cannot be disconnected should be taken off the hook and a "Do Not Disturb" sign should be placed outside the door. The lighting in the room should be soft or indirect if possible, and direct sunlight on the subject avoided. Optimal room temperatue is an important consideration since many subjects have heightened awareness and sensitivity to changes in heat and cold.[2] It may be wise to have a blanket handy for subjects who feel chilly, and where temperature cannot be adjusted easily.

A comfortable chair, preferably a recliner, is desirable for the subject in order to enhance physical relaxation and to reduce pressure on relaxed neck muscles. The pull of a 14-pound head on relatively weak neck supports often leads to feelings of neck strain or stiffness.[1] Soft piped-in music or "white noise" can be a soothing background for the hypnosis session, if available.

There are big differences between the ideal set-up for conducting an investigative hypnosis session and real world limits as they exist. Fortunately, in either case, most hypnotized subjects are able to adapt readily to a wide range of environmental experiences encountered. It doesn't seem to matter significantly whether the hypnosis is done in a soundproof room or in a fire house with clanging bells and sirens, if these stimuli plus the subject's responses are utilized to enhance the state of relaxation and hypnosis.

Electronic recording should begin prior to the subject coming into the hypnosis room and be continuous throughout the hypnosis session until the subject has left. This provides a complete record for investigative and possible court purposes. Videotape is desirable if available. The tape recorder should be used in plain sight, with extra cassettes handy and microphones in good working condition. The microphones should be properly placed for subject and hypnotist at the beginning of the session with an explanation as to the routine nature of the taping of hypnosis sessions. Any anxiety the subject may have about being recorded usually dissipates about ten or fifteen minutes into the session.

Although release forms may be utilized with investigative hypnosis subjects, they are not legally binding. In fact, they may raise unnecessary anxiety in the subject because of the implication of possible negative effects contained in the notices. To date, the only state law requiring informed consent by the subject for investigative hypnosis purposes is Oregon.

If feasible, it is desirable for investigative hypnotists to work in pairs using a team concept. One acts as the hypnotist/operator and the other as the recorder/evaluator at that particular session. This allows for consultation and feedback during the hypnosis session. The roles can be reversed in subsequent cases.

In general, relatives or close friends should not be present during the hypnosis session with the exception of cases with very small children who may require the presence of a parent.

It is desirable to brief others who may be present for the investigative hypnosis session about what will occur and what the process involves. They should sit in the back of the room behind the subject, out of the line of sight and out of the immediate context of the hypnosis transactions. On occasion, these observers may also go into hypnosis spontaneously as a result of observing the induction and deepening procedures. This is only a problem if an observer has to take notes or be aware of the subject's behavior during the hypnosis session. If so, it may be necessary for the hynotist to excuse himself temporarily with his subject while quietly dehypnotizing the observers, suggesting that they remain consciously alert during the rest of the session.

Unless the case investigators present are trained in investigative hypnosis techniques and in objective questioning nuances, it is probably better if they write out any questions they may want to ask the subject. The hypnotist should ask them rather than have the detectives directly communicate with the subject and risk the charge of introducing bias or unnecessary suggestion into the session.

Everyone who will be in the room during the hypnosis session should be introduced to the subject and the roles of each should be explained carefully. The operator should inquire of the subject about bathroom needs, wearing of contact lenses, and prior medical or psychological treatment. The possible length of the hypnosis session and procedures to be utilized with the subject should also be reviewed. In general, it should be kept in mind that the subject in hypnosis is a live, functioning person, who is aware of what is happening and who requires the same courtesies and considerations given to a nonhypnotic subject. In this connection, it is probably better to avoid talking back and forth with detectives present, and ignoring the subject as if the person were not hearing anything. With permission, the subject should be addressed by first name. When there is doubt about any of the subject's reactions or behavior, the hypnotist can get the answer very simply by asking the subject what is happening.

Most motivated subjects will relax noticeably after the hypnosis induction process beings. This reduces initial anxieties and uncertainties and enables the operator to proceed to the goal of information eliciting.

References
1. Cheek, D.B. and LeCron, L.M. *Clinical Hypnotherapy.* New York: Grune & Stratton, 1968.
2. Teitelbaum, M. *Hypnosis Induction Techniques.* Springfield, Illinois: Thomas, 1965.

CHAPTER 34
ADMINISTRATION AND COORDINATION OF AN INVESTIGATIVE HYPNOSIS PROGRAM

It is desirable that the administrator of a department investigative hypnosis program be involved in the project design from the beginning. This will tend to increase administrative support by reason of emotional investment and result in a fair program evaluation. It is also suggested than an outside consultant-faculty panel of hypnosis experts from the local community, including university and private practice professionals, be assembled to teach and consult.

Heavy financing of the project is usually not necessary since it can be done in-house with some volunteer help from the outside consultants. These health professionals are usually quite interested and very willing to participate in this kind of program. It allows them an exciting change of pace activity. Some minor expenses for text books and suitable recording equipment may be necessary.

The program concept should be cleared through the City Attorney and/or District Attorney's offices in order to forestall any potential legal questions that may be raised later on. In general, there have been no major legal bars to developing and implementing an investigative hypnosis program within a law enforcement agency. No special liabilities are involved.

Getting administrative approval to go ahead with the program may be somewhat difficult and time-consuming. Administrators are generally pragmatic skeptics whose first reaction to the idea of officers using hypnosis may be one of horror or joking. However, with written support from hypnosis authorities in the community, from legal experts and by in-house behavioral science staff, the administration will likely be willing to give this type of program a trial on a pilot basis.

If the physical facilities are available, it is preferable to assign a room for investigative hypnosis use and to furnish with appropriate lighting, chairs and recording equipment. If this is not feasible, hypnosis can be done almost anywhere else.

Selection of personnel for the hypnosis unit should include

parameters such as investigative background and expertise, track record, interest in and motivation for participation in the program, good interpersonal skills, and a liking for and consideration of other people. Personal competence rather than rank level should be a primary criterion.

The training of selected personnel can be accomplished either in-house or at an outside training seminar that has been evaluated as effective and pertinent. For agencies desiring to established an in-house unit with several hypno-investigators, it may be cost-effective to send at least two people for training outside the department, then have these people later become trainers of others for the unit when sufficiently experienced.

It is important that each investigative hypnotist continue his or her education by in-service or outside means. This may involve attending additional seminars, reading appropriate books and articles, joining the national society for investigative hypnosis, and participating in advanced seminars and workshops.

A program administrator or coordinator should be appointed to centralize referrals for hypnosis within the agency. Detectives in geographic areas can then call the hypnosis coordinator for evaluation of a particular case and assignment of hypnosis personnel when appropriate. On occasion, case investigators will attempt to set up a hypnosis session very rapidly because they feel that time is crucial or because they may want to avoid additional leg work. For either reason, it is generally not desirable to hurriedly arrange for hypnosis sessions since time is not a big factor and the case investigator should do his homework before calling on the investigative hypnotist.[1]

It is desirable for all hypnosis program personnel to engage in public relations work within the department and in the community. This involves giving talks and orientation workshops to judges, attorneys, investigators, and community members in order to educate and inform them about the myths and misinformation of investigative hypnosis and the realities of what can be accomplished. Statements to the media should be made carefully, avoiding exaggerations, sensationalizing, or misstatements of fact. It should be made clear that hypnosis is not a panacea but merely an additional tool that may enhance investigative results.

In small agencies, where there may be only one investigative hypnotist, that person should avoid working on his own cases. It is more desirable to call in a consultant or use an investigative hypnotist from another agency in order to avoid charges of bias or undue suggestion.

The administrator should establish the parameters for the kinds of cases suitable for hypnosis referral. This may depend on the size of the department, and the number and kind of crime cases in that jurisdiction. In large urban agencies, it is likely that hypnosis will be reserved for major crime cases such as homicides, rapes, kidnaps, and major robberies. Smaller departments will be able to utilize investigative hypnosis in additional, less serious types of crimes.[1]

The administrator may also decide on whether the investigative hypnotist should be on a full-time or added-duty basis. Presently, at the Los Angeles Police Department the hypno-investigators perform hypnosis as an added duty which is squeezed in between regularly assigned responsibilities. If possible, each agency should have a least two investigative hypnotists trained so that they can work as a collaborative team and assist each other with in-service training and continuing education.

The program administrator may have to make a decision in particular cases as to whether an investigative hypnotist from within the department should be used, or whether an outside consultant be called in to do the hypnosis. The decision may hinge on the particular kinds of trauma suffered by the victim and the special expertise which may be required in the case. Consultants may be desirable in complicated cases involving small children or with subjects having psychiatric or other kinds of problems.

The program administrator should have questionnaire forms sent out within 30 days of each hypnosis session to the commanding officer of the division to which the investigative hypnotists are assigned. This will likely ensure the prompt return of the completed questionnaire form with important data about the case. These forms should include anecdotal reports from the hypnotists on particular problems or unusual situations encountered so that they can be shared in training sessions.

When outside agencies request investigative hypnosis assistance in a particular case, it is recommended that that agency be asked to send the request in writing to the chief of police and address questions such as the amount of time required, the limits of liability, and any compensation that will be involved if the hypnosis is done on an off-duty basis. Working on outside cases can constitute a drain on agency resources and personnel since it can be very time consuming if court testimony is involved.[2]

References

1. Milwee, S.C. The hypnosis unit in today's law enforcement. *The Police Chief.* May 1979, 65-70.
2. Nielsen, Captain Michael. Personal Communications.

CHAPTER 35
EXPERIENCES AND PROBLEMS OF AN INVESTIGATIVE HYPNOTIST

Like beginners in the other professions, new hypno-investigators will experience varying amounts of anxiety about doing hypnosis with witnesses and victims of major crimes. This early tendency toward high anxiety may last for a period of six months to a year and will usually abate with increased experience and self-confidence.

The investigative hypnotist will gradually develop his own style with favorite techniques. It will likely be a composite derived from many models and information inputs, enhanced by his or her own refinements. The beginning hypno-investigator also will likely discover that hypnosis work with the subject is fatiguing and demanding, both physically and psychologically. While the hypnotist is working hard, the subject is comparatively relaxed and unconcerned about the passage of time. It would probably be wise to not schedule more than two hypnosis sessions in any one day in the early months of practice because of the draining effect and loss in efficiency.

It is important to orient and educate the officers and detectives who are potential referrers for investigative hypnosis. Tending to view hypnosis as black magic and shying away from it is no more unusual for uninformed criminal justice professionals than it is for the general public. On the other hand, some may have an over-inflated notion of the power of hypnosis and expect too much from a hypnosis session. Success tends to breed success and referrals for hypnosis will increase mainly by word of mouth when there has been a payoff in a difficult case. Because hypnosis is not a truth detection technique, it is important to point out that independent corroboration is highly desirable if not necessary in most instances.

There may be a temptation for hypno-investigators to use hypnosis for entertainment purposes or for symptom removal of family or colleagues, who tend to equate hypnosis with therapy or stage tricks. These applications would be outside of the specialized area of investigative hypnosis and contraindicated.

Some investigators may attempt to utilize hypnosis as a shortcut alternative to thorough investigation. The investigative hypnosis program should not be used for this purpose. The session should be scheduled only after the usual thorough investigation by the case detective. If sufficient information is obtained from witnesses on routine interrogation or interview, then hypnosis is really not necessary. In many instances, it is requested as a last resort because of the dearth of leads from witnesses.

Case investigators may want to rush into a hypnosis session thinking that recall is likely to be better immediately after the crime event. However, it is good practice to allow sufficient time for the subject to settle down, institute adequate defenses, and develop some emotional balance prior to the hypnosis session. The time lag should not affect the witness' ability to recall significant details.

The investigative hypnotist should get a brief narrative from the case investigator, look at the crime reports, both initial and follow-up, and have a good idea of the time frame, crime event and information desired. It is important to recognize that from the witness' point of view, there is no absolute truth since everything is relative to the perceptual viewpoint of the subject.

Witness certainty is no absolute measure of accuracy. One incident involved a boy who ran up to a getaway car after a parent was killed. He memorized the license number and then went back in the house and wrote it down. He was convinced it was accurate; however, the number he wrote down didn't check out and it was later found that in his excitement he had reversed two of the digits.

It is helpful to know what the case investigator has told the subject about hypnosis. In this connection, it would be desirable for the investigative hypnotist to develop a handout for detectives to be used in briefing potential subjects for investigative hypnosis. This information should include what hypnosis is, what it isn't, and some brief mention of the status and expertise of the hypnotist.

In deciding on a location for the investigative hypnosis session, subject comfort should be a strong consideration. If the subject will be uneasy at a police facility or if the crime has occurred in the patient's home, which is now associated with traumatic events, these locations should be avoided.

Because the crime location can be described verbally during the hypnosis session, it usually isn't necessary to physically take the witness back to the scene. However, there may be exceptions in special instances where a return to the original location may be an added memory jogger.

The subject's motivation is primary and it is sometimes difficult to evaluate this under hypnosis. One incident involved a state prison convict who claimed to have heard key information about the murder of a police officer from other convicts. He volunteered for a hypnosis session and was brought from prison to a police facility. Under hypnosis he gave "quotes" of seeming key details in this unsolved homicide. It was subsequently found the the information he gave was manufactured and that his real motivation was to have a day out of prison with better food and scenery.

The beginning investigative hypnotist may tend to view each case in terms of his own success or failure. The reality is, that if the hypnosis session is conducted properly, it is up to the subject whether useful information is elicited or not. If the subject has information that does not emerge during the investigative hypnosis session, it is the subject who "failed" and not the hypnotist, assuming that there has been optimal opportunity provided for the subject during the hypnosis session.

The hypnotist should avoid the word "try" with the subject since the work implies that failure is a strong possiblity. Descriptions of the investigative hypnosis session and wording by the hypnotist during the session should be in positive terms rather than negative.

There may be special problems with rape victims because of the nature of their trauma. The victim may now fear men in general and have massive anxiety about reviewing the hurtful event. This can be compounded by misinformation given to the subject by relatives. In one case, a rape victim was told by her sister that a big needle would be used by the hypnotist to inject chemicals so that she would forget what happened and also forget her own identity. Much work was needed to overcome the fear that resulted from this bizarre misinformation.

Should repeat sessions be scheduled with hypnosis witnesses? In practice we have found, that in most instances, a single session is adequate if the information is available to begin with. However, in cases where the subject may be overly anxious or may lack adequate motivation, it may be desirable to schedule an additional session with appropriate post-hypnotic suggestions for improved motivation, relaxation, and security. During the hypnotist's beginning practice, it is less likely that the subject will be resistant and more likely that the hypnotist will unwittingly make errors of omission or commission. It is interesting that subject resistance generally decreases as the hypnotist's skills improve.

Fear of retaliation by a witness can negatively affect motivation. In one case, a man observed his wife being raped in their bedroom by four men, who also threatened to kill him if he said anything about it. Prior to the hypnosis session, the witness said that he was positive he couldn't pick any of these men out of a line-up or from photographs, but indicated his eagerness to go ahead with the hypnosis. Needless to say, his fear of retaliation was stronger than his more conscious desire to cooperate.

With child subjects, it is useful to check with the parents in advance about terminology for the genitals and sex acts so that pet words and phrases the child will understand can be used during the hypnosis session.

In one interesting case, a rape victim stuttered badly in her normal consciously alert state. However, under hypnosis during the investigative interview, her speech was perfectly normal. In this situation an appropriate referral for hypnotherapy might be made.[1]

Another interesting case involved a 21-year old woman who was raped by 12 men and savagely beaten. In the hospital and paralyzed from the neck down, she agreed to hypnosis and during the interview as the incident was revivified, she moved her supposedly paralyzed arms up to a defensive position in front of her face. Unfortunately, this disturbed the hospital administrator who was present, since, medically, arm movement wasn't supposed to be possible. He banned further hypnosis interviews with this particular subject. In this connection, it is desirable to check local laws on in-hospital interviews for victims since many jurisdictions have parameters which are broader than this hospital administrator was aware of.[1]

In some instances, family members present during the hypnosis session may "hitchhike" into hypnosis along with the subject. In one situation, the subject, whose favorite relaxing position was lying on the floor with his head propped up on his hand, easily went into hypnosis. His verbally aggressive wife, who had previously expressed strong disbelief of "this garbage" of hypnosis, was seen sitting on the couch with arm levitated, in an apparently deep hypnotic state. After dehypnotization this lady again affirmed her disdain of hypnosis and its uselessness.

Subjects may react emotionally and develop a runny nose and tears. As with a nonhypnotized witness, the subject can be given a kleenex with a suggestion that the nose be wiped. Appropriate reassuring comments can also be made.

Some subjects may go into a deep state of hypnosis and become either inarticulate or hard to understand. They may also develop a longer response lag, stretching out the length of the session. In some cases, asking the subject to repeat an unintelligible word or phrase may help, but it may be necessary to suggest the subject come up to a lighter state of hypnosis where articulation and responsiveness can be improved.

Before finishing the investigative hypnosis interview, the operator should give the subject an opportunity to talk about anything that has not been discussed. "Is there anything else you would like to tell me that I haven't asked you?" Occasionally, this yields added information since some subjects in hypnosis know there are additional details they would like to mention, but feel it is either too much trouble or not important since they haven't directly been asked about them.[1]

References
1. King, Lieutenant Richard. Personal Communications.

CHAPTER 36
CHECK LIST OF PROCEDURES WITH A WITNESS

Preliminary Activity

1. Review case information including crime reports. Have briefings with case investigators, get time frame of crime, estimate likely length of hypnosis session.
2. Arrange for consultant if desirable, either to conduct the hypnosis session or be present as back-up.
3. Make brief outline of the areas of information sought: vehicle, conversations, descriptions of suspect, weapons, etc.
4. Logistical arrangements. Arrange time and location for hypnosis session, whether police facility, home or other place. The environment should be as relaxing as possible.
5. Get background information and check on any physical or emotional problems of the subject. Consideration of hearing difficulties, epilepsy, contact lenses, medications, etc.

Hypnosis Session

Pre-induction Phase

1. Tape or video recording equipment in plain view; explain taping procedures and get subject's reaction.
2. Introduce those present. Explain the role of each person — police artist, case investigator, recorder/evaluator, etc.
3. Exclude family members or friends except in case of small child or special situation.
4. Check on physical comfort: lights, temperature, eye glasses, bathroom needs.
5. Begin rapport building. Discuss mutually interesting topics as a warm-up. Discuss misinformation and misconceptions. Give brief explanation of mind as dual recording system and hypnosis as retrieval technique. Check the subject's motivation and reinforce if necessary. Give subject preview of what is to follow in order to demystify and to provide the initial expectations of the subject for the hypnosis session. Answer subject's questions. Decide on induction techniques for this subject.

Induction Phase

Possible techniques: Eye fixation; Spiegel Eye Roll; abdominal breathing; muscle relaxation.

Deepening Phase

Possible techniques: Count from ten to zero, go down elevator, escalator or stairs (after checking for fears); arm levitation and rigidity, five to ten times deeper with arm lowering; hands as magnets or arms rising and falling (use as convincers); fractionation or confusion or eyes opening and closing (resistant subjects); imagery (beach scene, etc.).

Information Eliciting Phase

Set the scene and time frame of the crime. Use permissive, self-paced recall as subject is able to handle.

Possible techniques: Induced dream — 2 minutes on clock to dream and review event subconsciously to aid later recall; TV technique; ideomotor finger signals (check license information) — use with poor imagers; age regression; composite drawing with artist or Identi-kit; posthypnotic suggestions to enhance subsequent recall or prepare for follow-up session; case investigators may frame questions, preferably in writing.

Dehypnotization Phase

Consider needs for follow-up session; give desired posthypnotic suggestions for later relaxation, anxiety reduction, sound sleep and feeling more normal in every way. The subject can be told that over time it may be easier to deal with the crime experience in a more constructive way.

Remove all temporary suggestions given for hypnosis effect such as heaviness, lightness, etc. Leave only those suggestions intended to remain in effect posthypnotically.

Count the subject out of hypnosis — fully awake and alert, feeling clear-headed, refreshed, relaxed and perfectly normal in every way. "This will have been a most interesting experience for you."

Make arrangements for repeat session as desirable. Make referral for professional counseling or therapy assistance if indicated.

Allow sufficient time for complete dehypnotization to occur, keeping in mind the usual time lags possible.

Answer subject's questions and thank subject for cooperation and participation. Indicate that subject may call as necessary.

CHAPTER 37
RESEARCH NEEDS AND METHODS

Meaningful *in vivo* research in the area of memory and hypnosis is sparse. The work being done on crime cases by investigative hypnotists is breaking new ground and has the potential for making a highly significant contribution to scientific knowledge.[1] Investigative hypnotists need to take advantage of their unique opportunities by designing and implementing research-oriented projects and data collection instruments.

Much of this work may only require information that can be tabulated and presented in the form of percentages. Specific areas of research that have been suggested include a measure of the hypnotic responsiveness of the witness; how is "new" information defined? It is really new to all parties involved; how is this strictly "new" information validated and what is the success rate?[5] In this connection, it is as important to report failures as it is successes. Ultimately, valid accuracy parameters of hypnotized witnesses can be established.

In the area of memory research, almost all of the current theories are based on laboratory studies and very little is said about their relationship to real life. Nilsson[8] indicates that more consideration needs to be given to this problem. He points out that there has not been much value in the simple application of laboratory findings to the outside world. The alternative, of course, is real life research.

The controversy over memory as a cumulative stage-setting process as opposed to the view of memory as a system of records can be reconciled by integrating the two approaches. The cognitive system can be seen to work in a variety of modes, from comprehension, utilizing past learning as the background and focusing attention on incoming events, to remembering, where new input retrieval cues act as the background and attention is focused on reactivation of some encoded past experience.[8] This concept involves a multi-access and multi-checking method of memory retrieval with a variety of ways in which material can originally be encoded, and an equally large number of retrieval mechanisms. The common example of recognition of a familiar face or name but not remembering until an associative process has been gone through is a good example of double or multiple access retrieval modes.

The whole problem of eyewitness unreliability in regard to perceiving and remembering faces of suspects or others is readily accessible to the hypno-investigator interested in making a research contribution in this area.

Many interesting issues can be explored in related hypnosis research areas as well. The work of Lozanov[7] indicates that suggestion can be as effective without formal hypnosis induction, as measured by his studies in education and learning. Research comparing waking suggestibility and hypnotic suggestibility could be done very easily with witnesses in major crime cases.[6] This work could bear importantly on the controversy between the hypnosis-as-state or non-state theories, including any qualitative or quantitative differences.[10]

Other long-standing questions in hypnosis research that could readily be examined include the sample bias with volunteer subjects,[2] real versus simulating subjects,[3] the "hidden observer" with subjects having deep emotional commitment and highly charged motivational conflicts,[4] and the important issue of dual perception and encoding in traumatic crime situations. Hilgard points out that these experiments would contribute to the understanding of the baffling problems of attention and memory and that controversial issues on these points will ultimately be resolved through experimental methods.[3]

Although not all investigative hypnotists will be prepared to do sophisticated research on these questions, almost everyone can engage in data collection using questionnaires for the tabulation of results.[9] Those interested in more complex research questions are in a position to make a significant contribution in the important areas of memory, encoding and retrieval.

References

1. Burch, G.W. *Hypnosis, An Aid to Police Interogations.* Master's Thesis, California State University, Long Beach, June 1974.
2. Fromm, E. and Shor, R.E. (Eds.). *Hypnosis Research Developments and Perspectives.* New York: Aldine Atherton, 1972.
3. Hilgard, E.R. The domain of hypnosis with some comments on alternative paradigms. *American Psychologist,* November, 1973, 972-982.
4. Hilgard, E.R. *Divided Consciousness: Multiple Controls in Human Thought and Action.* New York: Wiley Interscience, 1977.

5. Hilgard, E.R. *Personal Communication,* March 1979.
6. Kline, M.V. *Clinical Correlates of Experimental Hypnosis.* Springfield, Illinois: Thomas, 1963.
7. Lozanov, G. *Suggestology and Outlines of Suggestopedy.* New York: Gordon & Breach, 1978.
8. Nilsson, L.G. (Ed.). *Perspectives on Memory Research.* Hillsdale, New Jersey: Lawrence Erlbaum Associates, 1979.
9. Ross, K. *Evaluation Study of the Los Angeles Police Department Hypnosis Project.* B.A. Project, University of Redlands, California, July 1977.
10. Spanos, N.P. and Barber, T.X. Toward a convergence in hypnosis research. *American Psychologist,* July 1974, 500-511.

CHAPTER 38
RESULTS TO DATE - SOME STATISTICS AND CASES

Pilot Project

Evaluation of the Los Angeles Police Department's one-year research demonstration project in investigative hypnosis, from June of 1975 until June of 1976, revealed some interesting data.[11] During the year a total of 67 hypnosis sessions were conducted in criminal investigations. Forty of the cases were homicides, one was hit-and-run accident, three were attempted homicides, seven were robberies, one was a burglary, ten were sex crimes, one was a grand theft, one was a bombing, and one was a misdemeanor vandalism.

Most hypnosis sessions were conducted at police facilities; however, some were conducted at the subject's private residence or place of business. Examination of the 67 hypnosis sessions indicated that neither the location of the hypnosis session nor the type of crime involved significantly affected the results. Approximately half of the hypnosis subjects were male and half female. Subjects' ages range from seven to seventy-five years of age with a mean age of 28.7 years. The sex, age, race, or occupation of the subject appeared to have no significant effect on the outcomes.

Results for these 67 sessions revealed that new investigative leads were obtained in 77.6% of these cases and that the solution of 16.4% were attributed directly to the hypnosis information. The researcher, an experienced criminal investigator, estimated that less than 5% of these cases would ever have been solved without hypnosis.

Long-term Results

Recent follow-up data covering some 350 cases of investigative hypnosis done by hypno-investigators at the Los Angeles Police Department between June of 1975 and December of 1978 remain fairly consistent with the original pilot study findings. Of 348 investigative hypnosis sessions surveyed, 79.3% yielded additional information not previously available. Of this elicited information, 66.4% was considered to be valuable to the case investigator.

In attempting to corroborate the information from 295 cases, accuracy was unable to be determined in 48.8% of these cases at the time of the survey. However, the 151 cases where follow-up information was then available, yielded a 90.1% verification of the information elicited under hypnosis.

Of 354 cases sampled at the time of the survey, 31.9% were solved and 68.1% still unsolved. Of 113 solved cases, the case investigators attributed value to the hypnosis-elicited information in 65.5% of them.

Of 345 cases sampled, the hypno-investigators estimated that 33.4% of the subjects achieved a deep state, 39.1% a medium state, 19.7% a light state, and that 7.8% were likely not hypnotized at all.

The types of crimes represented by hypnosis sessions from June of 1975 through December of 1978 were as follows: homicides, 59.9%; robberies, 11.7%; rapes, 13.4%; burglaries, 3.5%; others, 11.5%.[8]

Some Typical Cases

On January 19, 1976 at 9:30 p.m., a 64-year-old motion picture publicist was discovered murdered in his Van Nuys, California home, shot once in the neck. No witnesses or motive for the crime could be established. A systematic door-to-door check of the neighborhood located a witness who saw a suspicious vehicle in the neighborhood with its lights out shortly before the crime. The witness described the vehicle as a 1973 or 74 white Datsun pickup truck with a heavy-duty bumper. The vehicle contained three juveniles. The witness had looked at the license plate at the time, but could recall only that it started with a "7", had another "7" in it somewhere, and perhaps a "4". The witness was not able to recall any additional information, but agreed to a hypnosis session.

Under hypnosis the following additional information was obtained: The heavy-duty bumper was silver in color and had a red and blue "safe-tee" emblem on it; there were no dents or scratches observed on the vehicle; the word "Datsun" was written in large black letters on the tailgate; there was a small mirror on the left side; the vehicle had small chrome hubcaps; there were black rubber mud flaps behind the rear wheels and the vehicle had a "Datsun" license plate frame. There appeared to be beads or some object hanging from the rear-view mirror inside the vehicle. The complete license number was recalled as 70774W.

A Department of Motor Vehicles check confirmed that the license number was registered to a 1974 Datsun pickup truck at a local address. A stake-out on the vehicle led to a subsequent arrest of three juveniles who confessed to the crime. All of the information obtained under hypnosis was corroborated with the exception of two points. First, there was not a "Datsun" license plate frame, and second, nothing was hanging from the rear-view mirror. However, it is possible that a crack in the front windshield directly in front of the mirror could have been mistaken for something hanging from the mirror when viewed from the rear. The solution of this case was attributed essentially to to hypnosis.[11]

On January 8, 1975 a man returned to his south Los Angeles apartment at 11:20 p.m. and found his wife dead in the bathroom, nude and bound. He untied her and carried her to a bedroom, placing her on a bed and covering her with a blanket. In shock, he waited a considerable time before calling the police. During the interval he wandered from room to room picking up and putting away things found lying around.

When questioned by police he was unable to accurately describe the position of his wife's body, or what he had done before calling them. Autopsy disclosed that death was caused by asphyxiation due to strangulation with a minimum of damage to the victim's neck. There was no forced entry of the apartment or no unusual noises heard by neighbors. Though the husband was an initial suspect, it was established that he was working at the time the death occurred. Investigators, at a dead-end, decided some ten months later to use hypnosis to get additional information the husband might have forgotten.

Under hypnosis he was able to accurately recall the position of his wife's body and how she was tied. He described moving specific objects from and around the body and putting them away. This information and subsequent consultation with experts at the coroner's office enabled detectives to determine that this death was a sexual suicide, either accidental or intentional. Without hypnosis, the case would likely be in the unsolved file.[11]

On June 23, 1974, just after midnight, the sheriff of Polk County, Georgia, answered a burglar alarm with one of his deputies. They spotted a suspected truck and forced it to the side of the road. The sheriff got out to investigate, but as he approached the truck, the driver pulled a gun and started firing. The sheriff was killed outright, the deputy wounded in the leg and the truck disappeared. The wounded deputy could give only a vague description of the suspect and the truck. At a dead end, the chief of police decided to try hypnosis. Utilizing the TV technique, the hypnotist asked the deputy to describe everything that he saw. He was able to describe the suspect, including dress, appearance and description of vehicle.[5]

In 1976, in Chowchilla, California, the largest mass kidnapping occurred with the abduction of 26 children in a school bus by three masked gunmen. They were driven to a gravel quarry a hundred miles away and put into an abandoned trailer truck buried six-feet underground. Fortunately, some 16 hours later, the captives were able to dig themselves out and were rescued. Questioned by the FBI, they could not provide identifying information about the suspects. Hypnosis was utilized with the bus driver, who, with the zoom lens approach during the TV technique, was able to recall all but one digit of the license plate on the kidnapper's white van. This information was helpful in apprehending the three suspects.[4]

A recent Texas case involved the "traveling rapist". This suspect would go from door to door from about 3:00 a.m. to 9:30 a.m. looking for access. When an open door was found he would go in, rape and assualt his victim if she were a small female. One victim in Hereford was stabbed 13 times and left for dead. After the assault she could not remember anything about the suspect. However, under hypnosis, she was able to assist an artist to make a composite drawing and recall everything that the suspect had said and done during the crime event. When the suspect was later apprehended, the information elicited under hypnosis was compared with other facts and essentially corroborated. Subsequently, the suspect confessed to a number of murders and 65 rapes.[9]

One June 26, 1977 at a Los Angeles Airport area hotel, four men and two women, Continental Airlines flight attendants, were found, pistol-whipped and battered with exercise barbells by a suspect who also raped one of the stewardesses, who suffered a skull fracture. Descriptive information about the suspect was very limited when the victims were questioned initially. Under hypnosis, a composite drawing was done with the aid of the police artist. Subsequently, additional victims were flown into Los Angeles from around the nation for a line-up, where the suspect was identified.[7]

RESULTS TO DATE — STATISTICS AND CASES

On September 29, 1978, a 15-year-old girl was hitchhiking from San Francisco Bay Area toward Corona, California to visit her grandfather. She was picked up by a man in a van who raped and sexually abused her, after tying her up. He then chopped off both of her forearms with an axe and stuffed her body into a drainage tunnel. The victim played dead and was finally able to crawl out, stop a vehicle, and was taken to a hospital. When questioned by detectives she could recall only sketchy information about the traumatic event.

Under hypnosis, the victim was able to recall the suspect's name, other useful conversation and assist in the making of a composite drawing. Much of the information elicited under hypnosis was later corroborated by other witnesses. The suspect was subsequently convicted of two counts of rape, two of oral copulation, sodomy, kidnapping, and attempted murder.[12]

In this case, the Stanislaus County detectives performing the hypnosis with the victim had completed their basic investigative hypnosis training only several weeks prior to the occurrence of the crime.

In the first criminal court case involving hypnosis with witnesses in Maricopa County, Arizona, the rape suspect was described in detail under hypnosis including two tattoos. The information was later corroborated and the suspect convicted.[6]

The Biehler case in Los Angeles involved four homicides, two of which were 10 years in the past. Memory enhancement of witnesses using hypnosis led to a conviction on all four murders.[1] This case is interesting in that, in spite of the long time interval after the first crimes were committed, witness recall with hypnosis was successful. It appears that the factors of time and intoxication do not preclude the possibility of successful information retrieval with investigative hypnosis techniques.[10]

A recent landmark case for state district courts in Texas involved a homicide and the use of hypnosis with a surviving witness. A psychiatrist hypnotist, but without specific investigative experience, testified that the use of hypnosis ruined the credibility of the witness. A psychologist testified to the correctness of the session conducted by a local sheriff. The suspect was given an 50-year sentence.[2]

References
1. Anderson, P.B. Murder suspect accused of vice motive at trial. *Los Angeles Times,* November 13, 1976.
2. Campbell, B.V. Hypnotist's role tops testimony. *Lubbock Avalanche - Journal (Texas),* April 1979.

3. Floan, K. Hypnosis gains respect as an investigative tool. *The Kansas City Times,* December 16, 1977.
4. Hatton, K.L. Hypnosis takes hold as a legitimate police tool. *The Plain Dealer* (Cleveland), February 13, 1978.
5. Hypnosis for witnesses. *Newsweek,* August 5, 1974.
6. Kauss, L. Hypnosis jogs the subconscious memory and is gaining importance as a tool for criminal investigation. *The Phoenix Gazette,* December 1, 1978.
7. Kendall, J. Attacked airline employees arrive to view L.A. lineup. *Los Angeles Times,* September 23, 1977.
8. Nielsen, M. Personal Communication, March, 1979.
9. Patrick, P. Hypnosis credited in rape suspect's capture. *Lubbock Avalance - Journal,* July 2, 1977.
10. Reiser, M. Hypnosis as an aid in a homicide investigation. *The American Journal of Clinical Hypnosis,* 1974, *17,* 84-87.
11. Ross, K. *Evaluative Study of the Los Angeles Police Department Hypnosis Project.* B.A. Project, University of Redlands, California, July, 1977.
12. Vollmer, T. Seaman guilty in mutilation, rape of girl. *Los Angeles Times,* March 24, 1979.

CHAPTER 39
A REPRESENTATIVE CASE

On February 9, 1975 a 19-year-old waitress was abducted by three men while she was waiting for a bus on a corner in Van Nuys, California. She was taken through the Angeles National Forest to a desert area near Indian Springs where she was repeatedly attacked and abused sexually by all three men. After being badly beaten with fists and the butt of a gun, she was finally released in a semi-hysterical condition. She was able to remember very little to tell investigators about the suspects or their vehicle.

Under hypnosis, the victim was able to assist the police artist make composite drawings of all three suspects. In addition, she remembered names used during the 10 to 12-hour crime event as well as additional conversation and vehicle description.

Subsequently, the three were identified from the composite drawings made under hypnosis and corroborative evidence obtained. The judge, in handing down maximum sentences of 10 years to life on multiple counts of robbery, rape, sodomy and oral copulation, recommended that they never be released from prison. He said, "The viciousness of the attack on this victim was more perverse and brutal than any this court has ever seen, except possibly in some homicide cases...she obviously is still suffering from emotional problems as a result of the degradation and savage beating...and it is doubtful she will ever be able to lead a normal life."[1]

References
1. Farr, W. Trio sentenced in brutal rape case. *Los Angeles Times,* July 22, 1976.

HANDBOOK OF INVESTIGATIVE HYPNOSIS

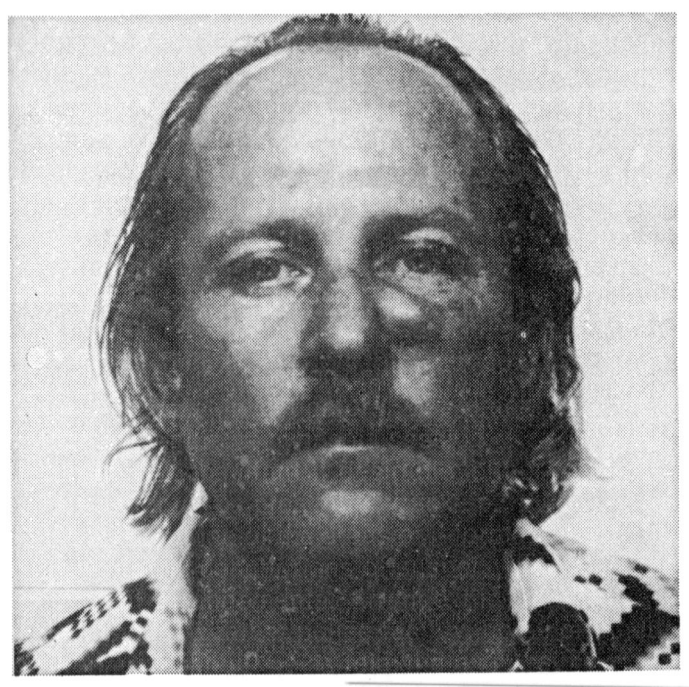

Composite drawing and photo — Suspect #1

A REPRESENTATIVE CASE

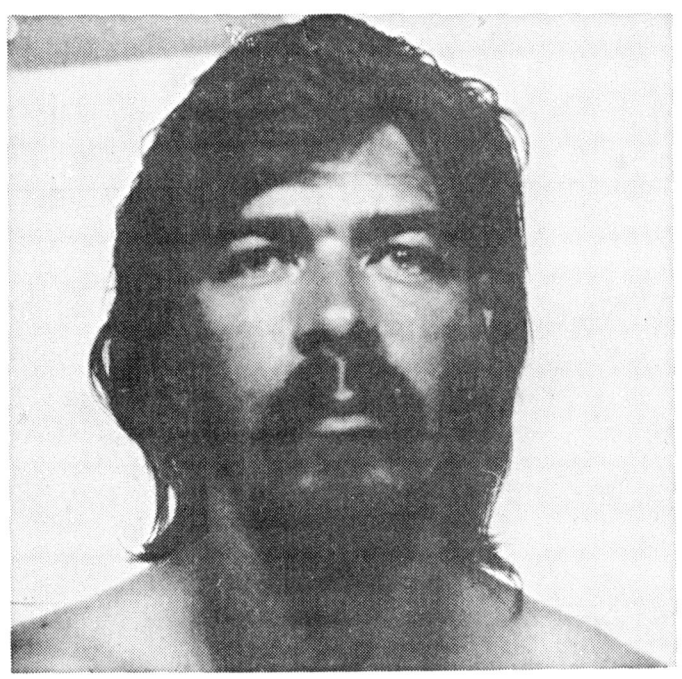

Composite drawing and photo — Suspect #2

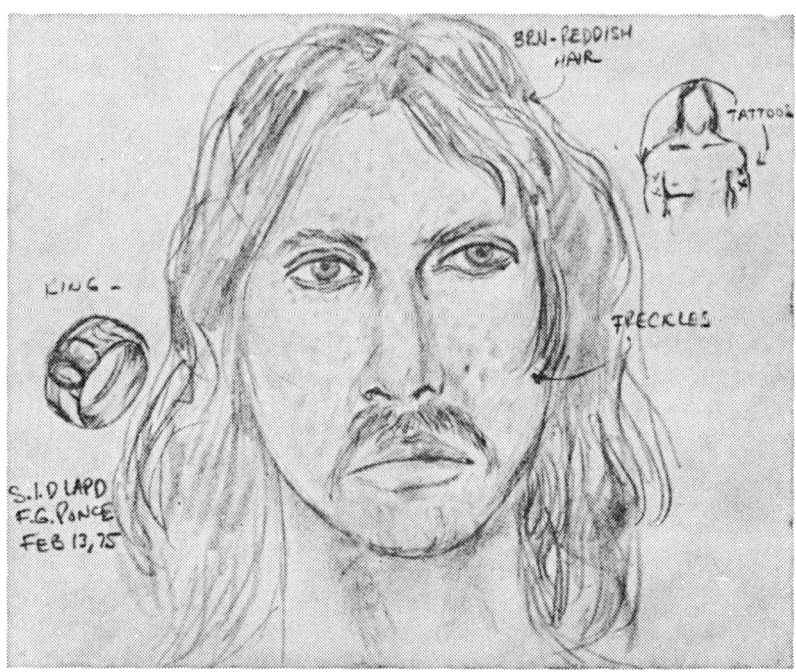
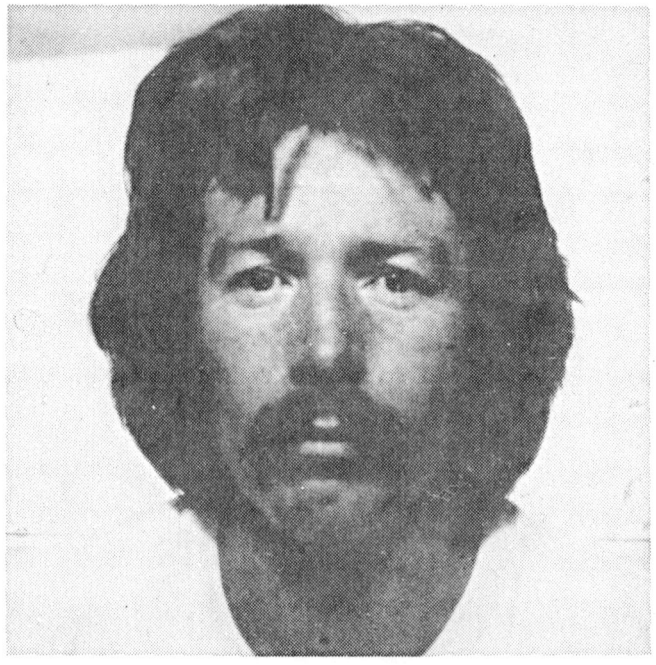

Composite drawing and photo — Suspect #3

CHAPTER 40
TRANSCRIPT OF A HYPNOSIS SESSION

HYPNOTIST: This is November 9, 1978, a hypnosis session with Miss Dee. Present are Investigator R, Investigator K, and Artist Fernando Ponce. Dr. Reiser is the hypnotist, session conducted at the Venice station this date.

HYP.: Hi, do you want to sit over here? I'm Dr. Reiser, Department Psychologist with LAPD. I think you met Mr. Ponce, and of course you know Detective R. First I'd like to put this mike around you because we routinely record each session so we can go back later and review it and see if there is anything we need to take another look at. Okay? Fine. What name do you like to be called?

SUBJECT: Dee.

HYP.: Dee. Okay.

HYP.: What about your physical and emotional health. Are there any problems in those areas that you're aware of?

SUB.: Well, I've been seeing a therapist for about a year on and off.

HYP.: Did that have any connection with this crime event?

SUB.: No.

HYP.: That was prior to that.

SUB.: Yes.

HYP.: Okay.

SUB.: It had to do with my marriage.

HYP.: Okay, fine. Any other physical problems that you are aware of?

SUB.: Well, I've got a bad back, that's about it.

HYP.: Okay, but you are not taking any medication.

SUB.: Okay, Valium sometimes, Elavil sometimes.

HYP.: Do you know what dosage it is?

SUB.: Um, Elavil I think is 25 milligrams, Valium, 10. I

	don't have much of a tolerance for tranquillizers.
HYP.:	Okay, fine. What do you know about hypnosis?
SUB.:	Nothing except what I've seen on T.V.
HYP.:	Oh oh. (laughing)
SUB.:	(laughing)
HYP.:	You mean the swinging pendulums and stuff like that?
SUB.:	Uh huh.
HYP.:	Well, we don't really do that. As a matter of fact, let me tell you just a couple of things about it and if you have any questions you can ask me. But, hypnosis is really a state of relaxation and an altered state of consciousness wherein you're not asleep, you're not unconscious, you know everything that's happening all the time and you can come out of hypnosis if you should want to at any time. Nobody is controlling you, it really works in getting you relaxed to the point where the attention you pay to peripheral or surrounding things gets focused more centrally on to what we're talking about.

Because of your relaxed state, you are able to tap subconscious levels of the mind more easily. Your brain doesn't have to work with processing a lot of the information it does when your eyes are open. It's really a very simple physiological and psychological process. Do you have any questions about that? As we get into it, I will explain step by step what to do in order for you to experience hypnosis. Now the reason we use hypnosis in crime cases is that we find in an overwhelming number of cases, because of the relaxation and the ability to tap subconscious levels of the mind, the witness or victim to a crime may have much better recall.

We find when we check things out that the recall very often is fairly accurate and we corroborate them by further investigation. It does help to improve the person's memory, particularly very emotional or traumatic things. Where you are very upset at the time they're happening and you would want to push things out of your mind because of the painful nature of what happened. In that connection let me say this, that you will not

TRANSCRIPT OF A HYPNOSIS SESSION

	be asked or pressured into dealing with anything under hypnosis or remembering anything that you don't feel comfortable with. You may remember as much or as little as you would like. If under hypnosis you remember something that later on, when you're out of hypnosis, you don't feel comfortable with, you're free to forget it again if you want to.
SUB.:	Is it easy to forget?
HYP.:	It will happen automatically.
SUB.:	Yeah?
HYP.:	With no conscious effort on your part. Your subconscious mind will take care of that. There are defense mechanisms that we all have operating to protect us and they operate without any conscious effort on our part at a subconscious level.
	Another thing, I understand that this crime involved some sexual activities as well as some brutal physical kinds of things. We're not interested in that and we're not going to go into a lot of the nitty gritty details of it unless for some reason you would like to, or you have a need to do that. Okay?
	We are interested in and we are going to focus on the identity of the suspects in the case. That's what we're interested in. So you don't need to worry about being embarrassed or being asked questions that are going to be painful because I'm not going to do that. Okay?
	Anytime I ask you something that you feel is painful, embarrassing, or uncomfortable, tell me. You will be able to talk even though you are in hypnosis, just as you are talking now.
SUB.:	Am I going to know that I'm in hypnosis?
HYP.:	Yes, you'll know it, though it may not be what you're expecting. Many people, the first time under hypnosis, are really surprised that they're aware of what's happening because no matter how many times you tell them that it's not being asleep or unconsious, they are expecting to be zonked out in some fashion. And you will not be. Okay?
SUB.:	Okay.
HYP.:	So, we can do one or two things during the session

SUB.:	that I think will be interesting to you to let you know that you indeed are in hypnosis even though you are aware of what's happening all the time. All right? Okay.
HYP.:	Okay, now, let me tell you exactly what we are going to do so there are no secrets. There is no mystery or no secrets to this procedure, it's very open and very plain. When we begin, the first thing that we'll do is I will make suggestions to you in order for you to experience the state of hypnosis. Okay? And all you have to do is follow the suggestions that I give and experience what you will experience. If you are motivated and you are cooperative and really want to assist then you'll experience these things. Okay? If at any time there's a problem that you are experiencing please tell me about it because even with hypnosis I can't read minds. Nobody else can either.

Okay, once you're in the state of hypnosis I will ask you to recall the non-sexual part of the contact that you had with these suspects at the time that it happened so that you can refresh your memory, revisualize that so it becomes clearer and more vivid to you. Then, after we do that for a period of time, I'm going to ask you to take the most vivid one. I understand there were two people involved in this case; I'm going to ask you to focus on the most vivid picture that you have and Mr. Ponce will begin a composite drawing, he'll ask you some questions about the person's appearance. Then Mr. Ponce will begin drawing an outline of the person and then at a certain point I will ask him, with your okay, to ask you some questions because he knows better what to ask you about drawing than I do because he's an expert in that and I'm not.

At a certain point, I may ask you to stay in hypnosis but open your eyes so you can see what he's doing after he has a rough drawing and make corrections, and you'll be able to keep the picture of this person in mind, the suspect that you have revisualized while you are in hypnosis, and you'll be able to look at the drawing and tell him how to make his drawing just as accurate as the picture

	in your mind of that person.
SUB.:	Okay.
HYP.:	And that's the procedure. We will do that with the two suspects.
SUB.:	Okay. Will I be able if I have a question, to ask you when I'm under hypnosis?
HYP.:	Sure.
SUB.:	Will I be able to ask you?
HYP.:	Oh yes, you can talk, you can ask questions, you'll be perfectly okay. The only thing you may find, as some people do, is that because hypnosis is so comfortable and so relaxing, that it becomes a little bit of an effort to talk, because it's like work. So you may find yourself feeling a little reluctant to talk, but you'll be able to talk, no problem. Okay? Any other questions?
SUB.:	No.
HYP.:	How do you feel right now?
SUB.:	A little bit nervous and a lot of anticipation.
HYP.:	That's normal. That's perfectly normal. Most people we work with feel exactly that way. And that's okay. How do you feel about the detectives apprehending these suspects and putting them in jail?
SUB.:	When it first happened to me I wasn't going to report it to the police, I just wanted it blocked out of my mind and to forget about it. And to a certain extent I still want that. I want it to be over and done with, but I realize that I have this sort of guilt feeling, that if I didn't do something about it, somebody else might get hurt and I don't want that to happen because of me.
HYP.:	Unfortunately, that's probably so, because, as you know, the kinds of people who do that usually don't do this once. The other thing is that if they're put in jail and sent to long prison terms, they can't harm anybody for a long time. You bring up a point that I want to mention also, that I think is important for you. We find with many of the people who have been brutalized by either rape or some other kind of physical assault, that going through the hypnosis session, might be a little scared about it and a little nervous. Afterward they tell us that they felt the experience was helpful to them. Some

	of the people have told us that they sleep better, that if they've had nightmares, they have fewer nightmares. That they feel more at ease with themselves, having dealt with these feelings.
SUB.:	I've been having a lot of nightmares but I can't recall any of them. I just wake up several times in the night and I feel like I'm dying or something. I feel really funny inside, like something's happened. And it's a physical feeling, it's not an emotional feeling. I don't understand that.
HYP.:	Well, I think there is also emotion involved in it. If there weren't, you wouldn't wake up in the state that you do from the nightmares, feeling a lot of fear and anxiety. Are you right-handed or left-handed?
SUB.:	Right.
HYP.:	Right-handed. Any other questions?
SUB.:	Uh, unh.
HYP.:	Okay, fine. I'm going to tell you how to feel and experience hypnosis now. Okay?
SUB.:	Okay.
HYP.:	Okay, are you as comfortable as you can get in that chair?
SUB.:	Yeah, I would probably be more comfortable with my legs crossed.
HYP.:	Well...
SUB.:	Is that all right? No.
HYP.:	It's a little easier because of the work that we'll be doing if you could keep them on the floor, if you don't mind, and if you put your hands on your knees like so, and just let them relax that way. That'll be okay. All right.
SUB.:	That's all right?
HYP.:	Yes, that's great. Okay, I'm going to put my finger on the top of your head, like so, and I'd like you to look up right, as if you're looking through the top of your head, like that. And you're going to look right at my finger, eyes all the way up. Higher, look up as high as you can, all the way, that's fantastic, good, good, good, more, more, more. Okay, that's good, pretty good, that's good. Once more, do it once more, all the way, up, as high as you can, come on, come on, you're doing well, all the way up, all the way up. That's a three, plus squint,

that's very excellent, that's fine. Now, take a deep breath, that's good.

Now keep your eyes closed, and as you let it out, just relax your whole body, let your body go nice and relaxed, just nice and relaxed...that's fantastic. Great. Okay, now I'd like you to breathe in deeply and exhale slowly, breathe in deeply and exhale slowly, that's good, that's good. And with each breath in, you are breathing in relaxation, and exhaling tension. And you can become more and more relaxed, more and more relaxed with each breath that you take. More and more relaxed with each breath that you take. You'll find yourself relaxing physically and mentally, your whole body and your mind relaxing more and more, all the time, with each breath that you take.

And let me explain, as you continue breathing that way, how this works because it's no mystery and as I said before, you can understand everything I'm saying and no matter how deeply you relax and go into hypnosis, you'll always be able to hear what I'm saying and answer questions or ask questions if you want to and know everything that's going on.

The deep breathing is important in hypnosis as it is in Yoga, meditation, Zen, and other relaxation excercises because it pulls more oxygen into your lungs. That oxygenates the blood and carries away carbon dioxide and other waste materials. It improves the circulation to your hands, your feet and your brain.

You may notice, after a few minutes, as many people do, a tingling sensation in your hands and your feet, and you may notice that your hands, your fingers, your toes, may feel warm and heavy or light and floating. Any of those feelings are perfectly normal as you continue relaxing more and more, with each breath that you take. And you are breathing in relaxation and exhaling tension, that's fine. Very, very good. Excellent.

I'd like you to relax all the muscles of your body, which will enable you to feel even more comfortably relaxed. And just let all of your muscles, large and small, all of your ligaments, tendons, go very, very relaxed, from the top of your head to the tips of your toes, very, very relaxed. From the top of your head to the tips of your toes, large and small, just continue relaxing more and more with each breath that you take, and that's fine. And you continue to breathe in relaxation and exhale tension, with each breath that you take, and you can feel the tension draining away as you relax more and more easily, and comfortably, and securely. And you notice a couple of interesting things happening as you relax.

You notice that your body quiets down, and the tension drains away, kind of like water running down-hill, gravity flow from the upper part of your body into the lower part, and from the lower part into your feet, from your feet, out of your body, into the floor, leaving you feeling more comfortable and secure and relaxed. With each breath that you take, relaxing more and more all the time.

You may notice too, as many people do, that as your body relaxes with each breath that you take, that your mind relaxes also, because with your eyes closed, and with you concentrating on what I'm saying, and listening to my instructions, your brain can slow down and relax. It doesn't have to work as hard, and it, in turn, sends relaxation messages to the nervous system, central nervous system, the autonomic nervous system, and the other parts of your body, all of your organs and muscles and tissues and cells, that it's okay to relax, slow down. So your heart rate slows down and your breathing and respiration slow down and your metabolism slows down.

All of these functions indicate a state of heightened relaxation, more and more comfortable and relaxed and secure. And it's a very, very pleasant feeling, as you allow yourself to experience that nice, drowsy, yet alert state of relaxation and hypnosis and it feels so nice. That's fine, and you're doing very nicely. Okay Dee, I'd like you to pay attention for a couple of minutes as you continue relaxing with each breath that you take.

I'd like you to pay attention to your left hand for just a moment, and you will notice some very interesting things as you pay attention to it. You'll notice that you can feel the fabric of your jeans through the fingertips of your left hand, and you may notice the quality of the fabric, the courseness of it, on your fingertips.

And it's even more interesting to notice, as you focus your attention on your left hand and fingers, that you can feel the heat from your leg coming through your jeans to your fingertips, you can sense the heat in your fingertips and that's kind of interesting because you didn't notice that before. And then you may notice, in a moment or so, that there will be an increased sense of warmth in your left hand as the circulation improves. You may notice a tingling sensation increasing in the fingers in your left hand in one or more of the fingers and you may notice, in a moment or two, that one or more of the fingers of your left hand will begin tightening up and twitching slightly. And your little finger is twitching slightly and that's fine.

And you may notice other fingers twitching also. And your ring finger is twitching now, and your middle finger and your forefinger and then your thumb. You may notice that all of the fingers of your left hand will begin feeling more and more weightless and light and then your hand, your fingers and your hand and your arm will feel lighter and lighter, and lighter and lighter and lighter, and more and more weightless.

From your fingertip, here (stroking), up your arm, all the way up to your shoulder, will now begin to feel lighter and more and more weightless and will be as if your hand and your arm are like a large balloon of your favorite color, filled with helium gas, which is lighter than air, allowing the balloon to float upward toward the blue sky, and the warm summer sun, and the white fleecy clouds.

There's a little seagull up there flying around in circles making his little cawing noise. And it begins to feel lighter and lighter and lighter and lighter, and you may notice then that one or more the fingers of your left hand will begin gently lifting upward, slowly at first and then faster, and faster and faster, as they feel lighter, and lighter and lighter. They're beginning to drift upward now, more and more, with each breath that you take, as they feel lighter and lighter and lighter and lighter. Drifting upward, that's fine, more and more weightless, more and more weightless, as it begins drifting upward, higher and higher and higher.

That's a very interesting experience you've had and you can feel some tightness in your arm as your subconscious activates the autonomic nervous system, the proper muscles, ligaments and tendons that will raise your hand and your arm with no conscious effort on your part required, and it's a very interesting experience. It's very interesting and quite normal and it's getting lighter and lighter and lighter and drifting higher and higher and higher and higher and higher as it feels lighter and lighter. And faster now, moving up a little bit more quickly, faster and faster as it feels lighter and lighter. That's fine, you're doing beautifully, very nicely, and now it can drift there all day long. It can drift there all day long if it wanted to and you wouldn't feel any tiredness at all in that hand and arm. It would drift there like that lazy, light, weightless balloon in that blue summer sky, feeling very very comfortable.

And you're doing very well Dee, you're doing an excellent job. I'm very pleased. Okay, in just a moment, I'm going to tug very lightly on your left wrist, and when I do, your left hand will become a fist and your left arm from your shoulder all the way down will stiffen up, get very stiff and rigid, your elbow will lock and your arm will feel like a rigid, tough, steel bar. Rigid, tough and unbending, and that will be fine. That will be an interesting experience also. That arm will be so steely and rigid and tough and unbending that I could hang on there if I wanted to, and it still wouldn't bend and that'll be perfectly fine (tugs on wrist). Okay, fine, rigid, tough.

That's excellent, great. Okay, I'm going to count to three, Dee, and when I reach three, I'd like you to very slowly begin lowering that steel bar arm about three degrees at a time, kind of like a cogwheel, a few degrees at a time, back to your leg, where it will again feel perfectly normal in every way, except that you may be at least five times as deeply relaxed as you are right now. You may be at least five times as deeply relaxed as you are now, and you'll feel very secure and comfortable and at ease and you'll have a very excellent feeling. One, two, three.

Perfectly normal in every way. If you'd like, you can open those fingers and allow them to relax on your leg, very normal, and you're very, very relaxed, very relaxed, and doing a fine job. Excellent. Okay, Dee, I'd like you to imagine yourself on the third floor of a building, and this can be an office building or any kind of building you like, whatever is comfortable for you. And you're going to be walking down three flights of stairs in this building. In a moment when I tell you, and when you get down to the basement of this building, there'll be a room there and it'll have a bunch of filing cabinets in that room, and I'm going to ask you to go into that room and look up something in one of the filing cabinets. But right now you are on the third floor of this building and I'd like you to see yourself in your mind's eye on the third floor and you're about to start down, walking down the stairs.

You can walk down fairly rapidly, and you see yourself now taking hold of the handrail and you are walking down the first flight of stairs, from the third floor to the second floor. You are halfway down, and you are three-fourths of the way down, and you are now approaching the second floor and make a little turn and then you start down the stairs that are going down from the second floor toward the first floor.

And you start down and you are walking down, toward the first floor, and you are halfway down, three-fourths of the way down, and you are down at the first floor. You make the little turn around the landing to start down the stairs going from the first floor to the basement. And you see yourself walking down the stairs to the basement and you are halfway down, and you are three-fourths of the way down and now you are down in the basement of the building. It's a well-lighted, comfortable basement. There's nothing scary about it, a perfectly comfortable, safe and secure, security building.

You see a door nearby, and that's the door to the filing room, that has the filing cabinets of memories. You open the door now, you are opening the door to the filing room of memories, and you're going into the room. You see a bunch of filing cabinets and interestingly enough, each one of these filing cabinets, Dee, has your name on it. And these are Dee's filing cabinets because these are all of Dee's memories.

Things that you remember, things that have gotten recorded, perhaps from the time you were born, all the way up to the present moment, and you notice that each of these filing cabinets has a date on it. I'd like you to look for the filing cabinet, a recent one, that has at the top of it November, 1978, and you see yourself in front of that filing cabinet with the label, November, 1978. In the top drawer of that cabinet, which you are pulling out now, there is a file, a manila folder, and on top of that manila folder it says 11-1-78.

Okay. In that folder is a videotape, a cassette videotape of everything that happened to you, everything that got recorded in your brain around that date of November 1, 1978. It's an exact, accurate and vivid recording of everything that you experienced and perceived, saw, heard, or felt on that particular date, perhaps beginning at midnight and running for about 24 hours. I'd like you to look over toward the far side of this file room and you'll notice a video cassette player on a table and above it is a TV screen that looks pretty much like a set that you've looked at before. It looks familiar to you and you know how to operate it easily.

Now this videotape of memory from that date is being put into the videotape player, being turned on, the TV set is being turned on. There's a very

TRANSCRIPT OF A HYPNOSIS SESSION

comfortable chair, much like the chair you're sitting in right now, with a high back. It's very relaxing and very comfortable to sit in that chair and in just a moment, when I count to three, the TV set is going to turn on and you're going to watch this videotape. It's going to be an exact replay of some of the things that happened on Thursday morning, November first at approximately 1:30 - 2:30 a.m., early in the morning on that date. You are going to be able to sit in your chair, very relaxed and comfortable, remaining objective and secure and comfortable and this will be like watching a documentary film on television. It will be kind of interesting.

You may be seeing yourself in that film or some other people in that film and it will be as if you are watching someone else and you'll stay in your chair relaxed and comfortable and at ease and able to watch that videotape accurately, vividly and in great detail and you'll be able to describe to me those things that we are interested in on that documentary videotape. Now, at any time we want to, we can stop the videotape. We can put it into slow motion, we can run it backwards, we can zoom in and have closeups on anything in any frame of the film of the videotape, whether it's a face or a car or a license plate or anything like that. As that zoom lens goes in on that object or person, it will become clearer and clearer and more vivid and accurate and you'll be able to see that and describe it in great and accurate detail, and that will be fine.

Okay, now, the videotape is now in the machine and the machine is turned on. You see yourself sitting in that comfortable chair, in front of the TV screen that's connected to the videotape machine. The TV screen is being turned on, the set is lighting up, and in just a moment you'll be watching the videotape. There is no need to describe, unless you feel like it or want to, any of the sexual activities specifically. You may focus your attention and describe the people, the appearance of the people and perhaps some of the things that are said if that's pertinent in the film, remaining objective and relaxed and comfortable knowing you are watching a documentary film, and that will be interesting to you. And if you talk about Dee, who is in this documentary film, you will say Dee is doing this or Dee says that, because you'll be watching Dee as if she is another person and she will be in this film, and that will be fine. One, two, three. . .the videotape is starting and I'd like you to describe to me what is happening. What's happening?

I'm just going to move your hair slightly so that I can see your face and that will be okay. Okay, you can talk to me now. Tell me what's happening.

SUB.: She's standing out by the beach.
HYP.: Okay, she's standing out by the beach.
SUB.: By a palm tree by the pavilion, not a tall one, just a little bit taller than she is.
HYP.: Okay, a rather short palm tree by the pavilion. Okay. What is happening now?
SUB.: The wind is blowing.
HYP.: Okay.
SUB.: It's cool out. She's got her arms folded.
HYP.: Uh huh.
SUB.: She's looking out at the ocean.
HYP.: Fine.
SUB.: She's thinking about something.
HYP.: Okay.
SUB.: Somebody's coming up behind her, but she doesn't hear them.
HYP.: Okay.
SUB.: It's two men.
HYP.: Okay.
SUB.: Two black men.
HYP.: Uh huh.
SUB.: They both grab her, one grabs her with his arm around her neck and face and puts his hand over her mouth.
HYP.: Okay.
SUB.: And grabs her shoulder.
HYP.: Uh huh.
SUB.: And the other one grabs the arms the way they are folded in front of her so that she can't struggle.
HYP.: I see.
SUB.: And her eyes are open wide and she starts crying.
HYP.: Okay.

TRANSCRIPT OF A HYPNOSIS SESSION

SUB.: And they start carrying her out on the beach and cross the bike path, she stumbles.
HYP.: Okay.
SUB.: And then they start dragging her out across the sand but she's not fighting. And she's still crying.
HYP.: Uh huh.
SUB.: They're talking to each other, but she can't hear what they're saying. She can only hear them, almost like a whisper but more like she can hear the movement of their mouths.
HYP.: Uh huh.
SUB.: And then they're out on the...there's a part on the beach where there are a lot of pilings, poles, sticking out of the sand and they were put there and they're behind that facing the ocean.
HYP.: Okay.
SUB.: And it's dark but there's still some light from the lights along the beach, the boardwalk.
HYP.: Uh huh.
SUB.: They let loose a little bit but she's crying and her hair's down in her eyes. The one guy that was holding her arms slaps her across the face.
HYP.: Uh huh.
SUB.: Not with an open hand and not with a fist but kind of just kind of semi-open. Now all of a sudden the other guy hits her in the back, the lower part of the back. She goes down on her knees. The one guy in front of her (crying).
HYP.: You can report on what you feel comfortable with. And you don't have to report or describe anything that you don't feel comfortable with, it's okay. It's okay.
SUB.: (Crying).
HYP.: Now I realize this is a very unpleasant thing to even watch on television because it's a very unpleasant kind of documentary to watch.
SUB.: (Crying).
HYP.: And it's okay to have feelings about it and you just let your feelings go as much as you want to and it's okay.
SUB.: (Continues crying).
HYP.: I'm going to put a handkerchief in your left hand and if you'd like to use it you can.
SUB.: The guy in front of her has his pants unzipped.

HYP.:	Okay.
SUB.:	And he grabs her hair on each side of her head just above her ears. And he forces himself on her.
HYP.:	Okay.
SUB.:	(Crying)...The jeans that she has on are old levis, the type that button up the front. The guy in back of her reaches around her waist.
HYP.:	If you would rather that we speed this videotape up for any reason and go past that we can, it's up to you. Would you like to do that?
SUB.:	Yeah.
HYP.:	Okay. Now I would like to stop, I'm going to stop this videotape and I'd like you to sit in that comfortable chair in the memory room and I'd like you to look at the videotape where I stop it and take a good calm accurate look at this person in front of Dee and you can see his face very clearly because of the light from the boardwalk, and when this videotape is stopped, you can take as much time as you need sitting in that chair in the memory room to look at that man's face who is in front of Dee in the videotape. Take as long as you need to see the face very very clearly, accurately and vividly with the frame stopped. I'd like you to describe it to me as you continue looking at it, seeing it clearly, accurately and vividly. Okay, I'm going to turn the videotape back to that point once more and stop it. Okay, now you have all the time in the world that you need to look at that frame of that man's face right in front of Dee, on the beach, and he's in front of her now and you can take all the time you need looking at the TV set and it becomes clearer and clearer and accurately vivid. Now would you please describe him.
SUB.:	(Crying)...He's got a green knit cap on.
HYP.:	Green knit cap on, okay.
SUB.:	His head is medium size. He's got, it looks like it would be long, bushy black hair, but it's pressed. His hairline comes, is lower, comes down low, comes to a point and he comes down.
HYP.:	Okay. Do you mean that he has a kind of low forhead?
SUB.:	Uh hum, and it's sunken in a little bit, not a lot.

TRANSCRIPT OF A HYPNOSIS SESSION

HYP.:	The top of his head is sort of sunken a bit.
SUB.:	The forehead.
HYP.:	The forehead. Okay.
SUB.:	It curves out toward his eyebrows.
HYP.:	Curves out toward his eyebrows. Okay.
SUB.:	He's got thick black eyebrows.
HYP.:	Okay, thick black eyebrows.
SUB.:	No hair, just maybe a little tiny hair in between.
HYP.:	All right. Very good.
SUB.:	His nose isn't broad, like most black men's noses.
HYP.:	Fairly thin nose?
SUB.:	Thin and it comes down, then comes out.
HYP.:	Uh huh, flares out toward the bottom? Toward the nostril?
SUB.:	Wide nostrils.
HYP.:	Wide nostrils but thin top.
SUB.:	Uh hum.
HYP.:	Okay. Is it pushed in at all toward the top or is it fairly straight?
SUB.:	Just a little bit.
HYP.:	Okay.
SUB.:	Just in here, it's pushed out a little bit (demonstrates).
HYP.:	Okay, that's fine, very good. Okay.
SUB.:	He's got not high cheekbones like mine, but a little bit less.
HYP.:	Okay.
SUB.:	His hairline comes down the sideburns, the hair is all connected, it comes down.
HYP.:	Uh huh, how far down is it?
SUB.:	Comes in like this (demonstrating).
HYP.:	Comes all the way down his chin towards his mouth?
SUB.:	And he's got a moustache.
HYP.:	Uh huh. Describe it.
SUB.:	The mustache starts not right under his nostrils, not in his nostrils. It comes down into his beard. It doesn't have, he's got full lips.
HYP.:	He has full lips, okay.
SUB.:	The thing that's more different about him than most black men is he's got smoothe skin.
HYP.:	Uh huh, okay, is it light, dark or medium?
SUB.:	A golden brown, I don't know, the light is not that good. But it's not black.

HYP.:	Okay. Take a look at the lips again on that TV set and describe those a little bit more if you would.
SUB.:	They're full lips but not fat. Not pouty.
HYP.:	Okay, are they both the same thickness or is one thicker than the other?
SUB.:	They're both about the same.
HYP.:	Okay.
SUB.:	The bottom lip doesn't protrude.
HYP.:	Okay. Fine. Now lets take a look at the TV set now and look at his ears. Describe his ears to me.
SUB.:	They're flat against his head.
HYP.:	Flat against his head. Okay, what about size?
SUB.:	Just normal ears.
HYP.:	Normal ears, okay. Now take a look at the chin on this person. Describe the chin.
SUB.:	I can't really tell with the hair on his face, but it comes down.
HYP.:	Is it round or pointy, or square?
SUB.:	Not round and not pointy, but just gradually tapers, sort of.
HYP.:	Okay, and the tip of his chin, what does that look like?
SUB.:	He's got hair on it.
HYP.:	Okay, it is a lot of hair or straggly hair or full hair? What does the hair look like?
SUB.:	It's like a tapered beard; it looks like it might come out about that much (demonstrates).
HYP.:	About a half inch or so, or longer?
SUB.:	No.
HYP.:	Just about a half inch or so?
SUB.:	Yeah. Maybe not that much.
HYP.:	Uh huh. So it's very short and thick. Okay. That's fine. Now direct your attention upward on the TV frozen frame and look at this person's eyes and you have all the time you need to describe his eyes to me. Very accurately and vividly.
SUB.:	He's got large, large eyes.
HYP.:	Okay, fine.
SUB.:	Sort of almond shaped, not deep set.
HYP.:	Okay. Are they light colored, dark colored? What do you see? What size are the pupils?
SUB.:	I can't see the pupils.
HYP.:	Can't see them. Okay. Could you describe the iris?
SUB.:	They're black. His eye color is black.

TRANSCRIPT OF A HYPNOSIS SESSION

HYP.: Eye color black. The iris of his eye is black around the pupil?
SUB.: Uh hum.
HYP.: Okay. Now I'd like you to just very slowly and calmly take a look at the total face of this person and see if there's anything about the face that strikes you, any scars, marks of any kind or anything that comes to your attention that you haven't yet mentioned, that could mention about his face.
SUB.: His skin tone.
HYP.: Okay, could you describe that.
SUB.: It's almost like when a black woman uses bleaching cream. There's little, not distinguishable blotches, but little, little discolorations.
HYP.: Okay. About how old is this person?
SUB.: Thirty, thirty-two.
HYP.: Thirty or thirty-two. Is this a large person, medium size, or small person?
SUB.: He's large. Not fat, but big.
HYP.: Big. Okay, how big is he, would you say? Take a good look.
SUB.: Six feet tall.
HYP.: Six feet tall. And about how much does he weigh, would you say?
SUB.: 180.
HYP.: About 180, and he's not fat. Is he well built?
SUB.: No, he's not, he's big, but he's muscular, not like a weight lifter, but big.
HYP.: Uh huh. Muscular and not built like a weight lifter.
SUB.: No. His muscles are big, he's in good shape, he's not flabby, not loose.
HYP.: Okay. I'd like you to take another look at this man's face on the TV set and mention anything else that we haven't yet talked about that you can notice about his face. What else do you see?
SUB.: He's, you can see a little bit of hair on his nose.
HYP.: A little bit of hair in his nostrils?
SUB.: Um hum.
HYP.: Okay. Fine. Anything else? Okay, excellent, that's fine. I'd like you now, Dee, to take another look at the total face in this frame on the TV screen. It's very vivid, you can see it clearly and accurately and there's no way that you would confuse this

face with any other face, it's so clear and vivid and accurate you could recognize it anywhere if you saw it again and that will be fine. And you are going to keep the image of this face in your mind and in just a moment I'm going to ask you to stay in hypnosis and you'll be able to open your eyes, remaining in hypnosis, and Mr. Ponce is going to show you a rough sketch he has made from your description.

You'll be able, with your eyes open, remaining relaxed, comfortable and secure in hypnosis, to look at his sketch and answer his questions. When he is finished and you are finished making your suggestions for his drawing to be more accurate and vivid, it will look as much like that picture that you have vividly in mind right now as it could possible look. Very vivid and accurate of this particular person who was there with Dee on the beach, very vivid, clear and accurate, in great detail and you'll be able to describe it and help him make that drawing extremely accurate.

I'm going to count to three and you can then open your eyes, remaining in hypnosis, very relaxed and answer Mr. Ponce's questions and help upgrade his drawing based on the picture that you will keep in mind clearly, vividly and accurately. One, two, three. You can open your eyes now. Just remain in hypnosis. Okay, just answer Mr. Ponce's questions.

ARTIST: Okay Dee, take a look at the drawing and I'd like you to tell me the features that need to be changed.

SUB.: The nose is a little bit smaller. They are not coming down this way. And a little bit thinner here.

ART.: Okay Dee, take a look at the nose. You may touch it.

SUB.: That's his nose. The hair in here came further in, in here (pointing).

ART.: Yes, uh huh, now where is that peak? Where is the peak that you see in the drawing?

SUB.: There. But it comes up here, and then it comes in a little bit here and then it goes back down.

ART.: Is that it?

SUB.: There's a little bit more hair showing and the cap

TRANSCRIPT OF A HYPNOSIS SESSION

ART.:	was more...(pointing).
ART.:	Toward the back.
SUB.:	To the back, but that was the way the cap was.
ART.:	You're doing fine, excellent. Take a look at the shape of the face. Now, tell me about the shape of the face. Is it correct? Are the sideburns correct too?
SUB:	Uh hum. You got the beard right, but it was more like this hair up here, darker.
ART.:	Darker, but the shape is correct? The shape of the beard too? Is the moustache correct?
SUB.:	Uh huh.
ART.:	Is the moustache touching the upper lip?
SUB.:	No. You know how some men have hair that comes all the way down to the little lines.
ART.:	Uh huh, okay. Now, the middle of the upper lip, the little part of the upper lip, is it pointed or rounded? This part? Pointed, ovular or rounded?
SUB.:	Curved around (pointing).
ART.:	Rounded?
SUB.:	Um hum. A little bit, but it almost comes to...
ART.:	Almost to a point. Okay. Do the lips protrude? Are they pointed out? Does the lower lip hang?
SUB.:	No.
ART.:	I'd like you to see what's different on the face. I can change it to make it very very accurate. Look at the ears. Were they closer to the head or are they properly placed?
SUB.:	Maybe shorter, that much shorter.
ART.:	Okay. Rounded ears? Take a look at these bones, those bones do they show very much or are they molded?
SUB.:	This part comes like...
ART.:	This part, does it come out or...
SUB.:	Um hum.
ART.:	Okay now, the same area, does it go in, under here?
SUB.:	Not in here.
ART.:	Is it a whole face right here, or somewhat sunk in?
SUB.:	No.
ART.:	It's like that. Okay. Take a look at the eyebrows. Look in this area of the eybrows. Are they protruding?
SUB.:	Uh huh, they came down like...

ART.:	Going this way. Now look at the eyebrows. Are they straight across like this, or curved?
SUB.:	They're more curved, and come down like...
ART.:	Very good. Are they dark?
SUB.:	Yes.
ART.:	Good. Now the nose. Is it deep?
SUB.:	No.
ART.:	Shallow. Okay. Now the ears, deep set? Okay, very good. Look at the shape of the eyes.
SUB.:	Um hum, but you could see his lower lashes.
ART.:	Okay. Do you see the upper ones too? See the upper lashes too? Look at the eyelid, the lower eyelid, does the lower eyelid show? The lower eyelid, does it show?
SUB.:	No.
ART.:	Okay, do you find any other differences in the eyes, that you would like to change?
SUB.:	His eyes were darker.
ART.:	Darker, and the...
SUB.:	Dark in here, all around like that, really black.
ART.:	Jet black. Okay. Now were the white of the eyes really clear, real white or were they yellowish, redish? Can you see that area?
SUB.:	They weren't white like our eyes.
ART.:	Uh huh. No redness? No yellow casts?
SUB.:	No. A little. Yeah, not yellow but pink.
ART.:	Kind of pink. Okay, does he show a crease along the eyes? Does he show a crease?
SUB.:	No.
ART.:	Okay. Are there any other changes you'd like to make?
SUB.:	There was one line, but I don't know, because he was frowning, like that...
ART.:	Uh huh. Was it a permanent line or just a temporary emotional line? Can't tell? There was a line here right in the depression of the forehead?
SUB.:	Yeah.
ART.:	Is the size of the forehead perfect? A little angle. Does he have any frown lines?
SUB.:	No.
ART.:	No frown lines. Any other lines around the forehead, in the face?
SUB.:	This eye had like that line...
ART.:	The eyelid. This line corresponds to the eyelid.

TRANSCRIPT OF A HYPNOSIS SESSION

SUB.: Uh huh.
ART.: Correct now?
SUB.: Yeah.
ART.: Okay. Now, how are the nostrils? The nostrils of the nose, the holes of the nose. Are they properly depicted?
SUB.: This one, larger.
ART.: Are there any hairs in that area? In the nostrils, hairs in the nostrils?
SUB.: It looks like that.
ART.: Okay. How close is this drawing?
SUB.: That's him!
HYP.: That's him. Is that the person? And you'd recognize him anywhere? Okay, very good.
ART.: Very good, great job.
HYP.: Okay, fine. You can just close your eyes again and go very, very relaxed. Just go nice and relaxed back where you were before. Take a good, that's it, a couple of good deep breaths and with each breath that you take just go back and relax, very, very deeply, where you were before, nice and relaxed and that's fine. Okay, very, very relaxed. Okay.

Now you're sitting in the chair in the memory room and you're in front of the TV set and we are going to run this videotape. I'm going to run this videotape, Dee, and at some point in this videotape you're going to see a clear picture of this second man, the one that perhaps was behind you for some of the time. But you'll have an opportunity in the videotape to see the face of this second man clearly and vividly and when that videotape reaches that second man's face, it will automatically stop and freeze on that frame of the second man. You'll be able to look at it, taking all the time in the world, all the time that you need to see that second man's face very clearly and vividly because the videotape will stop completely, freezing that man's face for as long as you need to look at it so that you can see it in all its detail, very accurately, clearly and vividly.

Okay, the videotape is going to run. You don't need to tell me about it, just watch it silently. Watch the videotape silently and when it reaches that second man's face, it will stop automatically. When it does you can allow your left thumb to raise up to let me know that the TV tape has stopped. The frame is frozen on the second man's face and you are looking at it. When that happens your left thumb can come up. And we can run the videotape in fast forward if necessary so it doesn't take quite as long as the actual time frame, alright? Fine, excellent. Okay. Did you want to say something?

SUB.: There's not any face.

HYP.: There's not a face? Okay, your thumb came up. Is the videotape stopped? What is it that you're looking at? What's on the screen? What's on the film?

SUB.: I can see the guy behind her. But I can't, she can't see him.

HYP.: She doesn't have to see him. You can see him. You are watching the film from your chair. Now what are you seeing? You can see more than she can.

SUB.: I can see what he's doing to her.

HYP.: Okay, we're not interested in that unless we can see his face and describe him, such as his size, his build, anything that he says, anything that would be helpful in identifying this person, that's what we want. Okay. Is this a large person, small person, medium size person? Take a good look. Tell me what you see.

SUB.: He's large, like the other man.

HYP.: Is he larger?

SUB.: Maybe a little bit larger. Just a little.

HYP.: A little bit larger than the first man. Okay, about six feet one or two maybe, something like that?

SUB.: Um.

HYP.: You said the first man was about six feet, is that right?

SUB.: Uh huh.

HYP.: And is he taller, heavier, broader? In what way is he larger, would you say?

SUB.: He seems stronger.

HYP.: Uh huh.

SUB.: But I can't see him.

HYP.: Okay, just relax now, just relax. We're going to rewind this videotape. All right we pushed the rewind button, it's going back, rapidly now, all the way back to the beginning. Okay, the machine clicks, it's rewound now. I'm going to push the start button. Okay, it's starting up again, now we're going to put it on fast-forward, now starting right from the beginning. Now, even though it's going fast-forward, you can see these scenes on the TV screen and it will automatically stop and freeze the frame when you can see this second man. Even if it's a split second, when you can see that man, that's all we need because we can freeze that frame in that split second and catch him right there, forever if we want to.

Okay, I'm going to push the fast-forward button so the videotape starts rolling at a faster speed and it will automatically stop when you can see that man's face, and when that stops, your left thumb can come up. It may even stop at an unexpected place, and that's okay. Just a glimpse is all we need to stop it and freeze it right there. Even a split second glance is enough, and we can stop it just like we take his picture with a poloroid camera. Okay, when the videotape runs out, your little finger on your left hand can raise up and let me know that the film has run out. Okay? Fine, you can relax it now. I'm going to push the rewind button once more, and rewind this tape once again. Okay it's rewinding, going all the way back. Okay, it's rewound.

This time, Dee, I'd like you to watch this videotape in slow motion. It's going to play in very, very slow motion. But even though it's in slow motion, it's only going to take two minutes of real time on the clock for this slow motion videotape to play from beginning to end. And I'd like you to pay attention to what is said, to the words and hear them clearly, any words that are said that you'll be able to tell me about. And I'd like you to pay attention to that second man. Any kind of description that you can give from this slow motion videotape about his size, his appearance, his speech, anything like that, you will tell me about as that slow motion tape is going on that particular spot.

Okay, I'm pushing the start button now. It's starting in slow motion and will take about two

	minutes in slow motion for this videotape to play. Okay. And you can just tell me if something is heard, if you hear something on that videotape. Or you can describe that second man in any way, you can tell me about it as it's happening. Okay, the tape is running in slow motion.
SUB.:	She can feel how strong he is.
HYP.:	Okay. Is she hearing words?
SUB.:	They're talking to each other by she can't...it's like whispers.
HYP.:	Okay. Let me turn the volume on the TV set up very, very high so that those low whispers become louder and louder as you're watching the videotape. Okay, the volume is way up now and see what you can hear and what they are whispering to each other. Maybe she can't hear it, but I'm turning the volume on the TV set up so that perhaps you can hear it. Okay.
SUB.:	It sounds like when your mouth is wet...
HYP.:	Uh huh.
SUB.:	And you make, when you're talking, when you're mouthing something you can hear the lips coming together.
HYP.:	Um hum.
SUB.:	And you can hear air coming out, but you can't make out what they're saying.
HYP.:	Okay, that's fine. That's fine, that's very good. Okay. The tape is continuing in slow motion and at any time now it's going to end very shortly. Any time now that you can see from where you're sitting in the chair, a description of the second person, from his build, his face, anything like that, you tell me what you're seeing.
SUB.:	The guy behind her does say one thing to her that...
HYP.:	Yes...
SUB.:	It's real dirty.
HYP.:	Okay, we don't need to go into that if it's not going to be helpful.
SUB.:	He doesn't have um, any detectible Negro dialect type, but he's strong.
HYP.:	Um hum.
SUB.:	And he's big. Sexually and physically.
HYP.:	Um hum.

TRANSCRIPT OF A HYPNOSIS SESSION

SUB.: And she can feel the hair on his legs.
HYP.: Okay. Okay, is she aware of a smell or odor from either of these two guys?
SUB.: From the guy in front. He's wearing a cologne.
HYP.: Okay, what does that cologne smell like?
SUB.: Um, it's, comes in a blue bottle.
HYP.: Comes in a blue bottle?
SUB.: Um hum.
HYP.: Is it a men's cologne?
SUB.: Um hum.
HYP.: And you've smelled it before?
SUB.: Um hum.
HYP.: And would you remember the name of the cologne?
SUB.: Um hum.
HYP.: Okay. I'm going to stop the frame. I'm going to run this videotape back and stop the frame on the first man again, the first man that was in front of Dee. Okay, and I'd like you to take a look at this first man and look at this first man's penis and tell me if he's circumsized or not. Okay, we're going to stop the frame on that particular picture of this first man. Okay, now take a look, the light is shining from the boardwalk and you can see him very clearly and tell me whether or not he's circumsized.
SUB.: No, he's not.
HYP.: He's not, okay. Okay fine, excellent, very good. Is there anything else that you saw on the several runs through of the videotape that we did not talk about before that you should mention?
SUB.: The first guy had on a jacket.
HYP.: Okay. Would you describe the jacket. Let's go back to that frame again with the jacket, with this first guy and we'll freeze the frame right there and you can take a good long look at it, as long as you need to describe it.
SUB.: He had on a plaid shirt.
HYP.: Okay.
SUB.: The jacket was like, um, the Air Force-style type jackets that zipped up the front, with a curved collar. But I don't know whether it's leather or whether it's, that shiny, vinyl-type material.
HYP.: It's either leather or vinyl. . .

SUB.:	Um.
HYP.:	What color is it?
SUB.:	It's dark, either dark green or black.
HYP.:	Dark green or black, but it looks Air Force-type to you.
SUB.:	Um.
HYP.:	Does that mean it has pockets. Slash pockets or patch pockets?
SUB.:	Um hum.
HYP.:	Slash pockets. Okay. And the color, take a look at the plaid shirt and tell me what the colors are in the shirt. Take a good long look at it. Do you see the colors? Okay.
SUB.:	The base color is white or creme color.
HYP.:	Okay.
SUB.:	And it's small. Small plaids.
HYP.:	Small plaids, okay. What about the other colors.
SUB.:	There are several.
HYP.:	Okay, which one is most outstanding?
SUB.:	Blue.
HYP.:	Blue is the most outstanding and it's mixed with other colors?
SUB.:	Um hum.
HYP.:	Okay. What's the next most noticeable color after the blue?
SUB.:	Red.
HYP.:	Blue, red, okay, and a couple of others?
SUB.:	Green.
HYP.:	Green, okay, fine. Okay, take a look at his trousers. What kind of pants is he wearing?
SUB.:	Jeans.
HYP.:	Jeans? Are they blue, or what color are the jeans?
SUB.:	They're faded.
HYP.:	Faded? Are they blue jeans or some other color?
SUB.:	Um hum.
HYP.:	Faded blue jeans?
SUB.:	Um hum.
HYP.:	Okay, take a look at his shoes. What do his shoes look like? No? That's okay, only if it's clear to you do I want you to describe it. That's okay, that's fine. Very, very good. Anything else now that you noticed on those runs through that you would like to mention, aside from the things that you have? And you're doing a fantastically good job and I'm

TRANSCRIPT OF A HYPNOSIS SESSION

very, very pleased. Anything else that you want to mention that you saw on those three runs through, Dee? Okay, fantastic. Okay, just relax now. Just let yourself relax, just go relaxed, real deeply relaxed. Take a good deep breath, good deep breath, and just go nice and pleasantly relaxed.

Okay, you're no longer in the memory room, you're out of there. You're back here in this room, you're feeling very, very secure and comfortable and normal in every way. Later on you will feel that this has been a very interesting and helpful experience to you and you may find, Dee, as many people do, that you will be able to deal with that very unpleasant, traumatic event much better in the future for having reviewed it this way.

You may find yourself sleeping better, feeling more relaxed and more comfortable with yourself. And any guilt feelings that you may have experienced for whatever reason will diminish because you will realize that what happened was not your responsibility, that it happened and could happen to anyone in certain circumstances. And that you don't need to feel guilty about it and that that experience did not change you in any negative way, that you are still the same person that you were before, just as worthwhile and valuable as you were before that experience happened and that those people didn't touch your inner self at all.

You're still the same person that you were before. And you may feel better physically and emotionally and spiritually and be able to come to terms with this experience in a way that you can feel comfortable with and feel secure about and that will be fine. And I think you'll find too that as this investigative process continues, you'll feel strong and up to it and able to cooperate with the investigators in a constructive way so that justice will be done in this particular case and that you can feel good about having played a very helpful role in that process, and that will be fine.

Okay, in just a moment I'm going to count up the the letter "E" and when I do, you can open your eyes and become fully alert and awake, out of the

hypnotic state, feeling clear-headed, refreshed, relaxed, perfectly normal in every way. Feeling good, having had a very interesting and good experience. The image of the suspect that you had in mind, you may keep in mind and this will have just merely refreshed your memory and as you said, you'll be able to recognize this person anywhere should you see him or his photograph or anything like that without any doubt. "A", coming alert slowly, "B", more and more awake, "C", more and more alert, "D", more and more, and "E", eyes opening, feeling very comfortable and good. Well, that was hypnosis. Now what do you think about that?

SUB.: It's weird, like living a dream.
HYP.: And yet you knew everything that was happening, didn't you?
SUB.: Yeah, but I didn't have that much control over it, as I thought I would.
HYP.: Well, you really did because a couple of times you gave indications of discomfort and I would rather have that.
SUB.: Yeah.
HYP.: But you feel pretty relaxed don't you?
SUB.: Um hum.
HYP.: Yes, that's how you feel as a result of hypnosis, very calm and relaxed. Any questions?
SUB.: I feel better.
HYP.: Yes, I think you did an excellent job. Okay? Do you have anything else? I'm going to turn this off at this point. This finishes the session at approximately 1522 p.m.; we started about 1345 this afternoon.

SAMPLE FORMS

The attached questionnaire is designed to elicit information regarding the use of hypnosis as an investigative tool and to assist in upgrading the Department's hypnosis program.

This questionnaire pertains to the hypnosis session conducted on _____ by _____.
The Investigator(s) who requested the session was
_____/_____
Type of crime _____
DR Number _____
Subject's name _____
It will be of great assistance if the concerned investigator would return the complete questionnaire within 10 days to:

Thank you for your cooperation.

1. To what degree do you estimate the subject was actually hypnotized?
   A. Not at all _____   C. Medium state _____
   B. Light state _____   D. Deep state _____
2. To what degree was the memory of the witness improved as a result of being hypnotized?
   A. Not at all _____   C. Moderately _____
   B. Slightly _____   D. Significantly _____
3. To what degree was any additional information elicited when the witness was in a state of hypnosis?
   A. None at all _____
   B. Some additional information _____
   C. Moderate amount of information _____
   D. A great deal of information _____
4. If any information was obtained as a result of hypnosis, either during, immediately after, or at some later date, how valuable do you feel that information was to the case investigator?
   _____ Extremely valuauble
   _____ Very valuable
   _____ Of some value
   _____ Of little value
   _____ Of no value
   _____ No new information was obtained
5. If any new information was obtained through hypnosis, how accurate was that information found to be?
   ___ Extremely accurate   ___ Inaccurate
   ___ Very accurate   ___ Accuracy unable to
   ___ Somewhat accurate   be determined
   ___ Not very accurate
6. Was the case solved?
   Yes _____   No _____
7. If the case was solved, how much value do you give to the information obtained through the use of hypnosis?
   _____ The case probably wouldn't have been solved without it
   _____ Extremely valuable
   _____ Very valuable

SAMPLE FORMS

_____ Of some value
_____ Of little value
_____ Of no value
_____ No new information was obtained

8. The subject's reaction to having participated in the Investigative Hypnosis Program was:

   A. Wished he hadn't _____
   B. Developed negative emotional after effects _____
   C. Felt emotionally relieved _____
   D. Derived significant emotional benefit _____
   E. Unknown _____

9. Would you recommend the contunued use of hypnosis as an investigative tool?

   Yes_____   No_____   (If yes, how many?_____)

11. How did you first become aware of the Department's hypnosis program?

    _____ A Department training session
    _____ A written Department notice
    _____ Word-of-mouth from other investigators
    _____ From a Department supervisor
    _____ Other (Specify)_____

12. If the use of hypnosis saved you time (investigative man-hours), please estimate how many.

    _____

13. Do you have an opinion, suggestion or recommendation regarding the Department's hypnosis program (Use the reverse side of this page if necessary).

    _____
    _____

14. If hypnosis assisted in the case being solved, please relate what part it played.

    _____
    _____
    _____
    _____
    _____

Investigator completing this questionnaire_____
_____ SERIAL _____
DATE _____ DIVISION _____
TELEPHONE _____

SAMPLE RELEASE FORM

I hereby agree, voluntarily and freely, to undergo hypnosis and interrogation under hypnosis in order to assist the personnel of the _____ Department with an investigation process.

I hereby waive any claim of injury or harmful effects in connection with this procedure.

NAME (Printed)_____
SIGNATURE _____ DATE _____
ADDRESS _____
              _____
WITNESS _____

CASE DATA SHEET

Date of Assignment_____
Hypnotechnician(s)_____
              _____
Case Investigator(s)_____
              _____
Case DR Number_____
Type of Crime_____
Date of Occurrence of Crime_____
Name of Witness or Victim Hypnotized_____
    Age _____

SAMPLE FORMS

Sex _____
Occupation _____
Previous Hypnosis   Yes_____   No_____
Nature of Involvement in Case_____
_____
_____

Reason for Hypnosis Referral (information desired)_____
_____

Additional or unusual factors in the case_____
_____
_____

Tape Number_____
Hypnosis Session Number_____
Date of Session_____
Time of Session_____
Approximate Length of Session_____
Persons Present During Session_____
_____

Information eliciting techniques utilized_____
_____

Estimated level of trance achieved
         light   medium   deep
Was new information obtained as a result of hypnosis?
    yes_____   no_____
If yes, explain in detail_____
_____

Hypnotechnician's evaluation of session
    extremely valuable   of no value
1   2   3   4   5
Comment: _____
_____

Case Outcome: _____
_____

If this was a repeat session with the subject, was additional information obtained? _____
_____

227

HANDBOOK OF INVESTIGATIVE HYPNOSIS

INVESTIGATIVE HYPNOSIS REPORT

CRIME DATA

TYPE OF CRIME	DATE & TIME OF OCCURRENCE	D.R. NUMBER
INVESTIGATORS		AREA, TEAM, EXTENSION

CRIME SUMMARY (INCLUDE INFORMATION DESIRED FROM SUBJECT)

SUBJECT DATA

NAME	SEX	DESCENT	DATE OF BIRTH	AGE
RESIDENCE ADDRESS	PHONE		OCCUPATION	
BUSINESS ADDRESS	PHONE		PRIOR HYPNOSIS ☐ YES ☐ NO	

NATURE OF INVOLVEMENT (INCLUDE UNUSUAL FACTORS & PRIOR HYPNOSIS DATA)

HYPNOSIS DATA

DATE & TIME OF SESSION	LOCATION	TAPE NUMBER	LENGTH OF SESSION
OPERATOR		RECORDER	

PERSONS PRESENT DURING SESSION

INDUCTION TECHNIQUES UTILIZED

DEEPENING TECHNIQUES UTILIZED

POST HYPNOTIC SUGGESTIONS GIVEN

ESTIMATED LEVEL OF TRANCE ☐ LIGHT ☐ MEDIUM ☐ DEEP ☐ NO HYPNOSIS INDUCED

HYPNOTECHNICIAN'S EVALUATION OF SESSION   VALUABLE 1 2 3 4 5 NO VALUE

ADDITIONAL COMMENTS (INCLUDE CASE OUTCOME IF KNOWN)

SAMPLE FORMS

INVESTIGATIVE HYPNOSIS REPORT (PAGE 2)

DATE OF HYPNOSIS SESSION	SUBJECT	D.R. NUMBER

HYPNOSIS INFORMATION SUMMARY

		Pre-Hypnosis	During Hypnosis	Verification
SUSPECT DATA	SEX			
	AGE			
	RACE			
	HEIGHT			
	WEIGHT			
	HAIR			
	EYES			
	CLOTHING			
	PHYSICAL ODDITIES			
	COMPOSITE MADE			
VEHICLE DATA	MAKE			
	YEAR			
	BODY STYLE			
	COLOR			
	LICENSE NO			
	EXTERIOR ODDITIES			
	INTERIOR ODDITIES			
WEAPON USED				
ADDITIONAL				

NOTE Use a separate summary page for each suspect involved

INVESTIGATIVE HYPNOSIS SURVEY
Date_____

1. Agency Name _____
2. Number of investigative hypnotists in your agency _____
3. What is the total number of cases in which your agency has utlized investigative hypnosis by law enforcement personnel? _____

4. Has your agency experienced reaction from the press? ___

5. Has your agency experienced positive reaction from the press? _____

6. Has your agency experienced adverse reaction from the public? _____

7. Has your agency experienced positive reaction from the public? _____

8. Has any subject claimed any adverse affects from hypnosis? _____
   If so, please explain. _____

9. Indicate the results gained through hypnosis: _____

10. In **each** case to what degree was any additional information elicited when the witness was in a state of hypnosis?

None at all _____
Some additional information _____
Moderate amount of information _____
A great deal of information _____

11. In **each** case, if any information was obtained as a result of hypnosis, either during, immediately after, or at some later date, how valuable do you feel that information was to the case investigator?

   ____ Extremely valuable   ____ Not very accurate
   ____ Very accurate   ____ Inaccurate
   ____ Somewhat accurate   ____ Accuracy unable to determined

13. Was the case solved?
    Yes _____   No _____

14. If the case was solved, how much value do you give to the information obtained through the use of hypnosis.

    ____ The case probably wouldn't have been solved without it
    ____ Extremely valuable   ____ Of little value
    ____ Very valuable   ____ Of no value
    ____ Of some value   ____ No new information was obtained

15. Comments: _____
    _____
    _____

Glossary

Abreaction - Emotional release or discharge resulting from bringing to awareness a painful or traumatic experience that had been forgotten (repressed).
Ambivalence - coexistence of two opposing drives or emotions toward the same person or goal. May be conscious or unconscious.
Amnesia - loss of memory.
    anterograde - amnesia for events after a significant point in time.
    retrograde - amnesia for events before a significant point in time.
Analgesia - absence of pain sensations.
Anesthesia - absense of sensation.
Apperception - perception as modified and enhanced by the individual's own emotions, memories and biases.
Association - relationship between ideas or emotions by contiguity, continuity or similarity.
Autonomic Nervous System - include sympathetic and parasympathetic divisions and innervates the cardiovascular, digestive, reproductive and respiratory systems - usually operates outside of conscious awareness.
Auto-hypnosis - self-hypnosis as opposed to hetero-hypnosis, induced by another person.
Catalepsy - generalized condition of diminished responsiveness. Small and large muscles get rigid and may remain in same position.
Central Nervous System - brain and spinal cord.
Cognitive - mental process of comprehension, judgment, memory and reasoning. Contrasts with emotional processes.
Confabulation - filling of memory gaps with imagined or distorted information.
Countertransference - the operator's conscious or unconscious emotional reaction to the subject, based on early family relationships.

GLOSSARY

De-hypnotization - assisting a subject from a hypnotic to a non-hypnotic normally alert state.

Dissociation - unconscious process which separates emotion and idea. May also refer to different ego states as in multiple personality or the altered states of consciousness in hypnosis.

Eidetic Image - unusually vivid and exact mental image; may be memory, fantasy or dream.

Hallucination - a false sensory perception.

Hypermnesia - greatly heightened memory and recall - opposite of amnesia.

Hypnoidal - light state of hypnosis akin to a reverie state.

Hypnosis - a state of increased receptivity to suggestion characterized by an altered state of consciousness. The degree varies from very light to very deep and usually includes relaxation.

Ideomotor - capability of muscles to respond immediately to thoughts, feelings and suggestions.

Indirect Suggestion - suggestion given in symbolic, metaphoric or analogic form.

Induction - the process of going into hypnosis or assisting someone into a hypnotic state.

Intrapsychic - that which takes place within the psyche or mind.

Kinesics - the study of body movement as a part of the process of communication.

Labile - pertaining to shifting emotions; unstable.

Mesmerism - an early term for hypnosis named after Anton Mesmer (1733-1815).

Misdirection of Attention - appearing to be focusing on one area with the intention of directing the subject into another.

Neurosis (psychoneurosis) - an emotional maladaptation arising from unresolved unconscious conflicts.

Post-hypnotic suggestion - a suggestion given during hypnosis to be carried out by the subject after being de-hypnotized.

Pre-inductive warmup - preparation before induction of hypnosis - includes explanation of hypnosis process and discussion of myths and misinformation.

Preconscious - thoughts not in immediate awareness but subject to recall.

Rapport feeling of confidence, trust and mutuality in the hypnotist-subject relationship.

Recall the process of bringing a memory into consciousness.

Regression - a partial or symbolic return to earlier times or patterns of reacting.

Repression - a defense mechanism, operating unconsciously that keeps unacceptable ideas, or emotions from consciousness.

Resistance - the subject's conscious or unconscious defense against bringing repressed material to light.

Screen Memory - a consciously tolerable memory that serves as a cover or screen for another associated memory that would be disturbing or painful if recalled.

Somnabulism - very deep state of hypnosis often with lessened responsiveness.

Subconscious - term that refers to preconscious and unconscious levels of the mind.

Suggestion - process of influencing an individual to accept less critically an idea, belief or attitude induced by the hypnotist.

Suppression - the conscious effort to control and conceal unacceptable thoughts, feelings or acts.

Trance - a state of diminished activity and consciousness.

Transference - the unconscious assignment of feelings and thoughts to others that were originally associated with important figures in one's early life.

Trauma - an extremely upsetting emotional experience.

BIBLIOGRAPHY

Adams, P. *The New Self-Hypnosis.* North Hollywood, California: Wilshire Book Company, 1978.
Allen, A.L. *Personal Descriptions.* London: Butterworth and Company, 1950.
Allison, H.C. *Personal Identification.* Boston: Holbrook Press, 1973.
Anderson, P.B. Murder suspect accused of vice motive at trial. *Los Angeles Times,* November 13, 1976.
Arons, H. *Hypnosis in Criminal Investigation.* Springfield, Illinois: Thomas, 1967.
A Syllabus on Hypnosis and a Handbook of Therapeutic Suggestions. Des Plaines, Illinois: American Society of Clinical Hypnosis, 1973.
Atal, B. Speech analysis and synthesis by linear prediction of the speech wave. *Journal of the Acoustical Society of America,* August 1971, 637-655.
Award winners for 1977. *The Police Chief,* December 1977, P. 22.
Baddeley, A.D. *The Psychology of Memory.* New York: Basic Books, 1976.
Barbara, D.A. *Your Speech Reveals Your Personality.* Springfield, Illinois: Thomas, 1958.
Barber, T.X. The concept of hypnosis. *Journal of Psychology,* 1958, *45,* 115-131.
Barber, T.X. Death by suggestion. *Psychosomatic Medicine,* 1961, *23,* 153-156.
Barber, T.X. *Hypnosis: A Scientific Approach.* New York: Van Nostrand Reinhold Company, 1969.
Barber, T.X., Spanos, N.P. and Chaves, J.F. *Hypnosis, Imagination and Human Potentialities.* New York: Pergamon Press, 1974.
Bard, M. and Ellison, K. Crisis intervention and investigation of forcible rape. *The Police Chief,* May 1974, 68-73.
Baudouin, C. *Suggestion and Auto Suggestion.* New York: Dodd Mead, 1922.
Beier, E.G. and Valens, E.G. *People-Reading.* New York: Stein and Day, 1975.
Benson, H. *The Relaxation Response.* New York: Morrow, 1975.
Berg, S. and Melin, E. Hypnotic susceptibility in old age. Some date from residential homes for old people. *International Journal of Clinical and Experimental Hypnosis,* 1975, *23,* 184-189.
Berne, E. *Transactional Analysis in Psychotherapy.* New York: Grove Press, 1961.
Berne, E. *Games People Play.* New York: Grove Press, 1964.
Bernheim, H. *Hypnosis and Suggestion in Psychotherapy.* New York: University Books, 1964.
Bernstein, L. Bernstein, R.S. and Dana, R.H. *Interviewing: A Guide for Health Professionals.* New York: Appleton-Century Crofts, 1974.
Bingham, W.V. and Moore, B.V. *How to Interview.* New York: Harper, 1959.
Biological Rhythms in Psychiatry and Medicine. Chevy Chase, Maryland: National Institute of Mental Health, 1970.
Birdwhistell, R.L. *Kinesics and Context.* Philadelphia: University of Pennsylvania Press, 1970.

Botwinick, J. *Cognitive Processes in Maturity and Old Age.* New York: Springer, 1967.
Bowers, K.S. *Hypnosis for the Seriously Curious.* New York: Jason Aronson, 1977.
Bowers, M. Hypnotic aspects of Haitian voodoo. *International Journal of Clinical and Experimental Hypnosis,* 1961, g, 269-283.
Bowers, P. Hypnotizability, creativity and the role of effortless experiencing. *International Journal of Clinical and Experimental Hypnosis,* 1978, 26, 184-201.
Braid, J. *Neurypnology.* New York: Arno Books, 1976.
Breuer, J. and Freud, S. *Studies in Hysteria.* New York: Nervous and Mental Disease Monographs, 1950.
Brodsky, S. *Psychological Training Techniques in Law Enforcement and Corrections.* Ann Arbor, Michigan: Center for Forensic Psychiatry, 1970.
Bromberg, W. *From Shaman to Psychotherapist.* Chicago: Regnery, 1975.
Brown, E., Deffenbacher, K. and Sturgill, W. Memory for faces and the circumstances of encounter. *Journal of Applied Psychology,* 1977, 62, 311-318.
Bryan, W.J. *Legal Aspects of Hypnosis.* Springfield, Illinois: Thomas, 1962.
Buckout, R. Eyewitness testimony. *Scientific American,* December 1974, 23-31.
Burch, G.W. *Hypnosis, An Aid to Police Interrogations.* Master's Thesis, California State University, Long Beach, June 1974.
Burgess, A.W. and Holstrom, L.L. Rape trauma syndrome. *American Journal of Psychiatry.* September 1974, 981-986.
Burgess, A.W. and Holstrom, L.L. *Rape: Victims of Crisis.* Bowie, Maryland: Robert J. Brady Company, 1974.
Burgess, A.W. and Holstrom, L.L. Sexual trauma of children and adolescents. *Nursing Clinics of North America,* September 1975, 551-563.
Burgess, A.W. and Holstrom, L.L. Coping behavior of the rape victim. *American Journal of Psychiatry,* April 1976, 413-418.
Burns, A. Changes in hypnotizability following experience. *International Journal of Clinical and Experimental Hypnosis,* 1976, 24, 269-279.
Cameron, N. *Personality Development and Psychopathology.* Boston: Houghtan Mifflin, 1963.
Campbell, B. Hypnotist's role tops testimony. *Lubbock Avalanche-Journal (Texas),* April 1979.
Cannon, W. *The Wisdom of the Body.* New York: Norton, 1939.
Caprio, F.S. and Berger, J.R. *Helping Yourself with Self-Hypnosis.* Englewood Cliffs, New Jersey: Prentice-Hall, 1963.
Charcot, J.M. *Lectures on the Diseases of the Nervous System.* London: New Sydenham Society, 1877.
Cheek, D.B. Unconscious perception of meaningful sounds during surgical anesthesia as revealed under hypnosis. *American Journal of Clinical Hypnosis,* 1959, 1, 101-113.
Cheek, D.B. and Le Cron, L.M. *Clinical Hypnotherapy.* New York: Grune & Stratton, 1968.
Conn, J.H. Cultural and clinical aspects of hypnosis, placebos and suggestibility. *International Journal of Clinical and Experimental Hypnosis,* 1959, 7, 1975-186.
Conn, J.H. Is hypnosis really dangerous? *The International Journal of Clinical and Experimental Hypnosis,* 972, 20, 61-79.
Cooper, L.F. and Erickson, M.H. Time distortion in hypnosis. *Experimental Hypnosis* (L.M. LeCron, Ed.). New York: Macmillan, 1952.

BIBLIOGRAPHY

Cooper, L.M. and London, P. Children's hypnotic susceptibility, personality and EEG patterns. *International Journal of Clinical and Experimental Hypnosis,* 1976, *24,* 140-147.

Coué, E. *How to Practice Suggestion and Autosuggestion.* New York: American Library Service, 1923.

Crasilneck, H.B. and Hall, J.A. *Clinical Hypnosis. Principles and Applications.* New York: Grune & Stratton, 1975.

Cumley, W.E. Hypnosis and the polygraph. *Police,* November-December 1959, p. 39.

Daim, W. *Depth Psychology and Salvation.* New York: Ungar Publishing Company, 1963.

Danto, B.L. The use of brevital sodium in police investigation. *The Police Chief,* May 1979, 53-55.

Darnton, R. *Mesmerism.* Cambridge, Massachusetts: Harvard University Press, 1968.

Davis, R.C. Physiological responses as a means of evaluating information. *The Manipulation of Human Behavior* (A. Biderman and H. Zimmer, Eds.). New York: Wiley, 1961, 142-168.

Deleuze, F. *Histoire Critique du Magnetism, Vol. II.* Pris: Hipolyte and Bailiere, 1812, p. 34.

Dellinger, R.W. Investigative hypnosis. Tapping your cerebral memory banks. *Human Behavior,* April 1978, 36-37.

Dermen, D. and London, P. Correlates of hypnotic susceptibility. *Journal of Consulting Psychology,* 1965, *29,* 537-545.

Derrick, C. Interrogation by hypnosis. *The Police Chief,* March 1959, 26-29.

Dhanens, T.P. and Lundy, R.M. Hypnotic and waking suggestions and recall. *International Journal of Clinical and Experimental Hypnosis,* 1975, *23,* 68-78.

Dieckmann, E. Hypnosis and crime detection. *Law and Order,* June, 1958, 37-40.

Dilloff, N.J. The admissibility of hypnotically influenced testimony. *Ohio Northern University Law Review,* 1977, *IV,* 1-23.

Dorcus, R.M. *Hypnosis and Its Therapeutic Applications.* New York: McGraw-Hill, 1956.

Dorcus, R.M. Recall under hypnosis of amnestic events. *International Journal of Clinical and Experimental Hypnosis,* 1960, *7,* 57-61.

Duckworth, J. *How to Use Auto-Suggestion Effectively.* North Hollywood, California: Wilshire Book Company, 1972.

Douce, R.G. Hypnosis: a scientific aid in crime detection. *The Police Chief,* May 1979, 60-61, 80.

Duke, J.D. Intercorrelational status of suggestibility tests and hypnotizability. *Psychological Record,* 1964, *14,* 71-80.

Eddy, M.D. *Science and Health With Key to the Scriptures.* Boston: Stewart, 1875.

Edmonston, W.E. Hypnotic age regression. An evaluation of role-taking theory. *American Journal of Clinical Hypnosis,* 1962, *5,* 3-7.

Ehrenreich, G.A. The influence of unconscious factors of hypnotizability. *Clinical Correlates of Experimental Hypnosis.* (M.V. Kline, Ed.). Springfield, Illinois: Thomas, 1963, 136-151.

Ekman, P. and Friesen, M.V. *Unmasking the Face.* Englewood Cliffs, New Jersey: Prentice-Hall, 1975.

Ellen, A. *The Intimate Casebook of a Hypnotist.* New York: New American Library, 1968.

Emotions and Physical Health. Metropolitan Life Insurance Company, 1959.

Erdelyi, M.H. and Kleinbard, J. Has Ebbinghaus decayed with time? The growth of recall (hypermnesia) over days. *Journal of Experimental Psychology: Human Learning and Memory,* 1978, *4,* 275-289.

Erickson, M.H. An experimental investigation of the possible anti-social use of hypnosis. *American Journal of Clinical Hypnosis,* 1958, *1,* 3-9.

Erickson, M.H. The confusion technique in hypnosis. *American Journal of Clinical Hypnosis,* 1964, *6,* 183-207.

Erickson, M.H. Pantomime techniques in hypnosis and the implicatons. *American Journal of Clinical Hypnosis,* 1964, *7,* 64-70.

Erickson, M.H. Deep hypnosis and its induction. *Advanced Techniques of Hypnosis and Therapy* (J. Haley, Ed.). New York: Grune & Stratton, 1967, 7-31.

Erickson, M.H. and Erickson, E.M. Concerning the nature and character of post-hypnotic behavior. *Modern Hypnosis* (L. Kuhn and S. Russo, Eds.). North Hollywood, California: Wilshire Book Company, 1974, 105-142.

Erickson, M.H., Rossi, E.L. and Rossi, S. *Hypnotic Realities. The Induction of Clinical Hypnosis and Forms of Indirect Suggestion.* New York: Irvington Press, 1976.

Erickson, M.H. Personal Communication, April 1978.

Esdaile, J. *Natural and Mesmeric Clairvoyance.* New York: Arno Books, 1975.

Estabrooks, G.H. *Hypnotism.* New York: Dutton, 1957.

Evans, F.J. An experimental indirect technique for the induction of hypnosis without awareness. *International Journal of Clinical and Experimental Hypnosis,* 1967, *15,* 72.

Farr, W. Trio sentenced in brutal rape case. *Los Angeles Times,* July 22, 1976.

Fast, J. *Body Language.* New York: Pocket Books, 1971.

Field, P.B. and Dworkin, S.F. Strategies of hypnotic interrogation. *Journal of Psychology,* 1967, *67,* 47-58.

Fink, D. *For People Under Pressure.* New York: Simon and Schuster, 1956.

Fisher, S. The role of expectancy in the performance of post-hypnotic behavior. *The Nature of Hypnosis* (R.E. Shor and M.T. Orne, Eds.). New York: Holt, Rinehart and Winston, 1965, 80-88.

Floan, K. Hypnosis gains respect as in investigative tool. *Kansas City Times,* December 26, 1977.

Frank, J.D. *Persuasion and Healing: A Comparative Study of Psychotherapy.* Baltimore: Johns Hopkins Press, 1961.

Frank, J. and Levinson, H. Report on non-conscious learning. *Academic Therapy,* Winter 1976-77, 133-153.

Frankel, F. *Hypnosis. Trance as a Coping Mechanism* New York: Plenum Medical Book Company, 1976.

Fricke, C.W. *California Criminal Evidence, 9th Edition.* Los Angeles, California: Legal Book Corporation, 1978.

Fromm, E. and Shor, R.E. (Eds.). *Hypnosis: Research Developments and Perspectives.* New York: Aldine Atherton, 1972.

Fross, G.H. *Handbook of Hypnotic Techniques.* South Orange, New Jersey: Power Publishers, 1974.

Furneaux, W.D. Hypnotic susceptibility as a function of waking susceptibility. *Experimental Hypnosis* (L.M. LeCron, Ed.). Secaucus, New Jersey: Citadel Press, 1972, 115-136.

Galwey, T. *The Inner Game of Tennis.* New York: Random House, 1964.

Gerber, S. Hypnotism - new weapon against crime? *This Week Magazine,* January 25, 1959.

Gerber, S.R. and Schroeder, O. (Eds.). *Criminal Investigation and Interrogation.* New York: W.H. Anderson Company, 1962.

Germann, A.C. Hypnosis as related to the scientific detection of deception by polygraph examination: a pilot study. *International Journal of Clinical and Experimental Hypnosis,* 1961, *9,* 309-311.

Gill, M.M. and Brenman, M. Hypnosis and Related States: *Psychoanalytic Studies in Regression.* New York: International Universities Press, 1959.

Gill, M.M. and Brenman, M. Data on the nature of the hypnotist. *The Nature of Hypnosis* (Shor, R.E. and Orne, M.T., Eds.). New York: Holt, Rinehart and Winston, 1965, 448-452.

Gill, M.M. Hypnosis as an altered and regressed state. *International Journal of Clinical and Experimental Hypnosis,* 1972, *20,* 224-237.

Goffman, E. *Interaction Ritual.* Garden City, New York: Anchor Books, 1967.

Gottschalk, L.A. The use of drugs in interrogation. *The Manipulation of Human Behavior* (A. Biderman and H. Zimmer, Eds.). New York: Wiley, 1961, 96-141.

Gruneberg, M.M., Morris, P.E. and Sykes, R.N. (Eds.). *Practical Aspects of Memory.* New York: Academic Press, 1978.

Haley, J. (Ed.). *Advanced Techniques of Hypnosis and Therapy. Selected Papers of Milton H. Erickson.* New York: Grune & Stratton, 1967.

Hammerschlag, H. *Hypnotism and Crime.* Los Angeles: Wilshire Book Company, 1957.

Hanley, F.W. Hypnosis in the court room. *Canadian Psychiatric Association Journal,* 1969, *14,* 351-354.

Harding V. State of Maryland. 246A. 2d 302 (Oct. 9, 1968).

Harris, T. *I'm OK, You're OK.* New York: Avon Books, 1967.

Hartland, J. *Medical and Dental Hypnosis.* Baltimore: Williams and Wilkins, 1971.

Hassel, C. The hostage situation: exploring the motivation and the cause. *The Police Chief,* September 1975, 55-58.

Hatton, K.L. Hypnosis takes hold as a legitimate police tool. *The Plain Dealer* (Cleveland), February 13, 1978.

H.B. 3125. Oregon Legislature, June 1977.

Hilgard, E.R. *Introduction to Psychology.* New York: Harcourt, Brace and World, 1962.

Hilgard, E.R. and Lauer, L.W. Lack of correlation between the CPI and hypnotic susceptibility. *Journal of Consulting Psychology,* 1962, *26,* 331-335.

Hilgard, E.R. *The Experience of Hypnosis.* New York: Harcourt, Brace and World, 1965.

Hilgard, E.R. *Hypnotic Susceptibility.* New York: Harcourt, Brace and World, 1965.

Hilgard, E.R. A critique of Johnson, Maher and Barber's "Artifact in the essence of hypnosis: an evaluation of trance logic." *Journal of Advanced Psychology,* 1972, *79,* 221-233.

Hilgard, E.R. The domain of hypnosis with some comments on alternative paradigms. *American Psychologist,* November 1973, 972-982.

Hilgard, E.R. and Hilgard, J.R. *Hypnosis in the Relief of Pain.* Los Altos, California: William Kaufman, Inc., 1975.

Hilgard, E.R. *Divided Consciousness.* New York: Wiley Interscience, 1977.

Hilgard, E.R. Personal Communication, March 1979.

Hilgard, J.R. *Personality and Hypnosis: A Study of Imaginative Involvement.* Chicago: University of Chicago Press, 1970.

Hollander, E.P. and Hunt, R. *Current Perspectives in Social Psychology.* New York: Oxford University Press, 1963.

Hull, C.L. *Hypnosis and Suggestibility: An Experimental Approach.* New York: Appleton-Century, 1933.

Hypno-induced statements: safeguards for admissibility. *Law and the Social Order,* 1970, 99-120.

Hypnosis for witnesses. *Newsweek,* August 5, 1974.

Jacobson, E. *Anxiety and Tension Control.* Philadelphia: Lippincott, 1964.

Jacobson, E. *Modern Treatment of Tense Patients.* Springfield, Illinois: Thomas, 1970.

Janet, P. *The Major Symptoms of Hysteria.* New York: Macmillan, 1907.

Janet, P. *Psychological Healing.* London: Allen and Unwin, 1925, p. 346.

Jersild, A.T. *Child Psychology.* Englewood Cliffs, New Jersey: Prentice Hall, 1960.

Johnson, A. Hypnosis and the law: a meeting of the minds. *Prosecutor's Brief,* March-April 1978, 34-36.

Johnson, L.K. *Memory Loss With Age: A Storage or Retrieval Problem?* Presented at the Gerontological Society, San Juan, Puerto Rico, Dicember 1972.

Kahn, R.L. *The Dynamics of Interviewing: Theory, Techniques and Cases.* New York: Wiley, 1957.

Kauss, L. Hypnosis jogs the subconscious memory and is gaining importance as a tool for criminal investigation. *The Phoenix Gazette,* December 1, 1978.

Kendall, J. Attacked airline employees arrive to view L.A. lineup. *Los Angeles Times,* September 23, 1977.

Kimmel, D.C. *Adulthood and Aging.* New York: Wiley, 1974.

King, Lt. R. Personal Communications.

Kline, M.V. *Freud and Hypnosis: The Interaction of Psychodynamics and Hypnosis.* New York: Julian Press, 1958.

Kline, M.V. Hypnotic regression: a neuropsychological theory of age regression and progression. *Clinical Correlates of Experimental Hypnosis* (M.V. Kline, Ed.). Springfield, Illinois: Thomas, 1963, 452-462.

Kline, M.V. *Psychodynamics and Hypnosis.* Springfield, Illinois: Thomas, 1967.

Kline, M.V. The production of anti-social behavior through hypnosis: new clinical data. *International Journal of Clinical and Experimental Hypnosis,* April 1972, 80-94.

Kline, M.V. *Clinical Correlates of Experimental Hypnosis.* Springfield, Illinois: Thomas, 1963.

Kline V. Ford Motor Co., Inc. 523 F. 2d 1067 (1975).

Kradz, M.P. *Psychological Stress Evaluator: A Study.* Ellicott City, Maryland: Howard County Police Department, 1971.

Kroger, W.S. and Fezler, W.D. *Hypnosis and Behavior Modification: Imagery Conditioning.* Philadelphia: Lippincott, 1976.

Kroger, W.S. *Clinical and Experimental Hypnosis, 2nd Edition.* Philadelphia: Lippincott, 1977.

Krystal, H. (Ed.). *Massive Psychic Trauma.* New York: International Universities Press, 1968.

Kubie, L.A. and Margolin, S. The process of hypnotism and the nature of the hypnotic state. *The Nature of Hypnosis* (Shor, R.E. and Orne, M.T., Eds.). New York: Holt, Rinehart & Winston, 1965, 217-233.

Kuhns, B. *A Study in the Use of Hypnosis to Subvert Polygraph Findings.* Unpublished Doctoral Dissertation, Newport International University, August 1978.

LaScola, R. Hypnosis with children. *Clinical Hypnotherapy* (D.B. Cheek and L.M. LeCron, Eds.). New York: Grune & Stratton, 1968, 201-211.

Lazarus, R.S. *Psychological Stress and the Coping Process.* New York: McGraw-Hill, 1966.

BIBLIOGRAPHY

LeCron, L.M. *Self-Hypnotism.* Englewood Cliffs, New Jersey: Prentice Hall, 1964.

LeCron, L.M. and Bordeaux, J. *Hypnotism Today.* North Hollywood, California: Wilshire Book Company, 1972.

LeCron, L.M. A study of age regression under hypnosis. *Experimental Hypnosis* (L.M. LeCron, Ed.). Secaucus, New Jersey: The Citadel Press, 1972, 426-438.

LeCron, L.M. *Experimental Hypnosis.* Secaucus, New Jersey: Citadel Press, 1972.

Leitner, K. *Scientific Hypnotism for Professionals.* New York: Stravon, 1953.

Levendula, D. The possible use of hypnosis in criminal investigation. *Criminal Investigation and Interrogation (S.R. Gerber, Ed.).* New York: W.H. Anderson Company, 1962, 335-346.

Levi, L. *Stress: Sources, Management and Prevention.* New York: Liveright, 1967.

Levinson, H. *Emotional Health in the World of Work.* New York: Harper and Row, 1964.

Levitt, E. et al. Testing the coercive power of hypnosis: committing objectionable acts. *International Journal of Clinical and Experimental Hypnosis,* January 1975, 59-66.

Lewis, H.R. and Lewis, M.E. *Psychosomatics.* New York: Viking, 1972.

London, P. *The Childrens' Hypnotic Susceptibility Scale.* Palo Alto, California: Consulting Psychologists Press, 1962.

London, P. and Cooper, L.M. Norms of hypnotic susceptibility in children. *Developmental Psychology,* 1969, *1,* 113-124.

London, P. and McDevitt, R. Effects of hypnotic susceptibility and training in response to stress. *Mental Health Digest,* May 1971, 39-43.

Lozanov, G. *Suggestology and Outlines of Suggestopedy.* New York: Gordon and Breach, 1978.

Luria, A.R. *The Working Brain.* New York: Basic Books, 1973.

Luthe, W. and Schultz, J.H. *Autogenic Therapy, Vol. I.* New York: Grune & Stratton, 1969.

Magonet, P. *Practical Hypnotism.* North Hollywood, California: Wilshire Book Company, 1957.

Maltz, M. *Psychocybernetics.* New York: Prentice Hall, 1960.

Marcuse, F.L. *Hypnosis: Fact and Fiction.* New York: Pelican, 1959.

Marks, J. *The Search for the "Manchurian Candidate." The CIA and Mind Control.* New York: Times Books, 1979.

McCleary, R.A. and Moor, R. *Subcortical Mechanisms of Behavior.* New York: Basic Books, 1965.

McCormick, C.T. *Handbook of the Law of Evidence, 2nd Edition.* St. Paul, Minnesota: West Publishing Company, 1972.

Meares, A. *A System of Medical Hypnosis.* Philadelphia: Saunders, 1960.

Meerloo, J. *The Rape of the Mind: The Psychology of Thought Control, Menticide and Brainwashing.* New York: World, 1956.

Melie, J.P. and Hilgard, E.R. Attitudes toward hypnosis, self predictions and hypnotic susceptibility. *International Journal of Clinical and Experimental Hypnosis,* 1964, *12,* 99-108.

Menninger, K., et al. *The Vital Balance.* New York: Viking Press, 1963.

Mental Illness and Law Enforcement. St. Louis, Missouri: Washington University, 1970.

Milwee, S.C. The hypnosis unit in today's law enforcement. *The Police Chief,* May 1979, 65-70.

Missildine, W.H. *Your Inner Child of the Past.* New York: Simon and Schuster, 1963.

Montgomery, J. The psychological stress evaluator in truth verification. *Assets Protection*, 1978, *3*, No. 1, 6-13.

Moore, R. and Lauer, L. Hypnotic susceptibility in middle childhood. *International Journal of Clinical and Experimental Hypnosis*, 1963, *11*, 167-174.

Moore, R.K. Susceptibility to hypnosis and susceptibility to social influence. *Journal of Abnormal and Social Psychology*, 1964, *68*, 282-294.

Morgan, A.H. and Hilgard, E.R. Age differences in susceptibility to hypnosis. *International Journal of Clinical and Experimental Hypnosis*, 1973, *21*, 78-85.

Mühl, A.M. Automatic writing and hypnosis. *Experimental Hypnosis* (L.M. LeCron, Ed.). Secaucus, New Jersey: The Citadel Press, 1972, 426-438.

Munsterberg, H. *On the Witness Stand*, 1908.

Nielsen, Captain M. Personal Communications.

Nilsson, L.G. (Ed.). *Perspectives on Memory Research*. Hillsdale, New Jersey: Lawrence Erlbaum Associates, 1979.

Notman, M.T. and Nadelson, C.C. The rape victim: psychodynamic considerations. *American Journal of Psychiatry*, April 1976, 408-412.

Olness, K. and Gardner, G.G. Some guidelines for uses of hypnotherapy in pediatrics. *Pediatrics*, 1978, *62*, 228-233.

Orne, M.T. The mechanisms of hypnotic age regression. *Journal of Abnormal and Social Psychology*, 1951, *46*, 213-225.

Orne, M.T. The nature of hypnosis: artifact and essence. *Journal of Abnormal and Social Psychology*, 1959, *58*, 277-299.

Orne, M.T. The potential uses of hypnosis in interrogation. *The Manipulation of Human Behavior*. (A. Biderman and H. Zimmer, Eds.). New York: Wiley, 1961, 159-215.

Orne, M.T. Can a hypnotized subject be compelled to carry out otherwise unacceptable behavior? *International Journal of Clinical and Experimental Hypnosis*, April 1972, 101-116.

Ornstein, R. *The Psychology of Consciousness*. New York: Viking Press, 1972.

Owen, C. Identi-kit enters its second decade. Ever growing at home and abroad. *Fingerprint and Identification*. November 1970, 11-17.

Palombo, S.R. *Dreaming and Memory*. New York: Basic Books, 1978.

Patrick, P. Hypnosis credited in rape suspect's capture. *Lubbock Avalanche-Journal*, July 2, 1977.

Pavlov, I.P. *Experimental Psychology*. New York: Philosophical Library, 1957.

Penfield, W. Memory mechanisms. *Archives of Neurology and Psychiatry*, 1952, *67*, 178-198.

Penfield, W. and Roberts, L. *Speech and Brain Mechanisms*. Princeton, New Jersey: Princeton University Press, 1959.

Penfield, W. *The Mystery of the Mind*. Princeton, New Jersey: Princeton University Press, 1975.

People V. Peters. 4th Crim. 5996, 1974.

Perry, C. Is hypnotizability modifiable? *International Journal of Clinical and Experimental Hypnosis*, 1977, *25*, 125-145.

Petersen, R.D. *The Police Officer in Court*. Springfield, Illinois: Thomas, 1975.

Petrie, S. *What Modern Hypnosis Can Do For You*. New York: Fawcett, 1968.

Physical Fitness for Law Enforcement Officers. Washington, D.C. Federal Bureau of Investigation, 1972.

Pierce, F. *Mobilizing the Mid-Brain*. New York: Dutton, 1924.

Podlesny, J.A. and Raskin, D.C. Physiological measures and the detection of deception. *Psychologicl Bulletin,* 1977, *84,* No. 4, 782-799.

Pribram, K.H. The neurophysiology of remembering. *Scientific American,* January 1969, 73-86.

Prince, M. *The Dissociation of a Personality.* New York: Longmans, 1925.

Prince, M. *The Unconscious.* New York: Macmillan, 1929.

Putnam, B. Some precautions regarding the use of hypnosis in criminal investigations. *The Police Chief,* May 1979, 62-64.

Raginsky, B.B. Hypnotic recall of air crash cause. *International Journal of Clinical and Experimental Hypnosis,* 1969, *17,* 1-19.

Raskin, D.C., Barland, G.H. and Podlesny, J.A. *Reliability of Deception,* Mimeo, 1977.

Recognizing and Supervising Troubled Employees. Washington, D.C.: U.S. Civil Service Commission, July 1967.

Regina V. Pitt. 68 D.L.R. 2d at 516.66 W.W. R at 403 (1967).

Reid, J.E. and Inbau, F.E. *Truth and Deception: The Polygraph Technique.* Baltimore: Williams and Wilkins, 1966.

Reiff, P. *The Triumph of the Therapeutic: Uses of Faith After Freud.* New York: Harper & Row, 1966.

Reiff, R. and Scheerer, M. *Memory and Hypnotic Age Regression.* New York: International Universities Press, 1970.

Reiser, M. *The Police Department Psychologist.* Springfield, Illinois: Thomas, 1972.

Reiser, M. *Practical Psychology for Police Officers.* Springfield, Illinois: Thomas, 1973.

Reiser, M. A note on the use of hypnosis in a police recruit training problem. *American Journal of Clinical Hypnosis,* July 1973, 65-66.

Reiser, M. Hypnosis as an aid in a homicide investigation. *The American Journal of Clinical Hypnosis,* October 1974, 84-87.

Reiser, M. Stress, distress and adaptation in police work. *The Police Chief, January 1976, 24-27.*

Reiser, M. Hypnosis as a tool in criminal investigation. *The Police Chief,* November 1976, 36-40.

Reiser, M. Hypnosis and its uses in law enforcement. *The Police Journal* (British), January-March 1978, 24-33.

Reiser, M. and Lowery, S. *A Comparison of Two Hypnosis Approaches for Weight Control Purposes.* Los Angeles Police Department, July 1978.

Reiser, M. *Investigative Hypnosis - A Developing Specialty.* Los Angeles Police Department (Mimeo), 1978.

Reiser, M., Ludwig, L., Saxe, S., and Wagner, C. An evaluation of the use of psychics in the investigation of major crimes. *Journal of Police Science and Administration,* March 1979, 18-25.

Reiter, P. *Antisocial and Criminal Acts and Hypnosis.* Springfield, Illinois: Thomas, 1958.

Reyher, J. *Hypnosis.* Dubuque, Iowa: William C. Brown, 1968.

Ringel, W.E. *Identification and Police Line-Ups.* Jamaica, New York: Gould Publications, 1968.

Roberts, D.R. An electrophysiologic theory of hypnosis. *International Journal of Clinical and Experimental Hypnosis,* 1960, *8,* 43-55.

Rodale, J.I. *Your Diet and Your Heart.* Emmaus, Pennsylvania: Rodale Press, 1969.

Rokeach, M. *Beliefs, Attitudes and Values.* San Francisco: Jossey-Bass, 1968.

Romanoff, R.A. A survey of case law (what the judges think of hypnosis). *Hyp-*

nosis Quarterly, 1977, *20*, 1-8.
Rosen, H. *Hypnotherapy in Clinical Psychiatry.* New York: Julian Press, 1953.
Ross, K. *Evaluation Study of the Los Angeles Police Department Hypnosis Project.* B.A. Project, University of Redlands, California, July 1977.
Royal, R.F. and Schutt, S.R. *The Gentle Art of Interviewing.* Englewood Cliffs, New Jersey: Prentice-Hall, 1976.
Sacerdote, P. Some individualized psychotherapeutic techniques. *International Journal of Clinical and Experimental Hypnosis,* 1970, *18,* 160-180.
Salzberg, H.C. The effects of hypnotic, post-hypnotic and waking suggestion on performance using tasks varied in complexity. *Clinical Correlates of Experimental Hypnosis* (M.V. Kline, Ed.). Springfield, Illinois: Thomas, 1963, 227-234.
Sarbin, T.R. and Coe, W.C. *Hypnosis: A Social Psychological Analysis of Influence Communication.* New York: Holt, 1972.
Schachtel, E.G. On memory and childhood amnesia. *A Study of Interpersonal Relations* (P. Mullahy, Ed.). New York: Hermitage, 1949.
Schafer, D.W. and Rubio, R. Hypnosis to aid the recall of witnesses. *International Journal of Clinical and Experimental Hypnosis,* 1978, *26,* 81-91.
Scheflen, A.E. *Body Language and Social Order.* Englewood Cliffs, New Jersey: Prentice-Hall, 1972.
Scheflen, A.E. *How Behavior Means.* Garden City, New York: Anchor Books, 1974.
Schein, E.H. The Chinese indoctrination program for prisoners of war. A study of attempted "brainwashing." *Psychiatry,* 1956, *19,* 152-168.
Schilder, P. *The Nature of Hypnosis.* New York: The International Universities Press, 1956.
Schneck, J.M. Henry James, George Du Maurier and Mesmerism. *International Journal of Clinical and Experimental Hypnosis,* 1978, *26,* 76-80.
Schneck, J.M. *Principles and Practice of Hypnoanalysis.* Springfield, Illinois: Thomas, 1965.
Schultz, L.G. (Ed.). *Rape Victimology.* Springfield, Illinois: Thomas, 1975.
Schwartz, G.E. and Shapiro, D. *Consciousness and Self-Regulation.* New York: Plenum Press, 1976.
Scott, E.M. Hypnosis in the courtroom. *American Journal of Clinical Hypnosis,* 1977, *19,* 163-165.
Segall, M. *The Questions They Ask About Hypnosis.* South Orange, New Jersey: Power Publishers, 1973.
Selye, H. *The Stress of Life.* New York: McGraw-Hill, 1956.
Senders, J.W. *Eye Movements and the Higher Psychological Functions.* Hillside, New Jersey: Erlbaum Associates, 1978.
Shor, R.E. Three dimensions of hypnotic depth. *The Nature of Hypnosis* (R.E. Shor and M.T. Orne, Eds.). New York: Holt, Rinehart and Winston, 1965, 306-321.
Shor, R.E. and Orne, E.C. *Harvard Group Scale of Hypnotic Susceptibility.* Palo Alto, California: Consulting Psychologists Press, 1962.
Shor, R. and Orne, M. *The Nature of Hypnosis.* New York: Holt, Rinehart and Winston, 1965.
Singer, J.L. and Pope, K.S. *The Power of Human Imagination.* New York: Plenum Press, 1978.
Sobel, N.R. *Eye-Witness Identification: Legal and Practical Problems.* New York: Clark Boardman Company, 1972.
Spanos, N.P. and Barber, T.X. Toward a convergence in hypnosis research. *American Psychologist,* July 1974, 500-511.

BIBLIOGRAPHY

Sparks, L. *Self-Hypnosis.* North Hollywood, California: Wilshire Book Company, 1973.

Spector, G.A. and Claiborn, W.L. *Crisis Intervention.* New York: Behavioral Publications, 1973.

Spiegel, H. An eye-roll test for hypnotizability. *The American Journal of Clinical Hypnosis,* 1972, *15,* 25-28.

Spiegel, H. *Manual for Hypnotic Induction Profile: Eye-roll Levitation Method.* New York: Soni Medica, 1976.

Spiegel, H. and Spiegel, D. *Trance and Treatment.* New York: Basic Books, 1978.

Spiegel, J.P. and Machotka, P. *Messages of the Body.* New York: The Free Press, 1974.

Spitz, R. *The First Year of Life.* New York: International Universities Press, 1965.

State of North Carolina V. Roger Lee McQueen. No. 92 Supreme Court of North Carolina, June 6, 1978.

Stevens, D. and Berlinger, L. *Special Techniques for Child Witnesses.* Seattle, Washington: Harborview Medical Center (Mimeo).

Stone, L.J. and Church, J. *Childhood and Adolescence.* New York: Random House, 1957.

Storr, A. *Human Aggression.* New York: Atheneum, 1968.

Stratton, J. The use of hypnosis in law enforcement criminal investigations. *Journal of Police Science and Administration,* 1977, *5,* 399-406.

Stukat, K.G. *Suggestibility: A Factorial and Experimental Analysis.* Stockholm: Almqvist and Wiksell, 1958.

Tart, C. *Altered States of Consciousness.* New York: Wiley, 1969.

Tart, C.T. Quick and convenient assessment of hypnotic depth: self-report scales. *American Journal of Clinical Hypnosis,* 1978, *21,* 186-207.

Taylor, L.L. Psychological stress evaluator (PSE). *IACP Police Law Reporter,* (no date).

Teitelbaum, M. *Hypnosis Induction Technics.* Springfield, Illinois: Thomas, 1969.

Test measure polygraph accuracy. *Law Enforcement Assistance Administration (LEAA) Newsletter,* March 1977, p. 21.

Tierney, K. *Courtroom Testimony.* New York: Funk and Wagnalls, 1970.

Tinterow, M. *Foundations of Hypnosis.* Springfield, Illinois: Thomas, 1970.

Ulett, G.A. et al. Hypnosis: physiological pharmacological validity. *American Journal of Psychiatry,* January 1972, 799-805.

United States V. Adams. 581 F. 2d 193 (1978). 581 Federal Reporter, 2nd Series.

Van Pelt, S.J. *Hypnotic Suggestion.* New York: Philosophical Library, 1956.

Virginia Researcher. Chartlottesville, Virginia, March 1975.

Volgyesi, F.A. *Hypnosis of Man and Animals, 2nd Edition.* Hollywood, California: Wilshire Book Company, 1968.

Vollmer, T. Seaman guilty in mutilation, rape of girl. *Los Angeles Times,* March 24, 1979.

Von Dedenroth, T.E.A. Trance depth: An independent variable in therapeutic results. *American Journal of Clinical Hypnosis,* 1962, *4,* 174.

Walker, N.S., Garrett, J.B. and Wallace, B. Restoration of eidetic imagery via hypnotic age regression. *Journal of Abnormal Psychology,* 1976, *85,* 335-337.

Wall, P. *Eye-Witness Identification in Criminal Cases.* Springfield, Illinois: Thomas, 1965.

Wallach, H. *On Perception.* New York: Quadrangle Books, 1976.

Walls, H.J. *Expert Witness.* London: John Long, 1972.

Watkins, J.G. Trance and transference. *Journal of Clinical and Experimental Hypnosis*, 1954, *2*, 284-290.

Watkins, J.G. Transference aspects of the hypnotic relationship. *Clinical Correlates of Experimental Hypnosis* (M.V. Kline, Ed.). Springfield, Illinois: Thomas, 1963, 5-24.

Watkins, J.G. Antisocial behavior under hypnosis: possible or impossible? *International Journal of Clinical and Experimental Hypnosis*, April 1972, 95-99.

Watson, G. *Nutrition and Your Mind. The Psychochemical Response.* New York: Harper and Row, 1972.

Watson, P. *War on the Mind.* New York: Basic Books, 1978.

Weinstein, M.D. Abrams, S. and Gibbons, D. The validity of the polygraph with hypnotically induced repression and guilt. *American Journal of Psychiatry*, February 1970, 1159-1162.

Weitzenhoffer, A.M. *Hypnotism: An Objective Study in Suggestibility.* New York: Wiley, 1953.

Weitzenhoffer, A.M. *General Techniques of Hypnotism.* New York: Grune & Stratton, 1957.

Weitzenhoffer, A.M. and Hilgard, E.R. *Stanford Hypnotic Susceptibility Scale. Paio Alto, California: Consulting Psychologists Press, 1959.*

Wells, W.R. Experiments in waking hypnosis. *Modern Hypnosis* (L. Kuhn and S. Russo, Eds.). North Hollywood, California: Wilshire Book Company, 1974, 45-55.

Wells, G.L., Leippe, M.R. and Ostrom, T.M. Crime seriousness as a determinant of accuracy in eyewitness identification. *Journal of Applied Psychology*, 1978, *63*, 3, 345-351.

West, L.J. and Deckert, G.H. Dangers of hypnosis. *Journal of the American Medical Association*, 1965, *192*, 9-12.

Whitlow, J.E. A rapid method for the induction of hypnosis. *Experimental Hypnosis* (L.M. LeCron, Ed.). Secaucus, New Jersey: Citadel Press, 1972.

Williams, S.G.W. Highway hypnosis: a hypothesis. *The Nature of Hypnosis* (Shor, R.E. and Orne, M.T., Eds.). New York: Holt, Rinehart and Winston, 1965, 482-490.

Wilson, R. Hypnosis: investigating the subconscious. *Police Magazine*, January 1979, 14-20.

Wolberg, L.R. *Hypnoanalysis.* New York: Grune & Stratton, 1945.

Wolberg, L.R. *Hypnosis: Is It For Your?* New York: Harcourt, Brace and Jovanovich, 1972.

Wolberg, L.R. *Medical Hypnosis, Volume I.* New York: Grune & Stratton, 1948.

Worth, J.W. and Lewis, B.J. *An Early Validation Study with the Psychological Stress Evaluator* (PSE). Lexington, Virginia: Washington & Lee University, 1972.

Wyller V. Fairchild-Hiller Corporation. 503 F. 2d 503 (1974).

Young, P.C. Antisocial uses of hypnosis. *Experimental Hypnosis* (L.M. LeCron, Ed.). New York: Macmillan, 1952, 403-406.

Young, P.C. Hypnotic regression - fact or artifact? *Modern Hypnosis* (L. Kuhn and S. Russo, Eds.). North Hollywood, California: Wilshire Book Company, 1974, 56-63.

Zinberg, N.E. *Alternate States of Consciousness.* New York: The Free Press, 1977.

INDEX

A

Abrams, S., 69
abreaction, 232
Adams, P., 127
additional session, 175
administration, 169
adult, 12
age regression, 5, 151
aids, mechnical, 122
aircraft accidents, 73
Allen, A.L., 88, 165
Allison, H.C., 88, 165
alpha waves, 8
altered states of consciousness, 8, 30, 110
ambivalence, 232
American Express, xx
American Medical Association, 5
American Psychological Association, 5
amnesia, 110, 114, 116, 232
  post-traumatic, 116
analgesia, 232
Anderson, P.B., 187
anesthesia, 232
anterograde, 116, 232
antisocial, 70
anxiety, 21
  neurotic, 22
apperception, 232
arms rising and falling test, 48
Arons, H. xxiii, 80, 140, 150
artist
  composite, 86
  police, 86
association, 232
  law of, 59
Atal, B., 69
authoritarian approach, 89
authoritative, 42
auto-hypnosis, 232
automatic nervous system, 9, 67, 154, 232
automatic writing, 152

B

Baddeley, A.D., 118
Barbara, D.A., 84
Barber, T.X., 39, 40, 45, 112, 182

Bard, M., 103, 104
Barland, G.H., 69
Baudouin, C. 58, 59
beach scene, the, 156
Beier, E.G., 84
Benson, H., 31, 33
Berg, S., 130, 131
Berger, J.R., 128
Berliner, L., 105
Berne, Eric, 11, 12
Bernheim, H., 5, 6
Bernstein, L., 84
Bernstein, R.S., 84
beta waves, 8
Bingham, W.V., 84
biofeedback, 8
Birdwhistell, R.L., 84
blackboard techniques, 161
body language, 81
Bordeaux, J. 57, 59, 101, 113
Botwinik, J., 131
Bowers, K.S., 33
Bowers, M., 45
Bowers, P., 49
Braid, James, 4, 6
brain, 7
brainwashing, 73
brain waves, 7
Brenman, M., 32, 40, 108
Breuer, Josef, 5, 6, 40
British Medical Association, 5
Brodsky, S., 29
Bromberg, W., 45
Brown, E., 80
Brunn, J.T., 118
Bryan, W.J., 141
Buckhout, R., 80
Burch, G.W., 181
Burgess, A.W., 104, 105
Burns, A., 49

C

Cameron, N., 29
Campbell, B.V., 187
Cannon, W., 22, 29
Caprio, F.S., 128
catalepsy, 232
catalystic approach, 89

cathartic method, 5
central nervous system, 232
centralize referrals, 170
cerebral psychology, 38
Charcot, J.M., 5, 38, 40
Cheek, D.B., xii, 11, 12, 35, 37, 57, 112, 114, 118, 119, 123, 153, 157, 168
Chiasson's technique, 54
child, 11
child subjects, 176
Church, J., 131
circadian rhythm, 17
Coe, W.C., 40, 77
cognitive, 232
composite artist, 86
composite drawing, 193
composite kits, 86
concentrated attention, law of, 59
condensation, 10
conditioned reflex, 31, 39
confabulation, 232
confusion technique, 121
Conn, J.H., 35, 36, 37, 45, 77
conscience, 19
conscious, 9, 15
consciousness, altered states of, 8, 30, 110
consultation, 76
contraindications, 34
controlled style, 103
Cooper, L.F., 118
Cooper, L.M., 49, 117, 131
coordination, 169
Cornell v. Superior Court of San Diego County, 133
corroboration, 87
Coué, E., 59
countertransference, 106, 232
Crasilneck, H.B., 96
creativity, 8
crisis, 22
crisis states, 102
Cumley, W.E., 67, 69
cybernetic, 7
cybernetic model, 114

D

Daim, W., 45
Dana, R.H., 84
dangers, 34
Darnton, R., 6

Davis-Husband scale, 97
Davis, R.C., 69
Deckert, G.H., 37
deepening phase, 179
deepening techniques, 55
defenses, 21, 23
Deffenbacher, K., 80
dehypnotization, 56, 233
dehypnotization phase, 179
Deleuze, F., 6
Dellinger, R.W., xxiii
delta waves, 8
demand characteristics, 32
demonstration project, 183
Department Psychologist, xix
depth categories, 97
depth classification scales, 97
Derman, D., 45
Derrick, C., 80, 150
Dhanens, T.P., 109, 112
diet, 15
difficult subjects, 119
Dilloff, N.J., 141
direct, 43
disorders, 25
'displacement, 10, 23
dissociation, 233
dissociation theory, 39
dominent effect, law of, 58
Dorcus, R.M., 79, 80, 114, 118
drives, 15
drugs, 68
Du Maurier, George, 34
Duckworth, J., 128
Duke, J.D., 49
Dworkin, S.F., 150

E

early history, 3
early warning signs, 27
Ebbinghaus, Hermann, 115
Eddy, M.B., 45
Edmonston, W.E., 153
educational uses, 73
Edward the Confessor, 3
Ehrenreich, G.A., 101
eidetic image, 233
Ekman, P., 84
elderly subjects, 130
electroencephalograph, 8
electronic recording, 167
Ellen, A., 124

Ellison, K., 104
emotional reactions, 104
entertainment, 173
environment, 15
episodic (redintegrative), 115
equilibrium, 18
Erickson, E.M., 113
Erickson, M.H., 71, 75, 76, 77, 84, 95, 96, 107, 108, 111, 113, 117, 118, 120, 124
Erickson's naturalistic techniques, 92
Ericksonian approach, 162
Esdaile, James, 5, 6
Estabrooks, G.H., 70, 71, 72, 74, 113
ethical issues, 60
Evans, F.J., 96
exercise, 15
experiences, 173
expert witness, 142
expressed style, 103
eye closure, 52
eye fixation, 52
eye roll, Spiegel, 54
eye-roll test, the, 48
eyes opening and closing technique, 89
eyewitness testimony, 78
eyewitness unreliability, 181

F

faith healers, 42
family members, 176
Farr, W., 189
Fast, J., 84
fear of revenge, 52
Fezler, W.D., 90, 96, 157
Field, P.B., 150
finger pull test, 47
Fink, D., 29
Fisher, S., 113
forms,
    questionnaire, 171
    release, 226
    sample, 223
fractionation technique, 120
Francis, I., 3
Frank, J.D., 12, 45
Frankel, F.H., 6, 101, 108
Franklin, Benjamin, 4

Friesen, M.V., 84
Freud, Sigmund, 5, 40, 44
Fricke, C.W., 150
Fromm, E., 181
Fross, G.H., 124
Furneaux, W.D., 113

G

galvanic skin response, 65
Galwey, T., 6, 74
Gardner, G.G., 131
Garrett, J.B., 153
Gates, Daryl F., xv
general adaption syndrome, 22
Gerber, S.R., xxiii, 80
Germann, A.C., 67, 69
Gibbons, D., 69
Gill, M.M., 33, 40, 108
Goffman, E., 85
Gottschalk, L.A., 68, 69
Greatrakes, Valentine, 3

H

Hadfield, 5
Haley, J., 96, 162
Hall, Dr. Edward, 83
Hall, J.A., 96
hallucination, 223
Hammerschlag, H., 70, 74
hand-levitation technique, 53
hands as magnets test, 48
hand clasp test, 47
Hanley, F.W., 141, 150
Harding v. State, 134, 141, 144
Harris, T., 12
Hassel, C., 74
Hatton, K.L., 188
head pressure technique, 162
Hell, Father Maximillian, 3
hemispheres, 8
hetero-hypnosis, 74, 125
"hidden observer", the, 9, 79, 152
highway hypnosis, 31
Hilgard, E.R., 9, 12, 29, 32, 33, 45, 49, 77, 79, 80, 81, 101, 113, 114, 118, 131, 152, 153, 157, 182
Hilgard, J.R., 50, 113, 131
history
    early, 3
    modern, 3

Hollander, E.P., 29
hologram, 114
Holstrom, L.L., 104, 105
homeostasis, 22
hormones, 15
Hull, C.L., 40
Hunt, R., 29
hypermnesia, 152, 233
hypersuggestibility, 39
hypnoanalysis, 5
hypno-investigator, xxii
hypnoidal, 110, 233
hypnosis, 30, 233
    auto, 232
    hetero, 74, 125
    highway, 31
    investigative, xix, xxii
    theories of, 38
    yardstick of, 100
hypnosis and the polygraph, 66
hypnosis legislation, 139
hypnosis survey, 230
hypnotic suggestions, 109
hypnotist, 35
    role of the, 32
hypnotist's motives, 44
hypnotizability, 46
hysteria, 38

I

Identi-kit, 86
ideomotor, 154, 233
    action, 31
    finger signaling, 155
ideosensory techniques, 154, 156
imagery, 56
    techniques, 90
imagination, 4
immobilization theories, 38
Imbare, F.E., 69
indirect, 43
    suggestion, 233
induced dream, 160
induction, 233
    methods, 52
    phase, 179
    techniques, 89
information eliciting phase, 179
International Association of Chiefs of Police Award, xx
interviewing techniques, 81
intrapsychic, 233

investigative hypnosis, xix, xxii
investigative tool, 132
involuntary responses, 154

J

Jacobson, E., 57
Janet, Pierre, 35, 37, 39, 40
Jersild, A.T., 29, 131
Jewett v. United States, 132
Johnson, A., 141
Johnson, L.K., 131
Jones v. State, 135

K

Kahn, R.L., 85
Katz, Ronald, L., xiii
Kendall, J., 188
Kimmel, D.C., 131
kinesic behavior, 83
kinesics, 233
King, Lt. Richard, 177
Kline, M.V., 6, 12, 49, 71, 74, 108, 182
Kline v. Ford Motor Company, 136, 141, 153
Kradz, M.P., 68, 69
Krauss, L., 188
Kroger, W.S., 6, 40, 50, 52, 57, 59, 74, 75, 77, 90, 96, 124, 141, 157, 162
Krystal, H., 105
Kubie, L.S., 33

L

labile, 233
La Scola, R., 131
Lauer, L.W., 49, 131
Law Enforcement Hypnosis Institute, Inc., xxi
law of
    association, 59
    concentrated attention, 59
    dominent effect, 58
    reversed effect, 58
laying on of hands, 58
Lazarus, R.S., 105
Le Cron-Bordeaux Scoring System, 98
Le Cron, L.M., 6, 35, 57, 59, 74, 101, 111, 112, 113, 118, 121, 123, 124, 125, 128, 153, 157, 168

legal aspects, 132
Leippe, M.R., 80
Leitner, K., 124
Levendula, D., 79, 80
Levi, L., 29
Levinson, H., 12, 29
Levitt, E., 74
Lewis, B.J., 68, 69
Lewis, H.R., 45
Lewis, M.E., 29
Liébeault, 5
line-ups, 163
London, P., 49, 64, 105, 131
long term memory, 115
Los Angeles Police Dept., xix, 62, 86, 171, 183
Lozanov, G., 6, 74, 109, 113, 181, 182
Lundy, R.M., 112

M

Machotka, P., 85
Magonet, P., 124
Maltz, M., 12, 118
Manson v. Braithwaite, 164
Margolin, S., 33
Marks, J., 74
McCleary, R.A., 12, 118
McCormick, C.T., 132, 141
McDevitt, R., 105
Meares, A.A., 40
mechanical aids, 122
Melie, J.P., 45
Melin, E., 130, 131
memories, 7
memory, 114
    long-term, 115
    screen, 234
    semantic, 115
    short term, 115
Menninger, K., 22, 27, 29, 108
mental health, 14, 17
Mesmer, Franz Anton, 3
mesmerism, 233
methods,
    induction, 52
military and intelligence
    uses, 72
Milwee, S., 172
mind control, 34
misconception, 34
misdirection of attention, 122, 233

Missildine, W.H., 28, 29, 59
modern history, 3
modulation or control system, 7
Montgomery, J., 68, 69
Moore, B.V., 84
Moore, R.K., 50, 118, 131
moral and legal standards, 60
Morgan, A.H., 131
motives, 14
motor output system, 7
Mühl, A.M., 153
Münsterberg, H., 78, 80
myths, 34

N

Nadelson, C.C., 105
nervous system, the, 8
neurohypnosis, 4
neurology, 7
neurosis, 233
neurotic anxiety, 22
Nielsen, M., 172, 188
Nilsson, L.G., 182
nonverbal technique (written), 91
normal, 17
Notman, M.T., 105

O

observation technique, 96
odors test, the, 49
office procedures, 166
Olness, K., 131
open-ended questions, 82
Oregon, 139
Orne, E.C., 101
Orne, M.T., 32, 33, 71, 72, 74, 80 153
Ornstein, R., 13
Ostrom, T.M., 80
Owen, C., 88

P

pantomime techniques, 96
Paracelcus, 3
parasympathetic division, 9
parent, 11
partial regression, 151
Patrick, P., 188
Pavlov, I.P., 39, 40
pencil drop test, the, 49

pendulum, 154
Penfield, Wilder, 8, 13, 118
People v. Busch, 133
People v. Ebanks, 132
People v. Marsh, 133
People v. Modesto, 134
People v. Peters, 135, 141
People v. Quaglino, 137
permissive, 43
permissive approach, 89
Perry, C., 50
personality development, 11
Petersen, R.D., 150, 165
phase,
    deepening, 179
    dehypnotization, 179
    induction, 179
    information eliciting, 179
    pre-induction, 178
photographs, 164
physical touch, 56
Pierce, F., 58, 59
pilot project, 183
placebo effect, 42
Podlesny, J.A., 67, 69
police artist, 86
polygraph, 65
    hypnosis and the, 66
Ponce, Fernando, 86
Pope, K.S., 118
positive hallucination, 32
possible harm, 76
post-hypnotic suggestions, 56, 109, 233
post-traumatic amnesia, 116
preconscious, 9, 233
pre-induction, 51
pre-induction phase, 178
pre-induction warmup, 233
pressure points, 123
Pribram, K.H., 114, 118
primary processes, 10
Prince, Morton, 39, 40
problems, 173
procedures, 178
projection, 23
psychoanalysis, 5
psychoanalytic theory, 40
psychodynamics, 9
psychosomatic disorders, 26
psychosomatic theories, 4
pupillometrics, 68
Puységur, Marquis de, 4

Q

questionnaire forms, 171

R

Raginsky, B.B., 74
rape, 102
rape trauma syndrome, 102
rapid techniques, 119, 122
rapport, 32, 233
Raskin, D.C., 67, 69
rationalization, 23
reaction-formation, 23
reality principle, 10
recall, 233
recall of significant details, 79
recognition 115
refractory subject, 119
Regina v. Pitt, 134, 141
regression, 233
    age, 5, 151
    partial, 151
    theory, 39
rehearsal technique, 95
Reid, J.E., 69
Reiff, P.,45, 118, 153
Reiser, Martin, xi, xiii, xv, xvii, xxiii, 6, 13, 14, 64, 74, 77, 79, 80, 114, 118, 162, 188
Reiter, P., 74
relaxation approach, 89
relaxation technique, 53
release form, 226
release forms, 167
repetition, 31
repression, 10, 23, 116, 234
research, 62, 180
research demonstration project, xix
resistance, 57, 84, 234
resistances, 32, 119
retrieval techniques, 158
retrograde, 116, 232
reversed effect,
    law of, 58
revivification, 151
Reyher, J., 33
Ringel, W.E., 88, 164, 165
Roberts, D.R., 40
Roberts, L., 13
Rodale, J.I., 29
Rokeach, M., 45
role of the hypnotist, 32

role playing, 39
Romanoff, R.A., 141
Rosen, H., 40
Ross, K., 182, 188
Rossi, E.L., 96
Royal, R.F., 85
Rubio, R., 141

S

Sacerdote, P., 96
Sacerdote's sculpture
  technique, 90
Salzberg, H.C., 109, 113
sample forms, 223
Sarbin, T.R., 40, 77
scale,
  Davis-Husband, 97
scales,
  depth classification, 97
Schachtel, E.G., 118
Schafer, D.W., 141
Scheerer, M., 118, 153
Schefien, A.E., 85
Schein, E.H., 74
Schilder, P., 40
Schneck, J.M., 37, 40
Schroeder, O., 80
Schultz, L.G., 105
Schutt, S.R., 85
Schwartz, G.E., 13
Scott, E.M., 150
screen memory, 234
secondary processes, 10
selection of personnel, 169
self concept, 16
self-hypnosis, 74, 125
Selye, H., 22, 29
semantic memory, 115
Senders, J.W., 69
sensory input system, 7
Shapiro, D., 13
Shor, R.E., 101, 108, 181
short term memory, 115
*Simmons v. United
  States,* 164
Singer, J.L., 118
sleep, 8
sleepy fingers technique, 130
Sobel, N.R., 80
social, 70
social uses, 73

Society for Investigative and
  Forensic Hypnosis, xxiii, 62
somnabulism, 234
Spanos, N.P., 182
Sparks, L., 128
Spector, G.A., 105
Spiegel, D., 96, 108, 118
Spiegel eye roll, 54
Spiegel, H., 48, 50, 57, 96,
  108, 118
Spiegel, J.P., 85
Spitz, R., 15, 29
standards,
  moral and legal, 60
state of mind, 132
State v. Jorgensen, 135
State v. McQueen, 138, 141
State v. Nebb, 134
statistics, 183
Stockholm syndrome, 73
Stone, L.J., 131
Storr, A., 29
stress, 21
stresses, 20
Stukat, K.G., 50
Sturgill, W., 80
subconscious, 11, 234
subject's motivation, 52
success or failure, 175
suggestion, 4, 234
  types of, 42
suggestions,
  post-hypnotic, 56, 109, 233
  waking, 109
subject,
  refractory, 119
subjects,
  difficult, 119
  elderly, 130
suggestibility, 42
suppression, 23, 234
surprise, 122
susceptibility tests, 46
Svengali, 34
sympathetic division, 9
symptom removal, 173
symptoms, 23
system,
  modulation or control, 7
  motor output, 7
  nervous, the, 8
  sensory input, 7
  unconscious, 9

T

T.V., 158
Tart, C.T., 33, 101
Taylor, L.L., 68, 69
technique,
    blackboard, 161
    Chiasson's, 54
    confusion, 121
    eyes opening and closing, 89
    fractionation, 120
    hand-levitation, 53
    head pressure, 162
    non-verbal (written), 91
    observation, 96
    rehearsal, 95
    relaxation, 53
    Sacerdote's sculpture, 90
    sleepy fingers, 130
    tension and relaxation,
        the, 123
    visualization, 121
    watch, the,
techniques,
    deepening, 55
    Erickson's naturalistic, 92
    ideosensory, 154, 156
    imagery, 90
    induction, 89
    interviewing, 81
    pantomime, 96
    rapid, 119, 122
    retrieval, 158
Teitelbaum, M., 52, 57, 73, 74, 89, 96, 113, 124, 139, 141, 150, 168
tension and relaxation technique, the, 123
test,
    arms rising and falling, 48
    eye-roll, the, 48
    finger pull, 47
    hands clasp, 47
    hands as magnet, 48
    odors, the, 49
    pencil drop, the, 49
tests,
    susceptibility, 46
theories,
    immobilization, 38
    of hypnosis, 38
    psychosomatic, 4
theory,
    dissociation, 39
    psychoanalytic, 40
    regression, 39
therapeutic uses, 73
theta waves, 8
Tierney, K., 150
time distortion, 114, 117
time door to memory room, 161
time lag, 43
Tinterow, M., 6
training, 170
trance, 234
trance logic, 32
transcript, 193
transference, 106, 234
    reactions, 35
    resistances, 106
trauma, 175, 234
Trilby, 34
truth detection, 65
truth serums, 68
turning-on-the-self, 23
types of suggestion, 42
typical cases, 184

U

unconscious ego systems, 9
United States v. Adams, 138, 141

V

Valens, E.G., 84
Van Pelt, S.J., 30, 33, 109, 113
victimology, 102
visualization technique, 121
voice prints, 67
voice stress analysis, 68
Volgyesi, F.A., 40
Vollmer, T., 188
Von Dedenroth, T.E.A., 101
voodoo, 42

W

waking suggestions, 109
Walker, N.S., 153
Wall, P.M., 80, 163, 164, 165
Wallace, B., 153
Wallach, H., 118
Walls, H.J., 150
watch technique, the, 122
Watkins, J.G., 70, 71, 74, 107, 108

Watson, G., 29
waves,
    alpha, 8
    beta, 8
    brain, 7
    delta, 8
    theta, 8
Weinstein, M.D., 67, 69
Weitzenhoffer, A.M., 40, 41, 50, 57, 96, 101, 105, 107, 108, 109, 110, 113, 124, 128, 162
Wells, G.L., 78, 80
Wells, W.R., 113
West, L.J., 37
Whitlow, J.E., 124
Williams, G.W., 33
Wolberg, L.R., 33, 41, 74, 113
Worth, J.W., 68, 69
Wyller v. Fairchild-Hiller Corporation, 136, 141

Y

yardstick of hypnosis, 100
Young, P.C., 74, 153

Z

Zinberg, N.E., 13
Zwerling, I, 64

ABOUT THE AUTHOR

Dr. Reiser is Director of Behavioral Science Services, Los Angeles Police Department and is also Director of the Law Enforcement Hypnosis Institute. A Training Analyst and Faculty member of the Los Angeles Institute for Psychoanalytic Studies, he is a Diplomate in Clinical Psychology of the American Board of Professional Psychology, a Fellow of the American Psychological Association, and a Past-President of the Los Angeles County Psychological Association and of the Los Angeles Society of Clinical Psychologists.

He is a founder of the Society for Investigative and Forensic Hypnosis, a member of the American Society of Clinical Hypnosis, the International Society of Hypnosis, and the Southern California Society of Clinical Hypnosis.

The author of numerous articles on police psychology, Dr. Reiser has written two books previously, *The Police Department Psychologist,* and *Practical Psychology for Police Officers.*